Rbod '99

LOST WORLDS

ALASTAIR SERVICE

COLLINS
14 St James's Place, London

Editors: Randal Gray, Susan Hill, Robin L. K. Wood

Designers: Anita Ruddell, Eddie Pitcher

Picture Researchers: Sheila Thompson, Moira McIlroy

Maps and Illustrations: Tom Stimpson

This book was designed and produced by
Marshall Cavendish Books Limited
58 Old Compton Street
London W1V 5PA

© Marshall Cavendish Limited 1981

Published by William Collins Sons & Co. Ltd
London · Glasgow · Sydney · Auckland
Toronto · Johannesburg

First published 1981

ISBN 0 00 216461 2

Set in Bembo

Printed in Hong Kong

33, 565 X

Picture Credits:
AAA Photo: 16, 126, 138
Aerofilms Ltd: 189
Agence Hoa-Qui: 176B
BBC Hulton Picture Library: 161, 167
Barnabys Picture Library: 48/9
Carlo Bevilaqua: 172
Bodleian Library: 11
Jean Bottin: 25, 40
British Museum: 101, 104/5, 113(B), 135
J. Allan Cash Ltd: 69(L)
Peter Clayton: 112, 133(T), 119, 167
Bruce Coleman Ltd: 4/5, 9, 24 (Prato), 89 (Jennifer Fry)
Douglas Dickins: 65, 66, 68(L), 68(R)
C. M. Dixon: 141, 148, 153
Elisabeth Photo Library London Ltd: 185(B)
Robert Estall Photographs: 144/5, 154, 155, 180/1, 191
Humphrey Evans: 110, 111, 114
Mary Evans Picture Library: 32, 50, 127, 174, 195
Explorer: 87, 90 (Louis-Yves Loirat), 162
Giraudon: 77
Ara Guler: 80/1
Sonia Halliday: 1, 163, 176, 178
Robert Harding Associates: 4/5, 8
John Hillelson Agency Ltd: 92/3 (Dr. Georg Gerster), 116 (Brian Brake)
Michael Holford Photographs: 9, 20(T), 20(B), 33, 34, 43 (Ianthe Ruthven), 52
    53 (Museum Fur Volkerkunde, Munich), 97, 100(T), 100(B) (British Museum),
    108/9, 114, 116, 117, 132, 133, 136, 139, 140, 164/5, 168/9 (Gerry Clyde),
    177, 185
Alan Hutchison Library: 143
Illustrated London News Picture Library: 58
Eugene Kusch: 194, 196
Mansell Collection: 26, 74, 79, 98, 102, 103
William MacQuitty: 112, 118
Marion & Tony Morrison: 12/3, 27
John Moss: 137
Andrew Moylan: 21
Ian Murphy: 124
Museum of Mankind: 54, 131, 142
National Museum: 152
Ann & Bury Peerless: 10, 72, 76, 190
Popperfoto: 56/7, 82, 91
Josephine Powell: 78/9
Courtesy of Queen Victoria Museum, Zimbabwe, Rhodesia: 128
Rapho: 55, 128/9, 151 (Michael Serraillier)
Royal Geographical Society: endpapers
Scala: 172(R), 173, 177 (Vision International), 198 (Vatican Museum)
Ronald Sheridan: 156/7, 160, 192/3, 197
Edwin Smith: 173
Vautier Decool: 6, 18, 19, 24, 25, 28/9, 35, 42, 44/5, 61, 63, 67,
    69(R), 86
Roger Viollet: 179
Zefa Picture Library: 37 (Karl Kummels), 38 (Gunter Heil), 84 (R. Waldkirch),
    120/1, 125 (J. Rushmer)

For Nicholas

Title page *A Pompeian couple
carved on the column capital of
an early Samnite house in the
city destroyed and preserved by
the Vesuvius eruption of
A.D. 79.*

Endpapers *The 15 lost worlds
covered in this book are located
on a British world map of 1782
just after Captain Cook's
voyages closed the First Age of
Discovery.*

Acknowledgements: *We would like to thank the following publishers for their kind
permission to quote from the books listed below*
Michael Joseph Ltd: *Still Digging,* Sir Mortimer Wheeler (London 1955)
Thames and Hudson Ltd: *My Archaeological Mission to India and Pakistan,*
Sir Mortimer Wheeler (London 1976)
Ernest Benn Ltd: *Excavations at Ur,* Sir Leonard Woolley (London 1954)
Frederick Muller Ltd: *Mesopotamia,* Jean-Louis Margueron (London 1965)
J. M. Dent & Sons Ltd: *Lost City of the Incas,* Hiram Bingham (Phoenix House,
                                                                London 1951)

National Archives of Zimbabwe: *The Journals of Carl Mauch 1869–1872,* trans.
F. O. Bernhard and edited E. E. Burke (Salisbury 1969)

We are grateful to the Rainbird Publishing Group Ltd for permission to
use the *Atlas of Ancient Archaeology,* edited by Jacquetta Hawkes (Heinemann,
London 1974) as reference for the map of Ur and to the Reader's Digest
Association for permission to use *The World's Last Mysteries* (1977) as reference for
the aerial view drawing of Angkor.

PREFACE

LOST CITIES AND lost civilizations have fascinated people of the developed western countries for well over a century now. These 15 were chosen partly for their own special interest, partly because they are scattered widely around the world and widely through the last 5000 years. Thus they serve well my desire, as an architectural historian, to explore and consider the similarities and differences of purpose or design in the great monumental buildings at the settlements built by our early cultures in such varying climates as peoples spread to all corners of the world. For this sort of exploration, I have tried in each chapter to bring the place and its monuments alive through plans as well as photographs, while telling what is known of the people and why they built the great structures that survive in ruins today.

A note about dating will be helpful here, for dates have long been the subject of controversy among archaeologists. In the Middle East very ancient written records have been found, such as the king lists of Egypt, which gave archaeologists a chronological framework of varying dependability in solar years for the rulers and their buildings. By comparing the style and manufacture of various man-made goods found in a site with others found elsewhere, a system called cross-dating was evolved—though that has often proved misleading. Since World War II, three more important techniques have been developed, using various things found on archaeological sites; the analysis of pollen, the measurement of the stage of deterioration of the thermoluminescence (phosphorescence produced by heat) found in all pottery, and analysis of the stage of decay of the radiocarbon found in all organic matter. Radiocarbon dating has provided the most sensational discoveries, for many places turned out to be much older than previously suspected. Then in 1967 an American chemist, Professor H. E. Suess, published the first of a series of papers showing an error in radiocarbon dates earlier than 800 B.C. He showed that dates before that should be yet older than then calculated and that the error got greater the further back the dates went—thus, a radiocarbon date of 4200 B.C. should be calibrated on an irregular graph curve and would give a 'correct' date of 5200 B.C. The extent and constancy of this correction by calibration is still controversial among archaeologists. Therefore the dates given, for example, in this book's chapters on Malta, Avebury and Stonehenge (all of which have been calibrated on Suess's curve published in 1970) are earlier than those given in many books and should be treated with some reserve.

I would like to thank Susan Hill for commissioning the book, Frances Kelly for negotiating it, Robin Wood and Randal Gray for editing it, Louisa Service for her company while visiting several of the sites, John Irwin for long discussions on his researches into the almost worldwide presence of the chambered mound, pyramid, *stupa* or temple-mountain, John Cox for his insights into early studies of the heavens, Jean Bradbery for her research assistance on six chapters, Sheila Thompson and Moira McIlroy for the picture research, Anita Ruddell for the book design and my secretary Jeanette Highsted and my brilliant typist Mrs. G. Horton for such painstaking work.

CONTENTS

INTRODUCTION

LOST WORLDS: the words have an evocative ring for most people. Various pictures may arise in the mind—a high plateau in South America inhabited by prehistoric creatures, a devastated planet hurtling away through space, exotic overgrown buildings discovered in the jungle, the privileged glamour of wealthy Edwardian society before the Great War of 1914–18, a continent with an ancient civilization submerged under the Atlantic Ocean. Among these many possible meanings, the lost worlds of this book were 'worlds' in the sense that each was once the centre of a largely self-contained way of life in the minds of those who lived there. They were 'lost' in that either the place itself vanished and was rediscovered later, or that knowledge of the culture and the people's reasons for building their monuments disappeared until archaeology and other sciences pieced some of it together again.

The search for lost worlds of the past is a recent pursuit in the thousands of years of mankind's development. A cool look at history seems to show that human cultures, at their most successful, drew on the available knowledge of the past to some extent in making their own monuments and artifacts. But they did not preserve outmoded buildings and they did not make great efforts to dig up ancient cities and study their remains. Traditionally, vigorous civilizations have demolished anything whose original use has passed and then built something else on the rubble—or moved their settlements when the conditions changed and dug new foundations for the future. Such attitudes are still with us—maximizing the profitability of land, flattening our High Streets to produce town centres of little individuality and on a scale unfit for the human spirit. We are dragged along into the future in the name of economic growth, of more prosperity and consumer goods, of more mobility and, in general, of progress. Yet why is it that the really worthwhile things—freedom from disease, violence, hunger, aridity of spirit, ignorance and unhappiness—seem to get further away, regardless of what political systems our countries follow, rather than nearer? Our great religions and political theories war with each other instead of co-operating and tolerating. Our science has produced weapons that could end all human life if the wars of ideas became overt and military. If there are more well-fed and healthy people than previously in the developed parts of our globe, there are also more starving and malnourished humans than have ever lived before in the world as a whole.

No wonder we look back to see whether earlier cultures did any better. We may look for clues about what tends towards human happiness and towards the well-being of most people in societies, or we may just indulge ourselves in nostalgia and escapism for a time. But men did not start their search for lost worlds for any of these reasons. Whatever the sense of wonder about unknown lands shown by ancient writers such as Herodotus and Diodorus Siculus, it was the riches of those far kingdoms that gripped their readers. Profit was the motive that drew the European explorers of the fifteenth century towards the unknown; profit through trade and even quicker profit through the plundering of other people's treasure. At first the chief treasure that men looked for was gold and other precious objects, usually to be melted

Previous pages *The 4000-year-old megaliths of Stonehenge remain one of the most baffling and awesome creations of mankind.*

Close-up of a Persepolis relief showing the Persian sculptor's stylized but lovingly detailed treatment of his subject.

Temple mountain in Mesopotamia—the Ziggurat of Ur. Because sun-dried bricks cannot resist water, the Sumerians produced kiln-fired bricks about 5500 years ago and gave such a protective layer to their greatest ziggurat.

down and sold as valuable metal and gemstones in bulk. The legend of El Dorado, the golden city somewhere in South America, haunted men's imaginations. But soon afterwards it became clear that the mines and the farmland of these new worlds were treasure too if they were exploited by settlers, and so the period of European empire building started.

From the start, the harsh exploiters of lands and people were criticized on moral grounds by other Europeans; the Spaniards' savage treatment of the Peruvian and Mexican natives is infamous, but the humanitarian protests in Spain—leading to royal edicts demanding better standards in the colonies—are much less well known. Other civilizing influences were at work, too. From the seventeenth century onwards an increasing interest in science and the arts initiated serious studies by antiquaries of ancient artifacts and buildings. And so, when Napoleon later set out to conquer Egypt, he took a team of artists and archaeologists to study and record the works of the Pharaohs.

The following decades saw the start of a blossoming interest in the most

ancient civilizations, for their remains harmonized well with the mood of the romantic movement. After Pompeii and Egypt, Mesopotamia started to fascinate the Europeans—for city after city emerged from the sand and revealed names familiar from the Old Testament of the Bible. By the end of the nineteenth century readers of illustrated magazines on both sides of the Atlantic were being presented with pictures of the Troy of Homer's *Iliad,* Angkor of the Cambodian empire, and the pyramids of the Maya and Aztec cities. And through the works of Rider Haggard and other novelists a whole romantic fiction of lost cities and lost worlds began to grow up, with explorers and archaeologists figuring as heroes.

Today the romance of lost worlds is still potent in our minds. Archaeologists may be scientists now, rather than adventurers and explorers in the mould of Heinrich Schliemann and Henry Layard—the discoverers of Troy and of Nineveh—but they still become glamorous figures on the television screen. Excavations have become meticulous and the analysis of finds now produces a phenomenal amount of information about those lost cultures. And

Temple mountain in Cambodia—Pre Rup step pyramid temple at Angkor. Built during A.D. 944–68, it was one of the last big Angkor temples to be made of plaster-covered brick. Visible at the foot of the steps is the ubiquitous phallic linga.

as the bulk of our knowledge grows, an overall picture emerges, blurred but with gradually increasing clarity, of the way human beings take the first steps to form the societies which change them from scattered families into organized civilizations—of the pressures which cause them to change, of their early beliefs about divine forces derived from observation of their surroundings, of the ways they invent to feed their increasing numbers, of the early monuments that they build, and of the mistakes that they make.

The 15 lost worlds or cultures described in this book cover a time span of 5000 years and a geographical span right around the world. They have been chosen to represent that spread in time and space, and to show both the wide similarities in many of their origins and buildings and the striking lack of similarity in some cases. The chapters are in a sequence that, in general, follows the sun around the world from Central America across Oceania, Asia and Africa to end in Western Europe and the legendary lost world of Atlantis. The cultures described have a surprising amount in common, either from shared ancestral roots that scattered certain patterns of behaviour and belief or perhaps in part because all areas of the world impose certain similar conditions if human societies are to succeed. Organized farming is an unalterable requirement for the growth of a civilization or culture. Early farmers almost always develop a religion apparently based on the powers of nature around them, but also on certain archetypal concepts apparently implanted in all human beings. Some type of wheat is the basic diet of most early farmers—rice came much later except for the people of the Indus civilization and a few others. Regardless of climate, societies in an early stage of development built frail dwellings for themselves which have often vanished completely, but lasting religious monuments were made of the most durable materials they could devise.

The astonishingly well-preserved baked clay brickwork of Mohenjo-Daro has kept many of the Indus city's walls standing.

The Oba of Benin rides in procession before his palace and city. The spires of the palace were topped by copper bird figures. This engraving from John Ogilby's Africa *(1670) has all the participants in royal pageants including midgets (in front of the Oba), leopards and an ivory horn-blower.*

The first sacred monument in a great many widespread cultures was a natural rock outcrop or a man-made mound—developing later into pyramid, barrow, ziggurat, *stupa, ahu*, stepped temple plinth, or temple mountain—the chamber within often used for burial as part of its role as a magnet for divine benevolence. The background for this sort of monument is probably a creation myth that occurs in varying forms in many parts of the world—as recounted in several chapters of this book—in which a deity places on the limitless seas a floating primeval female mound of earth, which is then pinned into a stable position by a male principle using a staff or some similar implement. Outcrops and chambered mounds are thus re-enactments of the creation, and suitable settings for rituals of death and rebirth. Hence, too, the recurring symbolic vision of a mountain at the centre of the world inhabited by a pantheon of gods that have noticeable similarities whether they are revered in the Americas, Greece or Cambodia. God-kings are another usual phenomenon, always with the responsibility to act as a link between the heavens and the people, and often required to build one of the local form of temple-mounds during each reign to reaffirm that link.

As for their ends, we tend to search for causes of the decline and disappearance of each culture with ominous thoughts about our own and perhaps a little hope that we may learn from their mistakes. Sometimes there may seem to be nothing there to learn—Pompeii was destroyed by a volcano, Angkor and Troy by invading armies, the megalith builders' culture by a change in the weather of all northern Europe. Sometimes the end was voluntary—the people of Zimbabwe simply moved northwards in pursuit of salt. In other cases the civilizations reached a peak and then slowly lost their vigour—Ur had degenerated long before the Euphrates changed its course and made life there impossible. We may feel helpless before such evidence of the cycles of history. But other cultures seem to have caused their own decline. The people of Mohenjo-Daro chopped down all the available trees and so deprived themselves of the timber on which their prosperity depended. The Easter Islanders overfarmed their small land until it became infertile. Here, perhaps, we can learn something.

Alastair Service

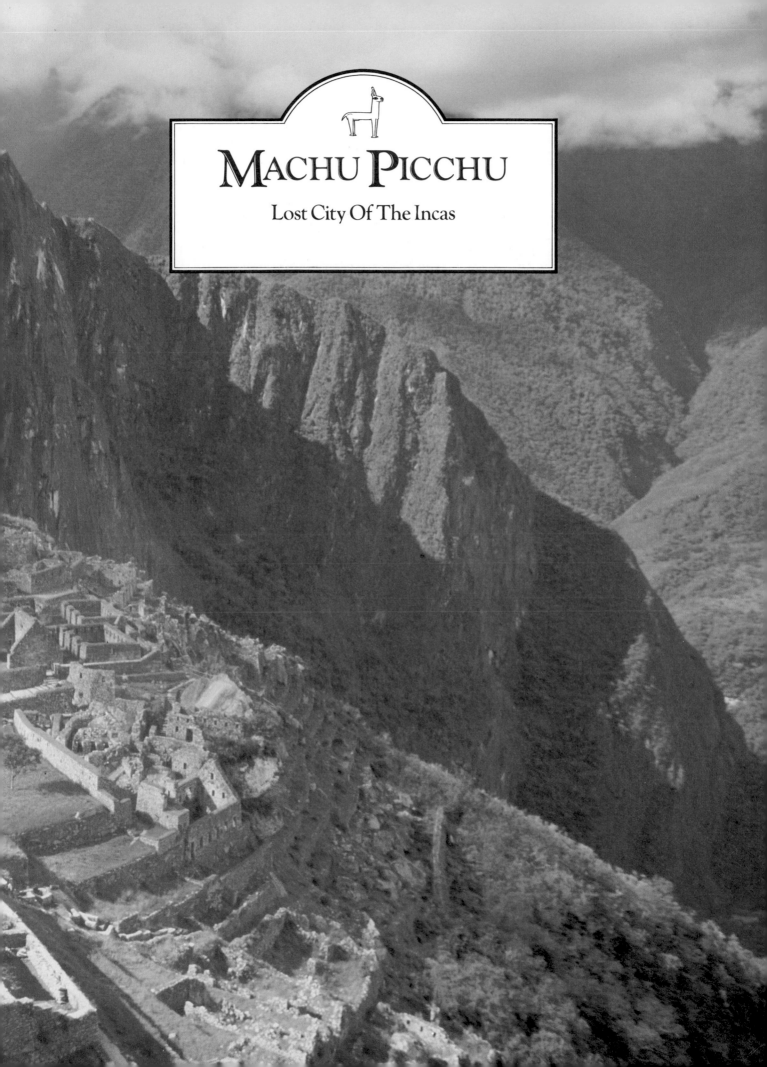

MACHU PICCHU

Lost City Of The Incas

THE SMALL TRAIN to Machu Picchu leaves the Peruvian town of Cuzco, the former highland capital of the Inca empire, early in the morning. Labouring up to a high pass, it crosses and starts the long descent through the valleys of the Andes to the canyon of the Urubamba river. The mountainsides are still stepped with the farming terraces built by the Incas centuries ago, and at the villages where the train stops the bowler-hatted and brightly dressed women, descendants of the Inca peasants, push on to the train to sell exotic breakfasts of their local produce. The mountains close in and the railway runs near to the Urubamba's water until the journey ends at a station where giant peaks rise steeply all around. Here, up a zigzag road that rises 450 metres (1500 feet) to a saddle between two mountains, lie the ruins of Machu Picchu, over 2500 metres (some 8000 feet) above sea level and one of the last retreats of the Inca rulers after the Spanish invasion of Peru in 1532.

It was a secret place, for its position was never recorded in the Spanish chronicles. Legend persisted over the following centuries that a last stronghold of the Incas had existed in the high Andean peaks. The search for the mountain hideout led to the discovery of Machu Picchu in 1911 by the American historian, Hiram Bingham.

Bingham was attracted to Peru by his admiration for Simon Bolivar, liberator of several South American countries from the Spaniards. Almost by chance, he became involved in an expedition into the little-known mountains where the last of the Incas had sheltered. Bingham then became intrigued by the elusive hints in local chronicles of a city called Vilcabamba. He raised funds in the United States by his contagious enthusiasm for the search and returned to Peru with a highly qualified American expedition. Various overgrown Inca sites were identified in the mountains around the Urubamba and Vilcabamba rivers, but the most dramatic moment came when Bingham climbed a precipitous slope with a local resident who had reported that there were remains on the hill. After an exhausting climb 'on all fours, sometimes holding on by our finger-nails', Bingham lay down to rest for some time, discouraged by the sight of nothing but thick vegetation at the top. Then he walked on along the saddle of Machu Picchu and made out, one after another, several stone buildings hidden by the undergrowth. Later, he returned with other expeditions to clear the branches and excavate the ruins.

Bingham concluded, wrongly it now seems, that this fortified town was the Vilcabamba of the persecuted Incas. In fact, the evidence published by the explorer Gene Savoy and also by John Hemming in his book, *The Conquest of the Incas,* suggests that the remote overgrown ruins of Espíritu Pampa, some distance away among the mountains, are those of Vilcabamba.

The significance of Machu Picchu among late Inca towns therefore remains elusive. What is beyond doubt is that the town contains some of the finest and best-preserved examples of Inca building craftsmanship and that it is located in one of the most beautiful settings in the world.

The great Inca civilization followed on from a long succession of different cultures for human settlements in Peru are known to go back to 3000 B.C. The great Chavín culture had flourished in the inland area north of Lima from a thousand years before Christ until the time when the Roman Empire was crumbling in Europe—a period of 1500 years. In the centuries before A.D. 1000 (in the period that saw Maya culture flower in Mexico 2100 kilometres—1300 miles—to the north), there followed the brick temples and skilled gold casting of the Mochica culture in northern Peru, while the people of the Ica-Nazca culture were drawing their gigantic designs—the Nazca lines—in the coastal desert to the south.

Previous pages *Machu Picchu occupies one of the most spectacular sites in the world and remained lost for nearly five centuries.*
The chapter symbol is a an Inca statue of a llama.

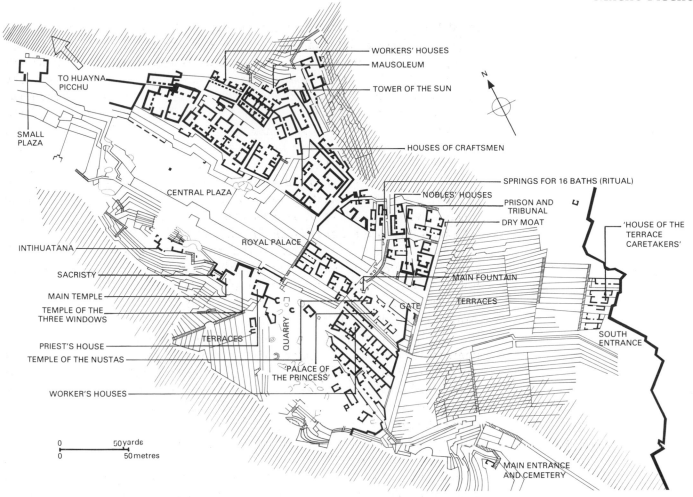

Machu Picchu's compact but intricate layout includes about 150 houses and 16 public baths in an area of 40 hectares (100 acres).

After that, the Tiahuanaco culture spread from the Andean lake of Titicaca throughout southern Peru, starting many of the technical and religious ideas that the Incas later developed. The same can be said of the Chimú people who submerged the Mochica in the north after A.D. 1000 and introduced mass industries, a good road system and a moon worship associated with their high step pyramids. Then, in about A.D. 1400, the Incas started to expand from the area around Cuzco.

According to their own legends, the Incas originated on an island in Lake Titicaca, where the Sun God created their first ruler, Manco Capac. The title of every ruler was the Inca (Son of the Sun God) and hence of the people they ruled. Manco Capac led his people north along the Andes in about A.D. 1000, founded the city of Cuzco and settled the land around it. The indigenous language of the Cuzco area was Quechua and the Incas spread it so effectively wherever they conquered that it still remains the dominant tongue among the Andean Indians.

Although the Inca expansion began earlier, their major empire-building surge started in the early fifteenth century. By 1450 they ruled all the Andes around Cuzco. Northern coastal Peru and southern Ecuador were taken in the years around 1470 and the empire spread into southern Peru, Bolivia and much of present-day Chile 20 years later. It spread farther to the north by the time the Spanish *conquistadores* arrived in 1532—11 years after they had conquered the Aztecs in Mexico. So the culture found by the Europeans was freshly in its prime, only established for half a century in its extended form.

Town is perhaps a more suitable word than city for Machu Picchu, the total area is not very large and the terraced land around the residential area could probably have supported only 500 people in times of strife when the

A llama stands proudly below the semi-circular Temple of the Ñustas, beside the road to the Central Plaza. Not only did the llama provide the Incas with meat, wool and milk but its dried dung was also used as a fuel.

produce of the valley below was not available. All the same, the quality of the architecture and other clues suggest that it *was* special, perhaps a place that their divine ruler, the Inca himself, would visit for short periods.

The approach to the ruins is across the agricultural terraces that occupy one end of the high shoulder of land between the peaks called Machu (old) and Huayna (new) Picchu. Five hundred years ago, the town was linked to the outside world by one of the royal foot-roads. The remains of that road can still be seen running high along the side of the Urubamba canyon, rising and falling in careful gradients. This was a side road in a network that laced the Andes.

The Inca road network spread, and still largely survives, from modern Colombia to Argentina and central Chile. Along the coast, the main north–south road covered 4000 kilometres (2500 miles), mostly across rather flat and arid desert. Dried mud was the only surface it needed, for the Andes draw the rain away from the coastal strip, but the track had walls on both sides to keep off the drifting desert sands.

The other key highway, the royal road of the Andes, is even more impressive. Even today it runs the length of what was once the Inca-dominated section of the vast mountain range for more than 4800 kilometres (3000 miles) through some of the most difficult terrain on earth—from central Chile, through Peru and on to north of Quito in Ecuador. The Andean road is carefully built, with a drainage system, and is stone-paved on those sections where water sometimes flowed across the track. Between the coast and the mountain highways, many roads, 160–320 kilometres (100–200 miles) long, completed the network.

Both of the long north–south roads were wide, unexpectedly so for the Incas did not use mounted animals. Like the other Amerindian peoples, they

had not invented the wheel or any drawn vehicle. On the coastal plain, the standard width was 7.3 metres (24 feet), while the mountain roads varied between 4.6 metres (15 feet) and 5.5 metres (18 feet). Where they crossed swamps, stone causeways were built. Where they met mountain gorges, suspension bridges up to 46 metres (150 feet) long were flung across the gaps, with wooden floors supported by ropes as thick as a man's body.

Llamas and men on foot were the chief travellers on the royal Inca roads and the control posts allowed only authorized traffic to pass. The width of the track had only one justification—in times of war or unrest in the empire, the Inca generals could move large numbers of troops along them at great speed to surprise and overwhelm the enemy. Those armies would be summoned by the messenger runners who, apart from general traders, were the most regular users of the roads.

The royal messengers are one of the most celebrated features of the Inca empire and rightly so, for their relays provided the quickest method of carrying detailed information before the invention of mechanized transport. The system was this. Each highway had a hut every 2.5 kilometres (1.5 miles) along its extent, each hut being occupied by two trained runners from nearby villages. These men kept alternate watch for any approaching runner, working on a rota of 24 hours. When a messenger arrived, he passed on a verbal message and a *quipu* or knotted rope. The *quipu* consisted of a number of coloured strings, each tied to the rope and each knotted in a way that had its own significance. Colour of string, type of knot and placing of the knot all had their own meaning, enabling quite complex information to be sent. But basically the *quipu* recorded numbers, rather than orders or any other verbal messages that accompanied them.

As soon as the next runner had received the *quipu* and the oral message, he

Agricultural terracing and reconstructed peasant houses at Machu Picchu. The grass thatched roofs were fastened with stone pegs fixed to the tall end gables. The terrace walls were built about 5 metres (15 feet) high and covered with a gravel base before soil from the valley was carried up the hillside.

would set off at a near-sprint towards the next hut along the road. Modern experiments on these roads have shown that a fit Peruvian Quechua Indian can still cover such a distance in under ten minutes (remarkable in these altitudes). The Spanish chroniclers plausibly tell of messages carried 2000 kilometres (1200 miles) in five days at heights of over 3000 metres (10,000 feet).

At the time of the Inca empire, terraces on the ridge of Machu Picchu would have been intensively cultivated. Today, the only living reminders are the occasional llamas and alpacas on the stepped levels or stone stairways. These were the main farm animals of early Peruvian people and of the Incas, and the llama in particular was the creature most closely identified with their lives.

The llama was the chief carrier of goods along the Inca highways, it could be eaten and it yielded good warm wool. A remote member of the camel family, the llama can carry a load of about 91 kilograms (200 pounds) for only 16 kilometres (10 miles) a day, but it can do that at any Andean altitude or in low-lying deserts. Its body can store enough water for several days' travel. It does produce usable milk and breeds prolifically.

The alpaca is about half the size of the llama and has a finer wool. But it cannot carry a load, nor can it leave the mountains. It was originally a cross-breed between the llama and the wild vicuña, the agile animal which has such soft wool that only the Inca and his nobles were permitted to wear it.

The seasons in Andean Peru are divided into a long rainy period, from October to April, and dry months, from May until October. During the dry season the Incas would repair or extend their terraces, building the sophisticated irrigation tanks and channels that are so important in such farming. In August the hand-ploughing would start, initiated by the Inca himself at Cuzco and by the local rulers in the provinces of the empire. The men would move backwards in a long row, turning the soil with poles with a foot-platform near the tip, while a row of women followed them, breaking the upturned clods and answering the men's rhythmic chants with their

own—almost everything was done communally in Inca peasant society. First the Inca's royal portion of the land was ploughed, then the portion for the Sun God and finally the terraces freshly apportioned every year to each family according to its number of children.

Many crops were planted in September, and October was a time of waiting to see whether the rain would come. If the weather stayed dry, llamas would be sacrificed, or even human beings on rare occasions. When the rain arrived, there was constant tending of the growing plants until the successive harvests of various crops between February and May. Again, the Inca's and the Sun God's shares were gathered first and stored or despatched to Cuzco. Then the people's own food was harvested, with votive offerings to the local pre-Inca gods before the families could bring home their year's supplies. The food produced by the Inca peasant included a rich variety of vegetables, many later adopted by the Europeans. Over 40 varieties of potato were grown at suitable altitudes and countless types of beans, including the types we call lima and runner. The great staple was maize, in its many forms, and there were other grains and tubers. In the low-lying parts of the empire, there were yams, manioc, sweet potatoes, peanuts, red peppers, pineapples and bread fruit—but it is unlikely that any but the ruling classes of Machu Picchu ever ate those. However, the people invented many ways of using their own local crops. The potatoes could be left out to freeze overnight, then pulped and dried into a flour that would keep indefinitely. Some varieties of maize were also suitable for flour, others for brewing into beer, and others again for eating boiled.

The farmers of the terraces around Machu Picchu had their plots close at hand, unlike some Inca villages. Just beyond the terraces here a flight of broad steps runs down the hillside of the saddle, with irrigation works within the stairway. On the far side of the steps is the wall of the town and from the top of the flight there is a good general view along the whole settlement. The steep slopes fall away to the valleys on both sides of the saddle on which it is built and the horizon is ringed with fierce peaks.

These houses were perhaps the homes of Inca nobles. They are made of the tough local granite shaped with stone hammers and possibly bronze chisels. This masonry is of the regular coursed pattern for important buildings rather than the other irregular, polygonal style. Several typical trapezoidal niches can be seen inside.

19

Above *Gold of the Chimú Empire that ruled in N. Peru for about a century before the coming of the Incas. The top item is a vase in the form of an animal god and the 11.5 cm (4½ in) diameter plate below shows the seed time for different crops round a central figure of the earth goddess.*

Right *Good stairways with drainage channels cut into the steps were essential to the life of Machu Picchu. Over a hundred stairways, some with 150 steps, link the city's many levels.*

From this point it can be seen that the buildings of Machu Picchu were piled up on small slopes on either side of an open plaza which runs, in broad terraces where the level changes, along the middle of the saddle for the whole length of the town. It can also be seen that this was a fortified place, unusually so for Inca towns, although the walls are not high. At the left-hand end of the town wall from this point there is a formal trapezoidal stone gateway where the royal road approached the town; this, the sole main entrance, was barred by a massive wooden gate. That trapezoidal shape—of straight sides tapering towards a narrow top—and the irregular sizes of the big stones that fit together so exactly, were the key themes of Inca architecture.

Machu Picchu has fine examples of Inca building, demonstrating the extraordinary techniques that the craftsmen developed with very primitive tools. The ordinary peasant house can be seen all over the terraces nearest to the main gateway of Machu Picchu. Usually the house was small, built to fit a couple and their children, but here and in other towns there are elongated houses for use by an extended family.

Built normally of rough stone walls, bonded by a liberal smothering of the mud called *adobe,* the peasant house had a roof of thick grass thatch, supported by wooden posts and beams inside. There was only one door and windows were rare; the door could be closed off by letting down a thick cloth suspended in a roll above the lintel. Within, men and women squatted on a floor of compressed earth, for there was no furniture in the European sense—no chairs, tables or beds. A fire in the middle of the floor served for cooking and for warmth, its smoke escaping gradually through the thatch, and the family slept on skins laid on the earth.

Wandering down the stairways connecting the stepped housing terraces of Machu Picchu, one can imagine them thronged with Inca peasants hurrying to the fields at daybreak. The people were, and are, quite short and broad, with huge chests and lungs. Their skin is a light brown, their heads rounded, with slanting eyes and a hooked nose (like most American Indians) in a wide face. Most of the women are muscular and share the men's ability to work or trot for long hours at high altitudes.

The ordinary people wore simple woollen clothes, a rectangular tunic with a head-hole—the men's with armholes too, the women's open at the sides—and belted at the waist. The women always wore shawls fastened with a metal pin. Over these clothes, a cloak of alpaca wool could be worn by both sexes against the cold. Most of them had decorated belts and other ornaments to wear at festivals, when the long hair of both sexes would be put up in complicated arrangements and head-dresses worn.

Discipline was rigid in Inca society from cradle to grave. At the age of 14, a boy put on his loin-cloth, and with it his manhood, with much ceremony. At 20 he was expected to marry. If he had no bride in mind, the *ayllu* (clan) council selected one for him and the couple were expected to start breeding as quickly and prolifically as possible. Among the young, unmarried sexuality was condoned as long as the young man gave help by working for the girl's father. After marriage, the peasants were expected to be monogamous—anyway, the *ayllu* made sure that husbands were worked so hard in gangs of 10 under a foreman that they had little energy for philandering. Ten of these foremen would come under a supervisor who was responsible to the clan chief or *Mallcu,* elected by the council of elders.

There was no conceivable way for the Inca peasant man to break out of his place in the social structure. For women there was just one chance. If a girl was exceptionally talented or attractive she might be taken from home by government officials and brought to Cuzco to become a *Ñusta;* these were the

Chosen Women, the specially educated group from whom the Inca and his nobles could choose wives or concubines.

The male Inca peasant went to work in the fields at dawn without breakfast. He returned in the mid-morning to eat the meal that his wife had prepared among her other household chores. After that he returned to the land, accompanied by the rest of his family at certain times of year. Their evening meal was eaten quite early, at around five o'clock. Then the family would usually gather around its own fire, squatting to listen to tales of their ancestors or the Inca legends and perhaps drinking the maize beer, which the women had prepared for fermentation by long chewing of the grain.

All Inca cooking was done by boiling and the food was served to the men on pottery plates as they squatted on the floor—there might be llama meat or one of the guinea pigs that all households kept running around. Different types of maize and potato gave some variety to the staple vegetables, but there was no escape from boiling as a way of cooking. When the men had finished, the women and children ate. When the *ayllu* chief ordered a village feast, the families brought their own food and squatted in long lines in front of their leader.

Life was very different for the nobles, some of whose dwellings at Machu Picchu were perhaps grouped below the peasant houses, around the building dubiously identified as the Royal Palace. These noble classes of the Incas provided officials who governed the empire at levels higher than the *ayllu* of the peasants. Many *ayllus* formed a district, many districts a region, many regions a 'quarter of the world' of the Incas. Each of these sub-divisions had a noble ruler and, at the top of this administrative pyramid, each 'quarter of the world' was governed by its *Apo,* responsible directly to the Inca himself.

For these ruling classes, life was luxurious but hard working. A noble male child was given a formal education in many things to prepare him for government. After puberty, a boy was given a personal girl of his own age to be his servant and concubine until, at 20, he was married off to a suitable head wife—extra wives were allowed to the nobles, but they were subservient to the first. Aristocratic dress was similar to that of ordinary people, but of softer wool and more richly decorated. The Inca himself wore only the finest robes of special cotton and the silky vicuña wool, sometimes with small feathers of many colours woven into the fabric so that it gleamed iridescently. And he wore each robe only once—they were burned when he took them off.

For the Inca was a god, the direct descendant of the Sun itself and ultimate owner of everything in his empire. His chief wife had to be his sister, so that their sons would keep the divine blood pure. If this was indeed his local palace that faces the central plaza of Machu Picchu, men of all ranks would come into his presence here barefoot and prostrated, carrying some symbolic burden on their backs. His divinity was very real in the minds of his subjects, for the Spaniards recorded that even the highest officials would tremble at his approach.

Every day and year was a ritual sequence for the Inca, from the moment of his coronation in Cuzco with the royal red fringe of wool wrapped round his head and his enthronement on the gold stool. When he travelled to the widespread towns of his empire, such as Machu Picchu, he was carried in a litter decorated with gold and silver, a canopy of jewel-studded gold above his head. These royal processions were made with vast retinues of soldiers, courtiers and Chosen Women. Behind the palace in Machu Picchu, there is a semi-circular temple of cyclopean masonry typical of late Inca work, huge stones of irregular size dressed to fit each other precisely. This temple is generally called the Temple of the Ñustas—from burials found in the hillside caves, Hiram Bingham concluded that Machu Picchu was especially dedicated to these Chosen Women.

Emerging from the Royal Palace into the long central plaza, one is in the heart of the Inca town. This open space probably combined the function of venue for the major festivals with that of market place. Markets were held three times in every lunar month and there was a year-long sequence of religious–cum–agricultural festivals. As there was no money, the markets gave the peasants a chance to barter any of their food, pottery or textiles that were beyond their own needs. In Andean markets they could get goods from the coast or from the Amazon jungle to the east—dried fish, seaweed food, dyestuffs, reeds, bright jungle feathers, rubber, cotton and the herbs and roots for their medicines.

The market days might be used for the announcement of royal decrees. If the day fell on one of the important festivals, there would be athletic games—uphill races and mock battles were popular—and ritual ceremonies. Men and women alike got drunk on the maize beer during these rites, as the Chosen Women danced or the priests led the assembly in hypnotic repetitive chants and shuffling dances until a state of ecstasy was reached.

At the core of Inca religion was the creator-god Viracocha. He had many titles and although he lived in the heavens, was believed to become visible at times of crisis. At the beginning of time, Viracocha created a dark Earth. Then he made a series of supernatural objects which themselves became deities—he lit the world by making the divine Sun and Moon rise out of an island on Lake Titicaca, formed the great Ocean and other things, then made mankind like himself and animals in many forms. Viracocha's great journey carrying his mighty staff, which follows in the myth, was marked by many incidents celebrated in Inca ceremonies and monuments, and after that he walked away across the Pacific.

For Inca men and women, the divine servants of the god played a greater

The Temple of the Three Windows. Excavation found nothing inside but the Central Plaza below was dotted with pieces of pottery. Were these offerings to the gods thrown through the windows?

The main temple of Machu Picchu, built of superbly cut ashlar. There is no evidence to suggest that this or any other temple in the city was roofed.

The distinctive Temple of the Ñustas built up from the natural granite behind the Royal Palace with each course of masonry smaller than the one below.

part in life than the creator himself. The Sun was the chief of these, but the female Moon and Earth, the Thunder, the Star gods and others were also important. In any case, religion as it affected ordinary people was apparently more a matter of divine organization of the farming and feast–day calendar, rather than of individual worship.

The chief religious buildings of Machu Picchu lie on and beside the hillock left of the main plaza, right above the gathering place. The main group of temples includes the so-called Temple of the Three Windows. The group consists of three large U-shaped enclosures of stone around a level space. The fourth side of this space drops away in a series of terraces, with a spectacular view of the valleys and the Andes beyond.

The enclosures show late Inca irregular cyclopean masonry at its most impressive, though the buildings are small compared with the great temples, palaces and fortresses of Cuzco. At the Inca capital, the fitted stones go up to a weight of 61 tonnes for a single carved rock. All these stones were quarried by pegs of wood that were driven into faults in the rockface and swollen with water. The stones were transported with rollers and levers, and the blocks were dressed with chisels of harder stone (despite the fact that the Incas could work metal). The bottom storeys of large buildings were always of solid stonework, the upper floors often *adobe* on a stone core, the roofs invariably of thatch. Paper and writing were unknown to the Incas, so their architects designed buildings by making models in clay. Literacy is not a requirement for precision engineering and design.

There is no sign that the temples were ever roofed; it seems more likely that they were built open to the sky and to the Sun God. We do not know the nature of the rites that took place here, but the architectural forms stir the imagination as one looks around the sacred place. As elsewhere, the stones are large near the ground, rising to smaller courses higher up. The Incas' favourite trapezium shape is everywhere—in the inward-leaning walls themselves, in the niches within those walls and in the unusual feature of the three windows punched right through the side of one temple.

The terraced hillock at whose foot the temples stand was itself probably part of the religious centre, for on top of it is an intriguing monument. Beside a small masonry temple, the bedrock emerges at the peak of the little hill and has been carved into a series of irregular steps rising to an almost square pillar. This was Machu Picchu's *intihuatana,* the hitching post of the Sun. Each year in June, when the sun reached its lowest point, an important rite in the Inca calendar was performed. With a gold chain fastened around the pillar of solid rock, a priest would ceremonially leash the sun to the Inca land to ensure that it did not fail to return on its journey up the sky again. We may imagine the crowds waiting in the long plaza below to make sure that the tying was properly accomplished. And we may imagine the drunken rejoicing when it was done, for the Incas thought mass intoxication the proper way to express communal joy!

On the far side of the main plaza from the *intihuatana,* another hill rises

The strange 'hitching post of the Sun' or intihuatana. *On the longest day of the year an Inca priest would 'leash' the sun to this rock with a gold chain as part of the festival of Inti Raymi. The pillar could also have been a sundial.*

with the remains of rows of houses and other buildings upon its terraced sides. On the far side of this hill the ground slopes gently away before, at the edge of the town, plunging almost vertically to the valley 450 metres (1500 feet) below. Here, it seems, was the monument Hiram Bingham stumbled on first when he discovered Machu Picchu. Among the bamboo thickets and dense trees, he suddenly found himself beside 'a semicircular building whose outer wall, gently sloping and slightly curved, bore a striking resemblance to the famous Temple of the Sun in Cuzco. . . . It followed the natural curvature of the rock and was keyed to it by one of the finest examples of masonry I have ever seen. . . . It fairly took my breath away. What could this place be?'

The rounded, so-called Tower of the Sun is roughly horseshoe-shaped and stands within a rectangular court formed by three walls of high masonry. These walls are pierced by trapezoidal niches, windows and a doorway facing the open side of the tower within the court. A window in the tower and the unwalled side of the court face out over the abyss of the deep valley and roughly east towards the rising sun.

The special importance of the Tower of the Sun is obvious, for it stands on a particularly sacred spot. Close beside the tower an opening leads into a rock-cut mausoleum beneath the building. The cave is cut into complex shapes, with a throne of solid rock and several cells opening off the main area. The tomb had been robbed when archaeologists examined it, but the position, the tower above and the fact that the internal walls of the cave were carefully encased in thin stone slabs are all indications that it was someone of very high rank.

Death was regarded in a very particular way by the Incas. An afterlife in a different dimension was assured, but for a long time after breathing ceased, the dead man or woman was felt to be present but unseen. If he was not to trouble those who lived on, his departure had to be marked with dance and chanting by the whole *ayllu*. When at last the spirit moved on to the next life, the body was wrapped in a shroud and entombed, sitting in the foetal position, in a hillside chamber with other dead members of the *ayllu*. His or her personal possessions and tools were arranged around the body.

Ceremonies were more complicated for the nobility, and for the Inca himself, the god king, the ritual was extraordinary. Upon his coronation, each Inca built himself a personal palace near the centre of Cuzco. When he died, that palace became his tomb. The dead king's body was embalmed and mummified, with its viscera stored in sealed jars. Then a prolonged feast was held, during which everyone became ritually drunk and the entire royal household of servants and women were strangled. A gold statue of the ruler was seated upon the royal stool in his palace, with the mummy and the remains of his household around it. Then the palace was sealed for ever—or rather until the Spaniards arrived and sacked every one of these sacred monuments.

So the mausoleum under the Tower of the Sun at Machu Picchu was not the resting place of any of the Inca emperors before the Spanish invasion. Yet it was an exceptional tomb and the discovery of two more cave–cemeteries down the mountainside gave rise to further speculation. For these tombs contained a total of about 100 bodies, 90 of which were women. Were they Sun priestesses, people wondered, or were they the Chosen Women of an Inca? We shall probably never know, but one intriguing possibility remains. After the Spanish leader Pizarro had the Inca Atahualpa executed in 1533 upon payment of an enormous ransom of a room filled with gold and silver, the throne went to a younger half-brother called Manco. The tale of Manco's resistance to the Spaniards is a heroic and tragic one.

A seventeenth century engraving of the luckless Inca Atahualpa. He wears the red royal fringe of wool round his head and the sun-disc on his chest. Atahualpa was garrotted by the Spaniards in Cajamarca's main square supposedly for plotting with an Inca army outside.

A few months after his accession as Inca, Manco appeared with thousands of foot soldiers and surrounded a handful of Spanish horsemen whom Pizarro was leading through the mountains to capture Cuzco. But Manco bargained with the Spaniards and soon found himself a captive monarch forced to watch while his false allies plundered the capital. He escaped and, mustering an army of perhaps 100,000 soldiers, vanished into the almost impenetrable Andes between the Vilcabamba and Urubamba rivers.

One day he suddenly reappeared outside Cuzco with his huge army. In the long siege and battles that followed, the Spaniards came near to defeat. But Manco could not retake the city and in the end he returned to the mountains to fight a guerrilla war from his new capital, Vilcabamba. That war continued for many years, to the frustration of the Spaniards. Then in 1541, Pizarro was assassinated by fellow *conquistadores* and Manco offered his protection to some of those who had killed the murderer of Atahualpa. He used these men to train his soldiers in Spanish fighting methods, but in time they became bored. Thinking that the death of Manco might bring them a pardon for that of Pizarro, they killed the last great Inca in 1544 over a game of cards. Three more Incas reigned before Vilcabamba was sacked and its last ruler dragged to execution at Cuzco in 1572, but Manco's death had marked the end of effective Inca resistance.

The Spanish chronicles say that Manco's body was embalmed amid great mourning by his people and taken to Vilcabamba. Nothing is said of his burial place and it may be that his tomb will be discovered if ever the true Vilcabamba is positively identified and excavated. But, looking out over the mountain tops from beside the Tower of the Sun and its mysterious mausoleum at Machu Picchu, the thought is irresistible that this was perhaps a worthy last resting place for that ill-fated hero.

The interior of Machu Picchu's mausoleum beneath the Tower of the Sun. Its position and design single it out as the tomb of some unknown high-ranking Inca. There are many other tombs inside and outside the city, natural caves often adapted by stone masons.

CHICHEN ITZA

Maya Ruins In The Yucatan Jungle

THE IMMENSE sacred *cenote* or Well of Sacrifice, just outside Chichén Itzá in south-east Mexico, lies at the heart of our picture of the Maya civilization. The Franciscan friar, Diego de Landa, told of his own visit to Chichén in a book written in 1566. Landa wrote of the stone causeway running from the plaza to the *cenote* 'about two stones' throws away. Into this well they have, and had then, a custom of throwing living men as a sacrifice to the gods in times of drought . . . they also threw a great many other things into it, such as precious stones and highly valued objects'. The modern legend that grew from such tales is of regular human sacrifice of beautiful Indian virgins, hurled off a cliff into the lake below.

The *cenote* is in reality an eerie place. It covers almost half a hectare (1 acre) and from its tree-covered edges the sheer limestone cliffs drop some 20 metres (65 feet) down to the water below. As a source of water in the dry Yucatán northern area, it was doubtless the original reason for the settlement here. But for perhaps a thousand years up to the Spanish conquest it was used chiefly for ritual purposes, the spiritual core of a great Maya sacred centre and the centre of pilgrimages from other parts of the Yucatán. The waters below look melancholy today and it is easy to imagine the victims and ritual objects dropping down from the small ruined temple on one side. So it must have seemed to the American, Edward Thompson, who started to dredge it in 1904.

Thompson was a strange character with an extraordinary life story. Trained as an engineer in Massachusetts, his imagination was lit by the idea of the Maya ruins as an outpost of the lost continent Atlantis. An article he wrote in a magazine attracted a backer who gave him money to visit the Yucatán and, almost unbelievably, the appointment as American Consul. Apart from fund-raising visits to the USA, Thompson stayed there from 1885 for over 40 years. He even persuaded one backer to purchase for him the ranch that included the ruins of Chichén Itzá. In the end the Mexican government confiscated the ranch as compensation for smuggled archaeological treasures and Thompson died penniless back in his own country. But by then his work was done. Apart from the discovery of some of the monuments smothered by vegetation, his lasting achievement was to reveal the reality behind the legend of the *cenote*.

With a derrick on the edge of the cliff and a dredge bucket, Thompson and 30 Indian workmen dragged up load after load of mud. During the first week in February 1904, two human bones were extracted. More bones, pottery and other objects followed. In December the first of many small gold figurines were found .Five years later the mud had been cleared to 12 metres (40 feet) deeper than the previous bottom of the pool and Thompson started to go down in a diving suit feeling along the crevices of the rock.

The true extent of Thompson's finds from the sacred *cenote* will never be known. He did not keep careful records and the objects were raided by tourists and others. The worst of these robbers was an Austrian engineer who lived nearby. This man, Teobert Maler, was obsessed with the notion that he was the true owner of the *cenote* treasure. He raided the discoveries frequently and his booty was never recovered. Later, his written complaint to the government helped to get Thompson thrown out. Thompson himself was far from blameless, for the deal with his financial backers involved payment of sorts, and visitors to Chichén Itzá returned to the USA with countless little packets over the years. Many of the objects in those packets can be seen today in the Peabody Museum at Harvard University in Massachusetts.

Over the years the dredge had brought up from the mud a variety of copper bells, stone chisels, ceremonial masks and weapons, many of which

Previous pages Chichén Itzá's Temple of the Warriors and the unique Court of the Thousand Columns stand in the middle of the Yucatan jungle.
The chapter symbol is a seated statue of Chac, the Maya rain god, with his offering bowl. More than a dozen such Toltec statues survive at Chichén Itzá, dating from the tenth century onwards.

Right The widely spread buildings of Chichén Itzá covering 10 square kilometres (4 square miles), clearly show it to have been a cult centre and not a conventional city.

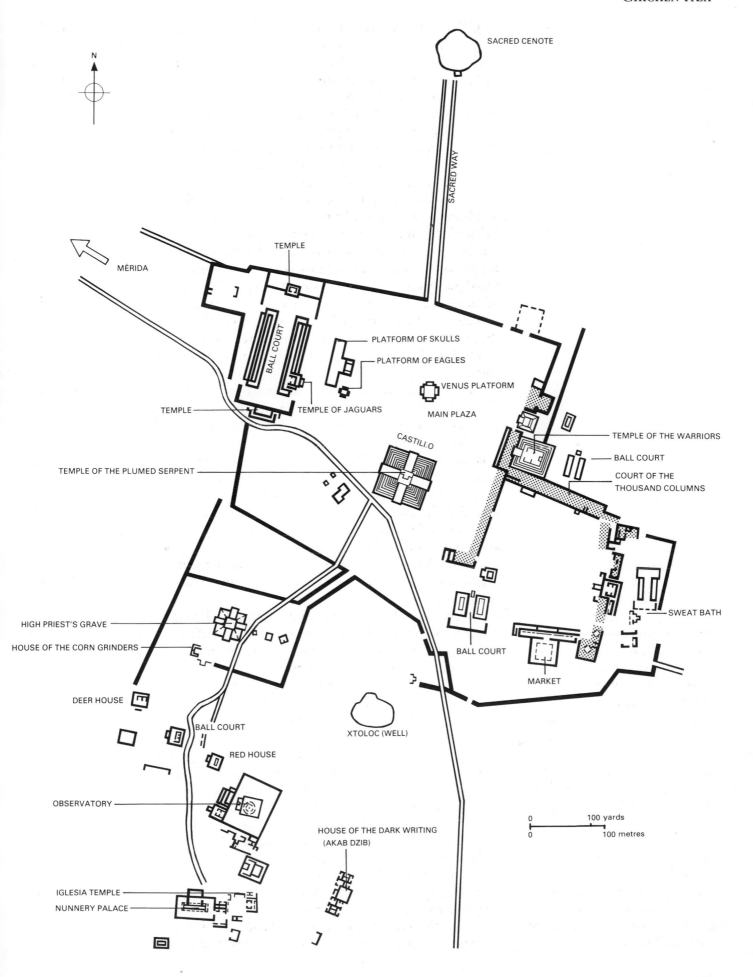

SACRED CENOTE

N

MÉRIDA

SACRED WAY

TEMPLE

PLATFORM OF SKULLS

PLATFORM OF EAGLES

BALL COURT

VENUS PLATFORM

TEMPLE

TEMPLE OF JAGUARS

MAIN PLAZA

CASTILLO

TEMPLE OF THE PLUMED SERPENT

TEMPLE OF THE WARRIORS

BALL COURT

COURT OF THE
THOUSAND COLUMNS

HIGH PRIEST'S GRAVE

SWEAT BATH

HOUSE OF THE CORN GRINDERS

BALL COURT

DEER HOUSE

MARKET

BALL COURT

XTOLOC (WELL)

RED HOUSE

OBSERVATORY

HOUSE OF THE DARK WRITING
(AKAB DZIB)

0   100 yards

0   100 metres

IGLESIA TEMPLE

NUNNERY PALACE

Above *A page from one of the three surviving Maya books. They were written on long strips of bark (deerskin was also used) and pounded into thin sheets to be stuck back to back. Both sides were coated in white lime for strength and as a base for painting. Pages were stuck together to form a folding book which was read in columns from top to bottom and left to right. Between the gods on this page, dealing with the 260-day religious year, are the glyphs (picture letters). Above them the dots and dashes are numbers (a dash=5). Maya writing still resists full decipherment; only a quarter of the 800 glyphs have been read.*

Right *The Castillo step pyramid seen from the forecourt of the Temple of Jaguars. The Jaguar was the symbol of the sun in the underworld and thus of the night.*

had been ritually broken before being sacrificed in the *cenote*. But the interest centred on the small gold figurines—formed from imported gold for there is no ore in the Yucatán—and on the human bones. These were from the skeletons of 8 adult women, 13 men and 21 children. Even allowing that as many skeletons again remained unfound or were smashed in the dredging, a total of less than 100 people over many centuries tells of human sacrifice as a rare event, perhaps for extreme crises. Nor is it clear whether these bones date from the Maya period at Chichén, or from the following period when the fierce Toltec from the north ruled the city and its ancient race.

A walk through Chichén Itzá is a journey through most of Maya history. The present road from Mérida, the modern capital of the Yucatán, divides the city into two. In general, the older Maya part lies to the south of the road, while the larger-scale Toltec buildings are to the north and so nearer to the sacred *cenote*. The ruined buildings are spread over an area of 10.4 square kilometres (4 square miles), with the main centre running 800 metres (880 yards) from north to south. Many of the ruins are still covered with bushes, but when the Spaniards arrived here in the sixteenth century most were well maintained by the people who remained from the high civilization of their ancestors.

The Spaniards moved into Maya territory comparatively late, for it was 1521 before they felt they had completed the subjugation of the Aztecs in the main part of Mexico to the north. They were in no hurry, for they did not expect to find great stocks of gold in the Maya lands. In this they were right, for gold was not used in Central America until around A.D. 1000, well after the end of the Classic Maya period. The Spanish conquerors found a land measuring some 800 by 650 kilometres (500 by 400 miles), inhabited by perhaps one or two million people. In 1545 some Franciscan friars arrived in the Yucatán to claim for Christ these long-lost tribes of human beings—or were they really human, it was debated? Four years later, the young friar, Diego de Landa, whose description of the *cenote* has already been mentioned, joined the mission. Fascinated though he was by the Maya life that he recorded so carefully, Landa was to supervise the worst atrocities on those people and the destruction of almost all their marvellous books.

The terrible burnings at Mani were the climax of the friars' campaign of 1562 against the Indians' relapse into paganism. After initial successes in imposing Christianity, the missionaries gradually discovered that their converts had countless idols hidden away. Landa, now in a position of high authority, began an investigation. He suspected that the ancient books, called codices, which the Maya treasured, illustrated with pictures of deities and written in a script of which he understood little, were cult objects too. At Mani, the Maya were tortured, maimed and even driven to suicide in the search for the idols and the books. The statues were smashed. As for the books, Landa coolly wrote later: 'we burned all of them, which they lamented to an amazing degree and which caused them great suffering'. Of all the codices, which told the story of the Maya race and its chronology, only three are known to survive today. The destruction at Mani completed the slow death of the Maya culture. After that, western civilization almost lost sight of its existence for over two and a half centuries, while the jungle grew over the great ruins of the Yucatán.

It was Jean Frédéric Waldeck's book *Voyage Pittoresque et Archéologique* (published in Paris in 1838), and John Lloyd Stephens' *Incidents of Travel in Central America, Chiapas and Yucatán* (New York, 1841), which awoke interest again. Stephens was an American diplomat and amateur archaeologist. With the English architect-artist Frederick Catherwood, he made two spectacular

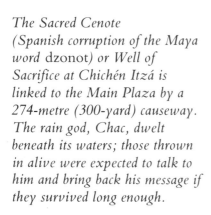

The Sacred Cenote (Spanish corruption of the Maya word dzonot) *or Well of Sacrifice at Chichén Itzá is linked to the Main Plaza by a 274-metre (300-yard) causeway. The rain god, Chac, dwelt beneath its waters; those thrown in alive were expected to talk to him and bring back his message if they survived long enough.*

expeditions to the Maya lands. He visited, and Catherwood sketched, the widely scattered sacred cities of Copán, Palenque, Uxmal and Chichén Itzá—all the most famous Maya centres except Tikal, an important site in the Maya lowlands. Stephens marvelled at the savagely steep and densely jungled country in which the Maya had built their cities. He came to realize, rightly, that these were not cities in the European sense. Stephens found no houses for ordinary people, no shops, no offices or commercial sectors. They were, in fact, sacred gathering places for the farmers in the surrounding region, consisting of a huge plaza of complicated form with various religious buildings around it. The people would journey there for the year's great religious festivals and perhaps for important market-days or council meetings. At other times the vast buildings and courts of these centres, such as Chichén Itzá, were empty except for the priests and some of the nobles.

It is difficult to identify anything at Chichén of the very earliest Classic Maya stage, for the monuments were rebuilt, or added to, many times. The first hunter-gatherers traced in the Yucatán are thought to have come there as long ago as 8000 B.C., but it was about 500 B.C. before the Maya culture became identifiable and 800 years later that its high period, the so-called Classic period, started. In A.D. 423 the Maya began to build Chichén, the greatest of their northern cities, in the comparatively level country of that part of the Yucatán. Some of the finest buildings (not necessarily the largest) date from the three centuries following A.D. 600, before the warlike Toltec arrived, a time when Europe was plunged in its Dark Ages.

The group of Classic period, purely Maya, buildings at Chichén is at the southern end of the complex—the opposite end from the sacred *cenote*. The most famous of the group are the so-called Nunnery palace, the Red House, the Caracol observatory and the small temple dubbed the Iglesia by the Spaniards.

The Iglesia is a small rectangular gem of a building, with bare stone walls at ground level, but rising to a deep sculpted frieze, then to a highly decorated roof 'comb'. These combs, carved ridges or free-standing walls of stone on the very top of buildings, are one of the great features of Maya architecture. Other characteristics are the high friezes of sculpture, the subdivision of decorated areas of wall into boldly defined quadrangular sections, and of course the typically terraced or stepped compositions of palaces and pyramid–temples. On the structural side, the Maya used well–dressed masonry, the stones cemented together and sometimes faced with stucco—they are exceptional among early American cultures in developing the use of cement. They employed the column and the pillar, and they built a variety of sophisticated corbelled arches without ever quite achieving a true keystoned arch.

The style of the Iglesia—and of the Red House, 183 metres (200 yards) further north—is called Puuc, for it grew up in the Puuc hills around Uxmal to the west of Chichén. The difference between the relative restraint of this Puuc style and the elaborate overall carving of its contemporary, the Chenes style, can be seen by comparing the Iglesia with the neighbouring annex to the Nunnery palace. This palace, which is also called the Monjas, is the largest of the Classic Maya buildings at Chichén, a tremendous 61-metre (200-foot) sweep of lower level, with massive walls and broad ramps of steps that rise to two further storeys. This may have been the early centre of the religious city and the setting for many of the rites to mark the year's important festivals.

In Classic Maya times the religion behind those rites had grown from man's general early concern with sustaining the order of nature into a complex system of personalized gods. Each of these gods apparently represented a natural force. Thus Kinich Ahau was the sun god and Chac the god of rain. Ah Mun was the important maize god, the reflection of the staple food of the Maya. Ek Chuah stood for merchants, Cizin for death and Ix Chel was the moon goddess. Each of these had a dual nature—good-evil, day-night, hot-cold and the like.

The small temple called the Iglesia with its rain god masks at the top and part of the Nunnery Palace to the right. Devout Spanish conquistadores in the sixteenth century thought the latter building was a convent.

The idea of an afterlife, in which everyone expected paradise, was important to the Maya, for there was no concept of social progress in their fixed society. They saw themselves very much as fitting into the balance of nature and so the appropriate gods had to be appeased for every act that disturbed other parts of that balance—even for the clearing of the forest for their maize fields.

The work of maintaining the natural order and its seasonal cycles was entrusted to a caste of priests. It was the priests' responsibility to fast and shed their own blood in the damp chambers within the temples for many days before the great festivals, then to conduct the ceremonies that would ensure the sequence of harvests, rainy seasons and the next cycle of the sun.

The priestly caste was an exclusive one and held a number of key roles in Maya society. To prepare for the festivals the priests decided on the appropriate ceremonies and sacrifices and performed them when the time came. To determine what rites were needed, they were learned in an abstruse system of astrology. At their astronomical observatory they prepared the most intricate calendars of past and future. They were the community's prophets and healers, with a wide knowledge of herbal and root remedies. Their voices were heard in civil debates and, by disposing of the cocoa harvest, they controlled the economy.

When the cocoa beans were gathered, they were delivered to the priests. Drinking chocolate was and still is a prized luxury in Central America and, while most of the beans were used for trade, the priests made sure that enough was kept for their own ritual cups of the drink. There is evidence to suggest that they took the hallucinogenic drug, *peyote,* too, perhaps as an aid to their prophetic powers.

As with other ranks in the Maya social structure, the priests were an hereditary class. They handed on their knowledge to their sons, who had to undergo novices' trials that included walking across red-hot coals. To prevent excessive inbreeding, the caste of priests intermarried with the nobles. These two castes provided an equivalent to the European church and state peerage at a social level between the supreme ruler of each community, who was both priest and noble, and the great mass of the ordinary people.

It was almost impossible to move from one level to another in Maya societies. There were a small number of artisan families, but the majority of the population consisted of agricultural peasants, living in organized village communities and giving occasional service to help build the latest of the great religious buildings, which the priests required in their sacred city. The skilled craftsmen doubtless supervised the design and construction of these monuments and the carving of the huge sculptural panels of figures or hieroglyphs. The engineering skill of these craftsmen varied a great deal. In some of the Maya buildings the mass of masonry shows an absurdly over-cautious approach to the roofing of chambers. In others, the use of columns and corbelled arches is very adventurous and light.

The roads built by the Maya were certainly daring and titanic in scale. The most notable example still exists and is the 96.5-kilometre (60-mile) causewayed stone road that starts at Coba and ends a few kilometres from Chichén Itzá. It is 9 metres (30 feet) wide and the road surface is 61 cm (2 feet) above ground for most of its length, rising to 2.4 metres (8 feet) in swamps or floodland. The big blocks of stone were cemented together and the road was apparently surfaced with cement as well. There are many other shorter stretches of road of this standard, one of them 29 kilometres (18 miles) long in a dead straight line. But what were they used for? The Maya had no wheeled vehicles and used no animals to pull loads. Men of importance were some-

Right Chichén Itzá's Observatory or Caracol likened by one archaeologist to a double-layer wedding cake put on top of its box. Archaeologists have used the Observatory to confirm the outstanding accuracy of Maya astronomical calculations which appear to have been made over a period of 384 years.

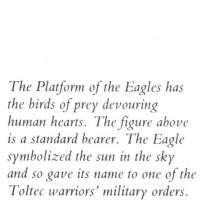

The Platform of the Eagles has the birds of prey devouring human hearts. The figure above is a standard bearer. The Eagle symbolized the sun in the sky and so gave its name to one of the Toltec warriors' military orders.

times carried in litters, but a good path serves better for that than a wide hard road. The date of these roads has not been precisely established, but they were probably built in the late Classic Maya period of A.D. 600 to 900, or perhaps early in the time of Toltec occupation.

The same approximate date can probably be given to the next major building moving north from the Nunnery palace through the ruins of Chichén Itzá. This, the Caracol observatory, has been a controversial building for archaeologists. For the Caracol is the most important of the observatories that stand as monuments to the Maya priests' study of time and the celestial bodies. Their view of time seems to have been very different from ours. It was seen in blocks or repeating cycles, rather than in a line stretching from the past into the future. Their calendar was of 365 days, made up of 18 months of 20 days, plus five odd days to complete it. Apart from this yearly cycle, they saw longer cycles of 52 years, complicated by other cycles of eclipses. These patterns were explored as far back as 400,000,000 theoretical years, and as far forward as 4000 years. Many of their books and the carved pillars, called *stelae* by archaeologists, were devoted to recording these blocks of time past and time future.

The object of these vast intellectual efforts is fairly clear. If time had repeating patterns, then it is reasonable to suppose that any stage of one period may share certain characteristics with the same stage of another. They came to see each day as being in a sense a god with a particular personality, who was carried through his course by a 'porter', again divine and with his own individual nature. Some were benign, others evil. If their return could be foreseen, so could good and bad times. And so the cycles of the sun, moon and planets must be observed and projected into the future.

The Caracol observatory, where the movements of the celestial bodies were recorded at Chichén, is a round tower on a giant three-stage platform whose detail is reminiscent of the Nunnery palace. The tower is climbed by a stairway that circles around it. In the chamber at the top there are sight-lines for sunrise on Midsummer Day and at the equinoxes, due east, as well as the other three cardinal points of the compass. Much of the architectural ornament on the tower, especially the serpent sculpture of the stairway rail, is in the Toltec style, so the tower of the observatory was at least embellished in their time, if not entirely built then.

Several hundred metres north of the Caracol lies a comparatively small temple-pyramid, named the High Priest's Grave by Edward Thompson, who extricated it from the jungle before he started work on the dredging of the cenote. Thompson discovered the entrance to this pyramid and made his way to a rock-cut chamber within, where he found five graves.

A little further east there is Chichén's other natural well, called the Xtoloc cenote, and one of the city's nine courts for playing the famous ball game which is described later. Beyond that is the so-called Market and the Court of the Thousand Columns unearthed by John Lloyd Stephens on his second expedition in 1842.

This is the part of the city thought to have been used for the more secular part of the Maya's activities during the major festivals. In this wide space many hundreds of people probably gathered to barter their produce and artefacts. They came here from the farming villages, which they had cleared from the forest for many kilometres around. Doubtless they travelled to Chichén in groups, for the Maya peasantry—which was certainly well over 90 per cent of the population—did everything in teams. There were teams to cut back the jungle and dig up the roots from the fields, teams to sow and reap the maize, teams to go hunting and teams to work on their priests' building projects.

In the villages of adobe huts with high thatched roofs, much the same today as they were then, the families brought up their children with a strictness that eliminated all signs of individualism. Births were occasions for village festivities, especially if a boy was born, for it was a male dominated society. On reaching manhood, each boy went through a trial lasting for weeks, shut in the cold stone cells deep inside the temples and instructed to wound himself so that he shed blood for the gods. Then, at the right moment, he was released into the daylight and his new adult world, reborn out of the darkness.

Just as the social hierarchy—priest and noble, craftsman, then peasant—was set and unchangeable from generation to generation, so the newly-wedded man went into a married life full of unbendable rules. The husband headed the household, laboured in the fields, hunted and took part in the village council. The woman started the day by making pancakes—called tortillas—from the blessed maize, boiled the black beans, ate after her husband had eaten, washed the cotton clothes and cleaned the hut. After her household labour was finished, she joined the other village women in the communal weaving of cotton cloth, the great creative outlet of Maya female society. Fine muslins and brocades were produced by these peasant societies, tie-dyed to achieve subtle effects.

The most spectacular of the textiles which these women produced, however, were not for them to wear. Peasant women were expected to dress very quietly in a skirt and oblong length of cotton cloth pierced for their head and arms. The fine clothing was reserved for the men. The usual male dress was a length of cloth wound between the legs and around the waist to form a tail of material in front, while the ubiquitous poncho was worn on the

Principal gods in the Maya pantheon. Itzamna, the chief deity (itzam means 'lizard' in Maya) who was god of the heavens as well of night and day, sits above Ah Mun the maize god holding a leafy maize plant.

Chac, the much sculpted rain god, sits in front of the Temple of Warriors at the top of the four-stage building (see picture on pages 28-29 and caption on page 30). It has been suggested that the offering bowl in his lap was for human hearts. One of the pair of magnificent serpent columns rises tail first behind him.

shoulder when not in use. The splendour of the material depended on occasion and social class.

Most classes practised the flattening of boys' heads by a board tied on top and behind. A flattened top to the head was part of the Maya criterion of beauty—male beauty, for female loveliness would have been a strange concept for them. They were, and are, a broad and rather squat people, with fleshy, hooked noses and wide cheek-bones. But if one can abandon European ideas of beauty, the handsome strength of Maya ideals can be appreciated. Their insistence on a pronounced squint of the eyes, often achieved by hanging a pendant from a child's forehead, makes this appreciation rather more difficult.

Body tattooing was another decoration favoured by the Maya. The peasants usually had small tattoos, but an aristocrat would often be patterned all over his body and his penis would be highly decorated. His clothing might include jaguar skins, fine textiles and feathers, topped by a fantastic head-dress and set off by artificial teeth of jade.

This description of Maya society and appearance is based on contemporary accounts by Spanish soldiers and missionaries in the sixteenth century, and it should be remembered that the Maya had then been under foreign domination by people from northern Mexico for many centuries. Mysteriously, after the great Classic period of about A.D. 400–800, the Maya abandoned the city around the year 900. They reoccupied and rebuilt it in A.D. 964, but were conquered 23 years later by the Toltec from the north.

The Toltec invaders were members of a noble family called the Itzá, who had left their native highland capital of Tula in northern Mexico after a period of internal struggle. These Toltec were a creative people, who, rather than destroy the old religious buildings, added to the sacred Maya city of Chichén. But they were a much more bloodthirsty people than the Maya, and it is likely that many of the ferocious rites attributable to the older culture were in fact introduced by the new rulers.

The new ceremonial centre of the city, now called Chichén Itzá after the Toltec family, was built in the area between the sacred *cenote* to the north and the Maya buildings to the south. Its great buildings, on a much grander scale than the Maya works, are grouped around a broad space known as the Main Plaza. Of this first Toltec, or Post-Classic, period after A.D. 987, the surviving buildings include the structures seen around the Market, the first floor of the Temple of the Jaguars (which almost amounts to a copy of the main temple in the Itzás' native city of Tula), the inner pyramid now under the Castillo and the Temple of the Warriors.

The Temple of the Warriors, with the magnificent colonnades of the Court of the Thousand Columns beside it, is one of the great works of Central American architecture. It is less dramatic than the tall Maya pyramids, but it has a spacious splendour of proportion that makes it particularly memorable. The temple rises in four stages, approached by a vast central flight of steps. On top of the wide step-pyramid is one of the largest covered temples built by American Indian civilizations. Its stuccoed timber roof has rotted and collapsed during the centuries of desertion, but the pillars of the interior and the feathered-serpent carvings of the stone entrance are finely executed and well preserved. (Curiously, the precise symbolism of the plumed serpent, found so widely in Mexico, has never been conclusively agreed.) The temple-pyramid complex here is strikingly like the pyramid of Quetzalcóatl at Tula, but the Itzá certainly outdid that model in the version they built at Chichén. Inside the pyramid is an earlier building, which may have been the first building put up by the Toltec after they established their capital here—its platform-altar, supported by 19 sculpted figures, was moved up to the rear of the top temple

Ek Chuah, the black god of merchants and of cocoa (the currency of all Middle America) with his trader's pack glyph, kneels above Cizin, the god of death with his skull glyph. Like all Maya gods, and there were 166 according to one post-conquest Spanish record, he had many names, guises and functions.

The gruesome relief with some of the original paintwork all round the Platform of Skulls, a rack of impaled heads. Real ones were once displayed on the platform. The finding of 14 skulls in four rows at the top of the Caracol stairway suggests that there was a dedicatory human sacrifice there too. But the Aztecs to the north far outdid the Toltecs in such practices.

when that was built in about A.D. 1150. Inside are some very fine murals.

Two hundred years after the arrival of the Itzá princes in Chichén, a second wave of Toltec invaders moved southward and took over the city. It is during these years after A.D. 1194 that the largest and most famous buildings of Chichén Itzá date. In the great space of the Main Plaza, three large stone platforms face the entrance to the Temple of the Warriors. These are the Venus Platform, named for its carving of a human head protruding from a serpent's mouth, a Toltec symbol of the planet Venus; the Platform of the Eagles, with the fierce sculpted birds eating human hearts; and the Platform of Skulls. The last of these, otherwise called the Tzompantli, has stone reliefs carved into racks of skulls and others showing sacrifices. It has often been assumed that the three platforms were used for various forms of the savage human sacrifices which northern Mexican tribes, such as the Toltec, undoubtedly carried out. Yet when the extensive excavations and restoration, financed by the Carnegie Institution, were started in 1923, the archaeologists found no trace of human remains around the platforms. They concluded that the bodies had been disposed of elsewhere.

The splendour of the Chichén Itzá ruins today owes much to the Carnegie restorations, for the forest had broken up the buildings to an extent far beyond the efforts of earlier workers, such as Stephens or Thompson. The huge step-pyramid that towers over the south side of the Plaza and over the rest of Chichén Itzá, known as the Castillo, had two of its sides restored to their original state by the Carnegie team and so can be appreciated much as the Toltec built it after A.D. 1194. This Castillo, with the small building on top of it, is the Temple of the Plumed Serpent, otherwise known as the Kukulcan. Rising in ten stages to a height of 23 metres (75 feet)—even that is only one-third of the height of the soaring pyramids at Tikal—the arduous climb to the top is rewarded by little more than a panoramic view. The inside of the small upper temple is not remarkable—the greater interior of the Castillo pyramid is in the older pyramid which it encases. The entrance to this is beneath the northern flight of steps. From there an inner stairway rises to a sizeable chamber, decorated with good carving and containing a splendid jaguar throne, painted red and studded with jade.

Across the open space from the Castillo, and past the Platform of the Eagles, the Temple of the Jaguars forms the western side of the Main Plaza. The lower part of this powerful building has already been mentioned as one of the first works after the Toltec conquest. The upper part of the temple, and the tremendous ceremonial Ball Court on its far side, date from the second stage of Toltec building, after 1194. The columns of this upper part, and the stone rail of the stairs leading up to it, repeat the motif of the plumed serpent. Inside the temple there is a damaged but recognizable mural painting, which seems to show Toltec soldiers laying siege to a Maya settlement.

From the upper terrace of the Temple of the Jaguars, one can imagine the Maya or Toltec priests watching the ball game in the court below. The precise rules of the game as played at Chichén Itzá are unclear, but a general idea can be obtained from the relief sculptures and other surviving descriptions, particularly the accounts by Spanish *conquistadores* of the version of the game played in other parts of Mexico. It seems that the game could be played by two teams of between three and nine players on each side, though the size of the main Chichén court seems to indicate larger teams.

The court is much bigger than others found at Chichén Itzá and elsewhere. It is 137 metres (450 feet) in length, with both sides bounded by high vertical walls for the greater part of that length. The tops of the walls provided grandstands for spectators. At either end of the court are unwalled areas and beyond these, two smaller temples face each other along the full length of the playing area.

Ball games were played with passionate intensity throughout Maya territories and further north, too. But the games on the giant Chichén court were probably the high point of festival days and may even have had religious significance. One can imagine big crowds of people gathered to watch the teams of players, while the priests conducted the ceremonies before the game started. The players would be dressed in splendid regalia, with massive padding on their loins as well as their elbows, hips and knees for they were not allowed to use their hands to hit the ball. This clothing can be seen in the wall sculpture.

At the start of the game the ball, of solid rubber weighing about 2.7 kilograms (6 pounds), was struck with knee, elbow or hip. It would rebound from one of the stone walls at great speed, to be hit again by another player. Large rings of stone project from the masonry walls on both sides of the court. To keep the ball in play at all, it was not allowed to touch the ground—to score, it had to be hit through one of the stone rings. The players would run and leap with dazzling speed, twisting to strike the flying ball with one of the permitted parts of the body. At the end, the winning team paraded in triumph. If the sculptured friezes around the the Chichén ball court are to be believed, the victors carried with them the bleeding decapitated head of at least one of the losing side. Death, for the Toltecs, was part of the game.

The main Ball Court lies on the edge of the centre of Chichén Itzá. Beyond it to the north there is only the forest and the causeway to the sacred *cenote*. The question that keeps recurring at the *cenote,* and elsewhere in Chichén, is about the differences and similarities between the Maya and the Toltec cultures. Were the human bones that Thompson dredged from the water all from the late Toltec period, or did those conquerors maintain an older tradition of human sacrifice? The accounts of the Spanish missionaries, and those written down by Indians themselves in the celebrated Books of Chilam Balam, tell of customs practised 600 years after the Toltec invasion, though the northerners left the Maya to their own devices again after a few centuries.

It is often impossible to sort out what was the legacy of the older civilization, but some things are clear. At a time when Europe was in confusion after the collapse of the Roman Empire, the Maya developed a culture remarkably advanced in some respects. Their masonry and architecture was splendid, their knowledge of mathematics startling and their textiles were refined. They devised the most expressive script of any American culture before Columbus, with characters that could express words or complex abstract ideas. Their records were written on stone or on a paper they invented, made from the bark of a type of fig tree. They made this paper into books, one of the few civilizations to do so. Their political system was durable and, despite occasional wars between their city states, reasonably secure.

Given such advances, the inventions the Maya did *not* make are almost equally extraordinary. They did not use animals for transport. They never quite developed a true arch. They did not discover the principle of balances or scales. Like the other Amerindian races, they had no knowledge of the wheel. They could not cast metal, so their swords and the tools that cut their intricate carvings were of stone. In many ways these 'deficiencies' make their achievements all the more impressive.

By the time that the Spaniards arrived the culture had long declined from its peak, and the newcomers soon extinguished it. Only the ruined stone monuments and the spectacular weaving of the Maya's descendants survived the arrival of the Europeans.

Typical wall sculpture from Chichén Itzá, a man's head in the jaws of a snake, from the Toltec period c. A.D. 1150.

EASTER ISLAND

Giant Stone Figures In The Pacific

EASTER ISLAND, with its carved birdmen and its rows of huge statues on platforms beside the sea, is an extraordinary case of a human civilization that was born and died in almost complete isolation. When the first Europeans visited the island during the eighteenth century, they wondered at the purpose of the hundreds of altar platforms around its shores. What beliefs inspired the islanders to sculpt the giant carvings and drag them from their hillside quarries to the coast? Why did each rank of stone heads face inland from their long altars, as if they had just landed from the sea? And why was there a taboo, or *tapu,* on the area surrounding some altars, but not others?

By 1860 the culture of Easter Island had almost disappeared after a protracted civil war had all but wiped out the inhabitants while the survivors were taken by slavers. So even today questions remain unanswered, though scholars and archaeologists have pieced together some bits of the puzzle.

Legend says the island was given its present form when Uoke, a supernatural giant, ranged across the Pacific Ocean. He levered up the islands with a vast pole, it is said, and pitched them into the deep. But when he came to Te Pito o Te Henua—the island at the centre of the world—he found that one part of it was of a rock too hard for his pole. So this triangular land formed by three volcanoes was left at the remotest eastern end of the Polynesian Islands, 1900 kilometres (1200 miles) beyond Pitcairn and 4000 kilometres (2500 miles) from Peru.

Uoke is perhaps an expression of the destructive forces—typhoons, tidal waves and erupting volcanoes—which beset the Polynesian people. The god who made the people themselves in the first place, known as Makemake in Easter Island, was a more benevolent but surprisingly fallible deity. Makemake is said to have created man because he was lonely. He saw his own reflection in water and thought how handsome he looked. A bird perched on his shoulder and Makemake was pleased by the combination, so kept his reflection and the bird together. Then he thought he would like to be able to talk to another creature more similar to himself. First of all he fertilized a stone with his semen, but that was unproductive. Then he fertilized water, but the result was fishes. At last he fertilized the earth and was delighted when mankind was the progeny of this union.

Makemake is probably the Easter Island equivalent of a more widespread Polynesian god called Tane, though their characteristics are not exactly the same. This remoteness from the rest of Polynesian culture is typical of Easter Island, for it seems that the community was the result of one settlement by boats in the years between A.D. 400 and 500, and perhaps a second around 1200, with only very occasional hints of outside influence after that.

There are two main theories about the origins of the Easter islanders. The holder of one was part Polynesian himself—from the largest of the scattered islands, New Zealand. In his Maori persona, named Te Rangi Hiroa, he was a dedicated scholar and advocate of Polynesian culture. As Sir Peter Buck—his father was Irish—he was a distinguished Member of Parliament and doctor of medicine. Later he gave up his career in New Zealand and devoted himself to Polynesian studies, holding the directorship of a museum in Honolulu until his death in 1951.

Buck's views about the origin of the Polynesians are still generally accepted. He believed that they were a Caucasian people who moved through South-East Asia into the Pacific islands at some remote time, though later than the broad-faced people of negroid type who inhabit Melanesia and much of Australia. Modern archaeology suggests that the Polynesian migrations from the west into the central Pacific began around 2000 B.C. Later arrivals of Mongol colonists from Asia brought about the mixture which can be seen in

Previous pages *One of the groups of Easter Island statues standing on their* ahu *platform of dressed stone and facing inland. The chapter symbol is a figure from an Easter Island wooden carving. It is thought to be a human face with a rat's body.*

the typical Polynesian face today, most numerous in Hawaii, Samoa and Tonga.

The other important theory has been propagated by one of the most remarkable men of our time, Thor Heyerdahl—a Norwegian scholar and explorer gifted with insight and a sweeping imagination. In 1936, soon after they were married, Heyerdahl and his wife lived for a year with the Polynesians in the Marquesas Islands, over 3200 kilometres (2000 miles) west of Easter Island. He was told the legend of how the first inhabitants had come from the *east,* from the direction of the American continent, with a king called Tiki. Later, in Peru, Heyerdahl heard of a pre-Inca legend there about a prince called Kon Tiki who was expelled from his domain near Lake Titicaca and sailed westwards with his people across the Pacific on a great raft. Soon after the end of World War II, Heyerdahl built a raft of the Peruvian type and sailed to the Polynesian Islands. The voyage and his book—*Kon Tiki*—made Heyerdahl famous, but he was careful to point out that it only proved that emigrations *could* have been made that way.

Europeans first contacted the Easter islanders in 1722, when a Dutch ship commanded by Jacob Roggeveen anchored there on Easter Day and gave the place its most commonly used name. Nearly 50 years afterwards, a Spanish ship arrived, named the place San Carlos and persuaded local leaders to inscribe documents of allegiance to Spain, sealed with their birdman hieroglyphs. Neither the name nor the allegiance stuck, for the island had little to attract colonists or traders. In 1774, the great English explorer, Captain James Cook, landed at the island on his second voyage and one place name on Easter is thought to commemorate the spot where one of his crew had his hat stolen by an islander. Cook's expedition carefully recorded what they found there, as did the French captain, the Comte de la Pérouse, in 1786. These four visits, slight though they were, give us a valuable record of Easter society in decline

Easter Island has an area of 116 square kilometres (45 square miles), scarcely more than a third of the size of Malta, yet its people managed to carve, transport and set up about 1000 statues in the course of 900 years. The 300 ahu groups of them dot the coast, facing inland.

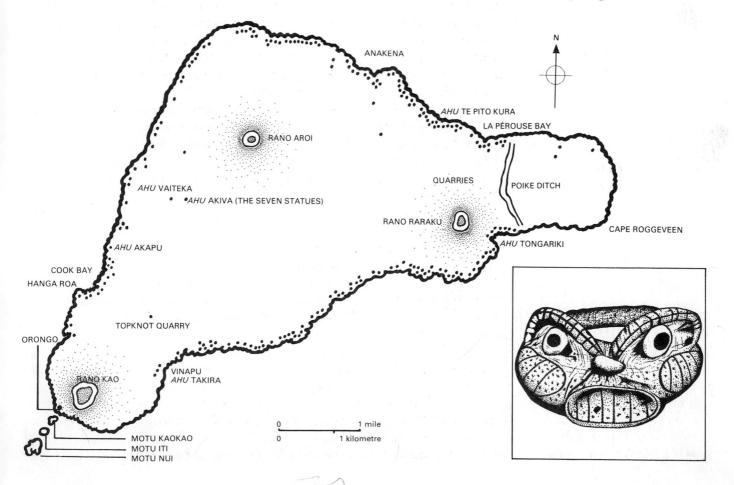

Some of the 50 giants on the slopes of the extinct volcano Rano Raraku. Anything from 50 to 300 man-hours is the modern estimate for the carving of such sculptures.

from the peak it had reached in the seventeeenth century.

By the time the European explorers came, Easter was a land of little fertility with largely barren soil. It was not so in earlier times, for archaeologists have found the foundations of huts whose roofs were evidently supported by branches so thick that they could not have grown in the conditions of recent centuries. It seems probable that the island reached by Polynesian sailors, 500 years after Christ, was fruitful and that the three freshwater lakes in the extinct volcanic craters made up for the total absence of running streams.

The oral legends of today's Easter islanders tell in surprising detail of the original settlement. The people came from Hiva, led by one of their sacred family or *ariki,* called Hotu Matua. Hiva may well be the Marquesas, where three islands still have that name combined with others. Alternatively, according to Heyerdahl's theory, Hiva would be Peru. Hotu Matua and his folk, using his *mana*—the divine powers which the *ariki* held for the benefit of

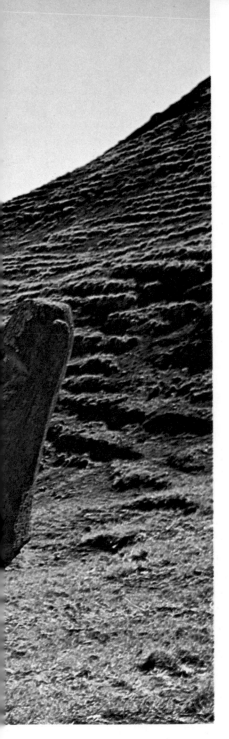

their people—duly arrived at the island. A house for Hotu Matua and his successors as *ariki* was built at Anakena, the lovely beach on the north side of the island where they had landed. The rest of the expedition soon occupied other parts of the little island, which is only 24 kilometres (15 miles) long. These groups evolved into eight clans (one of these later divided into three), each with its own territory.

Since Heyerdahl's archaeological expedition of the 1950s, the division of Easter Island's prehistory into three main periods has been widely accepted. The early period, from the settlement until about A.D. 1100, is vague. The middle period, between 1100 and 1680 saw the growth and culmination of a great culture in miniature. The decline of the society is described as late period, ending with the tragic slave raid by Peruvians in 1862 and the takeover by Christian missionaries.

The legends tell that the yam was brought by the Polynesian settlers, but they had to live on fish and sandalwood nuts while their plants were growing. The island was covered with a thick forest at the time, for pollen analysis has shown that palms and other trees grew there—though all have disappeared from the almost universal dry grassland which covers the soil today. Sugar cane, bananas, mulberries, a tuber called taro and sweet potato made up the crops grown in their forest clearings, for they had no grain. For meat, the settlers brought only chickens with them to vary the sea fish diet. They made nets, and fish-hooks of stone and human bone. Tools were made of wood or stone—notably basalt and the glass-like hard obsidian from the volcanoes. All cooking was done in an earth oven, as they made no pottery and their only vessels were gourds. The people wore little or no clothing—what they had was made from mulberry bark—but they put great effort into devising new types of feather hats.

In this early period many of the people lived in caves with a chamber containing a flow of molten lava for warmth. Others built houses in the style brought with them from Hiva—outline foundations of stone blocks had holes drilled in them to support arched poles, which were then thatched.

From very early times they built long platform altars on the seashore, with massive walls of dressed stone facing the sea and long ramps—studded with large round pebbles—running down on the inland side, levelling out into open courts. These 300 monuments are called *ahu,* and the oldest radiocarbon-dated example, *Ahu Tahai* near Hangaroa on the west coast, was built in about A.D. 700. Sometimes the structures had wing platforms at their sides and sometimes they were very large; *ahu* 2 of the group at Vinapu, built on the south coast around 850, is over 33 metres (110 feet) long and 3 metres (10 feet) high.

As far as is known, none of the 600 great statues on the island date from the early period. However, Heyerdahl's expedition did discover an extraordinary and powerful statue, 4.25 metres (14 feet) high, buried under debris. The primitive features and compacted force of this statue have led people to speculate that it may date from the first phase of the culture. As there are a few known statues on Polynesian islands far from Easter—although these are much smaller and less impressive—it is possible that Hotu Matua brought the idea of statues with him.

It does not appear that the statues were 'idols' in the sense that Europeans too easily use that term—that is to say, objects of worship in themselves. It is more likely that they were respectful monuments to beloved parents or older ancestors. And they were certainly the products of competition with other clans and other *ahu*-builders.

The eight clans derived from the original places of settlement on the island, later increasing to 10, each with its own territory. Within each clan, a

Members of the Comte de la Pérouse's Pacific expedition measure a top-hatted moai *in 1786, oblivious to an islander who is about to acquire a tricorn hat. Of all the presents the French brought, hats were the most prized by the islanders and there were not enough to go round. La Pérouse landed pigs, goats and sheep as well as some seed to try and improve the island's agriculture, but the hungry inhabitants ate all these before they could yield results.*

system of seniority controlled everything, including the position of chief. All the clans came under the spiritual leadership of the chief of the Miru clan, for he was the direct descendant of Hoto Matua. He was an *ariki,* keeper and dispenser of the divine *mana* that could make the land and its people flourish. This *mana* was a pervasive sacred force, as well as a magic power which its holder could use.

Religion was deeply embedded in the lives of the ordinary people. Seasonal festivals were celebrated with long hours of dancing and singing, sometimes by a special caste of boys and girls, sometimes by the assembled crowds. Both sexes enjoyed tattooing and painting their bodies fantastically for these feasts, and the women would make up their faces with care.

Other occasions were more solemn. There was a mysterious 'earth canoe' ceremony which involved rites around a long mound manned by a symbolic captain and crew. And there was the *paina,* for which a large figure of rough cloth—representing the host's dead father—was erected within a stone circle near his *ahu.* Surrounded by his clan, the son climbed inside the image and chanted lamentations and affectionate memories of the dead man.

The *paina* seems to have been separate from funeral ceremonies as such. For 'death' on Easter was a prolonged affair, often lasting for years after the dying person had stopped breathing. The body was taken to the family *ahu,* which was then declared taboo. While this order remained, no fishing was allowed near the *ahu* and fires must be 'smothered with grass'. The body, which was wrapped in a bark cloth, remained on the platform for up to three years, until the flesh was all gone and the death completed. Four relatives kept watch at any one time and they were likely to kill anyone who broke the sacred taboo or *tapu.* When the bones were clean they might be left on the platform or might be stored underground. At that time the *tapu* was lifted and a great family feast of chickens was held to celebrate the release of the dead person.

Most *ahu* were family affairs, but some—the larger ones in general—were those of chiefs, whose monument involved the honour of the whole clan. And it was from the competition between the 10 clans in the middle period that the magnificence of the Easter monuments grew. This had one extraordinary result—the spirit of aggression among human males found an outlet in statue-making which seems to have diverted Easter men away from war for many centuries.

The statues were memorials, it seems, 'living faces' in the words of the islanders, despite their frequent close likeness to each other. It is no accident that most of the *ahu* are along the shore, for time and again sacred ceremonies on Easter refer to the sea and the people's arrival from it. From the water's edge, the statues gaze hypnotically over the land, reminders of that first arrival. Much of their potency lay in the eyes, it appears, for only the eyes were not carved at the quarry before the huge works were transported to their *ahu.* When the statue was in place at last, its eyes were chiselled in and its full strength was unleashed across the island.

A few surviving early statues are of stone from various parts of the island—after that, all were quarried from the side of the volcano Rano Raraku towards the eastern tip. Volcanic tuff rock has the great quality of softness when quarried, hardening to great durability after some months in the open air. The great busts of the upper parts of human beings were quarried like the ancient Egyptians cut their obelisks—by carving down around them into the rock until, with most of their detailing completed, the final spinal join underneath was severed and the rock heaved upright. The system is clearly shown by half-completed statues (*moai*) in the Rano Raraku quarry.

Much has been written, and many vivid imaginations exercised, about the method of transporting the *moai* from quarry to their *ahu*. Some of these are more than 10 kilometres (6 miles) from Rano Raraku. Some writers have seen the transportation as the work of *mana,* others as a harnessing of high pressure vapour from the volcano. Sleds and bipods have been invented retrospectively to do the job, as have systems of encircling ropes with teams of heaving men trundling the upright statue while others steady it. This last fits in with accounts in the legends and with one piece of circumstantial evidence—on the slopes below the statue quarry at Rano Raraku there are dozens of statues, still blind-eyed, left scattered across the hillside when work stopped suddenly. These *moai* were apparently on their way to their intended sites and the majority of them are still upright.

If the stones were moved in the standing position, the puzzle remains just how the Easter people raised the hats or topknots which were originally on the heads of most. These topknots were of a different stone from the *moai* themselves, a dark red rock from the western side of the island. If the statues were carried horizontally, the topknots could have been lashed on top before raising—if they were moved vertically they must have been hoisted by some means. It is a tantalizing mystery to archaeologists and others alike.

In whatever way they were transported, the final effect of the statue-bearing *ahu* was one of the most overwhelming monumental achievements of mankind. During the civil wars which ended the middle period of Easter culture, all their statues were knocked over. But recently the archaeologist William Mulloy and others, with the help of the Chilean government which controls the island, have re-erected a number and restored their *ahu*.

Among the most celebrated *ahu* are those at Vinapu on the south-east shores. Here the masonry of the sea wall is drystone of a quality that is not found elsewhere on Easter Island, nor in many other places except in Inca Peru. Looking at this work, with great blocks of irregular size that fit each other like skilled carpenter's joints, one remembers the similarity between the Quechua word *kumar* and the Polynesian *kumara* for sweet potato. Is Heyerdahl right after all? Is it all coincidence or was there some trading contact between Easter and the Incas in the fifteenth century? It is slender evidence, for there are few other such links.

Some people have argued that another link with the Central American civilizations is provided by the island's birdman sculpture though most of that seems to date from the later period, after the end of statue making. The birdmen appear in carvings of wood and on rocks, especially near the ancient village of Orongo. Orongo was clearly an important village at the height of Easter's middle period with the population of the whole island at its peak of perhaps 10,000 people; advances in agriculture and fishing probably accounted for this growth. There are nearly 50 tightly-packed stone houses in the village, ruins of which have yielded radiocarbon dates of around 1500, so the village clearly dates from the great *ahu*-building years

Something happened very abruptly in about 1680 which made the Easter men stop making *ahu* and statues. *Moai* with their eyes uncarved have been found abandoned on their way to their *ahu,* while the quarry at Rano Raraku has many half completed statues and others only partly carved from the bedrock. One of these would have been far the largest ever made. Its height of 20 metres (65 feet) is almost double that of the tallest statue the islanders ever put up and the task of moving and erecting it would have been far beyond anything in the islanders' experience. Around these part-cut statues many stone-cutting tools were found scattered on the ground as if thrown down on the spur of the moment.

What caused this dramatic end to a craft perhaps centuries old? The

possibilities seem to be a natural disaster, invasion or civil war. Certainly, the climate seems to have changed, for when the Dutch ship arrived 40 years later there was a shortage of food and water, and the estimated population was only about 4000. So perhaps there had been famine, brought about by the people's obsession with building monuments to the neglect of farming. But if there is anything to the legends, there was certainly war on the island—probably for the first time.

The Easter Island stories, handed down by word of mouth from generation to generation, tell of a war between two groups. One, the 'long-eared' Hanau Eepe, may have been the descendants of the thirteenth century second wave of migrants to the island and the legends accused them in one version of giving arrogant orders or, in another account, of cannibalism. The other group, the 'short-eared' Hanau Momoko, turned on them and hemmed them in on the hill called Poike which forms the peninsula at the east end of the island. Here the Eepe built a series of defended ditches, whose remains can still be seen, across the neck of the peninsula. But the Momoko passed around both ends of the ditches, executed a pincer movement and killed all except one Eepe man. He was allowed to live, to marry and to breed.

Charcoal in one of the Poike ditches has been radiocarbon dated to about 1680, which fits well with the generation count handed down by the descendants of the one Eepe survivor. But who were the Hanau Eepe? All the statues have long ears, so perhaps they had subjugated the Momoko and used their labour for the big monuments. They may also have imposed peace on the island. For the Poike battle was followed by a continuing time of war, of decline in cultural achievements and apparently by a curious change of religious practices.

The late period in Easter Island, after 1680, saw a switch of attention from the statues and the commemoration of forefathers to the birdmen of the god Makemake and the sooty terns which contained their spirits. The carvings of birdmen on boulders and in wood, the sooty tern egg ceremony, the *rongorongo* tablets and the cyclopean round towers all seem to date from this late stage. The progress of change can be traced to some degree from European accounts. Roggeveen, in 1722, mentions the barren state of the island and the fact that the people lived in caves in fear of attack, but his description of the statues and their topknots implies that all were standing at that time. By 1774, Captain Cook reported, many of the *moai* had been felled. Vendettas and cannibalism plagued the island from this time on. A century later, when Christian missionaries arrived, not one of the statues on the *ahu* was upright after the wars between the clans.

During this period of bloodshed and disaster, the leadership of clans was often taken over by a *matatoa,* one of a caste of warriors which had grown up. Although there is no evidence that any of these *matatoa* ever actually ruled the whole island, the birdman cult was developed so that one of them took over a special position among the islanders each year. This post was called simply the *tangata manu,* the Birdman and the choice was made each September at the largest village, Orongo.

The houses of Orongo overlook the sea at the western tip of Easter, from the lip of the volcano Rano Kao. A couple of kilometres off the land there is a small island called Motu Nui. By tradition, the sooty terns were brought to Motu Nui once a year by Makemake to nest and breed their young. On a certain September day, probably the spring equinox, the *matatoa* of all the clans gathered with the priests on a beach north of the volcano for a great feast. There were chants, dances and readings from the *rongorongo* tablets—thick wooden planks densely covered with a lovely script developed in the island

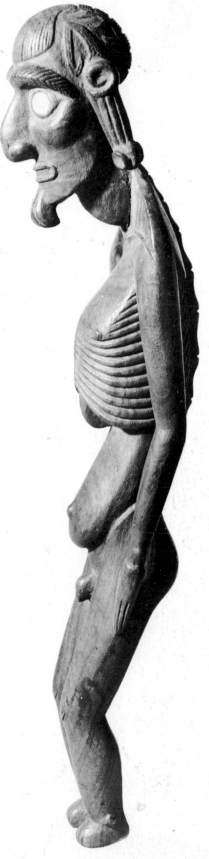

Above *One of 30 wooden ancestor-figures.*
Left *This statue was excavated from the debris of centuries and re-erected in 1956.*

A rongorongo tablet measuring about 21 cm (8½ in) long. Some 21 of these 'talking boards' have been found. A staff and four chest pieces also bear this Polynesian language, the only one written down. Until the French missionary Eugene Eyraud found the first after 1862, the remaining islanders had been using them as firewood. As a result too few have survived for a conclusive reconstruction of the language though the texts contain prayers, instructions to priests and island legends.

and unique to it. These tablets have never been conclusively deciphered, but it seems that the script of 120 symbols records chants about the deeds of Easter ancestors in a combination of pictographic and ideographic characters.

When the feast was finished, a procession made its way to Orongo, up the slopes of the volcano to cliffs which plunge 243 metres (800 feet) to the sea, with the islet of Motu Nui roughly opposite.

The *matatoa* and a crowd of ordinary people arrived at this place and passed the time with long chants while one servant of each climbed down the cliff and started the long swim to Motu Nui—in earlier times it seems likely that this was done by the warriors themselves. On the island, the servants searched among the rocks for the nests of the sooty terns and waited for the first egg to be laid. When an egg was found, the finder dived back into the sea with it and, while the *matatoa* on the cliff top tried to recognize the swimmer, laboured back through the breakers to the mainland. Then the servant had to climb the cliff again and deliver the egg to his master, who then became the Birdman. The chanting began again and the successful *matatoa,* who was now imbued with the spirit of Makemake and so subject to *tapu,* was escorted by the crowds to Rano Raraku—former quarry of the great statues—and isolated in a special house for his year of sacred office. And another relief carving—of a birdman with a bird's head on a human body—was added to the rocks of Orongo to commemorate him. The servants, who brought the spirit of Makemake through the sea, were not remembered.

This spectacular ceremony, whose age is not known, took place against a background of increasing murder and destruction in the late period. After the statues had been toppled, the *ahu* too were allowed to deteriorate even though burials in small stone chambers were still placed in them. Apart from the defended caves which replaced the oval houses as the chief dwellings, large round towers of drystone masonry—with corbelled chambers within—were built along the coast. These *tupa* are curiously reminiscent of the Scottish *brochs* and the Sardinian *nuraghi* built on the other side of the world 2000 years earlier, but the exact purpose of the Easter structures has not been proved.

By the first half of the nineteenth century, the arcadian life of earlier Easter people had degenerated into a dark age. The position of the Birdman for the year remained sacrosanct, but his relatives used it as an excuse for oppression of the other clans. By the 1850s, they would pillage houses at will, using the name of their *tapu* kinsman as their authority, and torture the other islanders to work the fields of the year's ruling clan. When a *matatoa* from another group won the annual race of the tern's egg, his relatives would avenge themselves on their predecessors in a continuing vendetta. There were deplorable instances of shootings when European ships made their rare visits to the island, but for once it seems that the foreigners were generally witnesses of a society's degeneration, rather than its cause.

The end of the process, however, did come from outside the island. In 1859 Peruvian ships began a series of slaving expeditions to Easter and, in December 1862, eight slave ships anchored off the beaches. The Peruvians set out sparkling trinkets on the shores at several points. When the islanders gradually emerged from hiding, the sailors suddenly surrounded them. After shooting those who used their stone spears to resist, they herded the rest to the boats and then into the holds of the ships. This one expedition captured about 1000 slaves, probably over half of the Easter population at the time, and took them to some islands off the coast of Peru. Within a few years, all but 100 had died there.

After vigorous protests by the Bishop of Tahiti, the Peruvian government shipped the survivors back to Easter Island in foul conditions. Only 15 were

One of the 150 birdmen carvings on the rocks of the Orongo cliffs. The birdmen have their hands clasped in prayer to the god Makemake. Below are the offshore islets of Motu Kaokao, Motu Iti and Motu Nui. The latter and farthest was the goal of the swimmers who would race each other to get a tern's egg and, sharks permitting, bring it back to their clan leader at Orongo. The winner's clan leader would become that year's Birdman (tangata manu). The last such ceremony was held in 1867 and the earliest known is placed in the fifteenth century.

alive when they got home and those few carried new diseases to the island, including smallpox. An epidemic followed and by 1877 there were only a few hundred Easter islanders left in the world, perhaps 200 living in Tahiti and 110 on their own island. The Christian missionaries who arrived there at that time were far more beneficial than their predecessors of earlier centuries in other countries. They persuaded the few surviving people to give up their violent customs and, although most of the old culture has now vanished from their daily lives, one can only feel that they have gained if their lives are compared with the regime under the late *matatoa*. Today, between 1000 and 2000 people live on Easter Island, most of them by fishing and small-scale agriculture, though tourism is a developing industry.

The example of Easter Island, as a self-contained civilization that rose and then declined tragically, has fascinated students of the patterns of human history. One picture of the whole process, put forward by the archaeologist Colin Renfrew in his book *Before Civilization,* may help us to understand the story. Renfrew sees the culture as one of many instances—in various parts of the world—of the evolution of human societies into 'chiefdoms' based on family groups, with established land boundaries. He suggests that the major *ahu* and the statues were the work of these chiefdoms in competition with each other.

This peaceful outlet for the aggressive instincts explains the success of the society, the growth of its achievements and its increasing population over several centuries. But when some factor or factors—deforestation, a reduction of rainfall, overpopulation and famine—upset the system, the people turned their desperation against each other. Rivalry became warfare and an apparently irreversible sequence of decline followed. If the missionaries had not arrived when the population had fallen from around 10,000 to little more than 100, the sequence might have continued to complete extinction. It is a process that may explain the fate of other civilizations described later in this book—total disappearance except for the ghosts in their stone monuments.

ANGKOR

Temple-Mountains Of The Khmer Empire

Previous pages Reflected in its broad moat stands Angkor Wat, the largest religious building ever constructed. Lost to the outside world for over four centuries, it was the masterpiece of the Khmer kingdom. Viewed here from the west, the decorated causeway crosses the peaceful, lotus-strewn waters to the towered entrance pavilion.

The chapter symbol is a Khmer dancer.

Henri Mouhot, the French naturalist, rediscovered the splendid ruins of Angkor while on an expedition into the interior of the Cambodian jungle in 1860.

Right A bird's eye view of Angkor showing the main examples of the 600 temples built between A.D. 800 and 1200. Angkor Thom, royal core of a city of 1,000,000 people, had 13 kilometres (8 miles) of walls.

THE FLORA AND FAUNA of the jungles of Cambodia were a source of wonder eagerly explored by French scientists in the nineteenth century, after their country had established its political domination over much of Indo-China. One of these scientists, Henri Mouhot, made an expedition into the interior in 1860 to study the plant forms that nature had evolved there. Walking along a narrow jungle path one steamy morning, he turned a corner and saw through the trees a fantastic tower of grey stone. As he moved forward, other towers appeared, grouped around the first. He had heard stories of overgrown temples in the area, but this was beyond all imagining. He had rediscovered Angkor Wat, the largest temple in the world, lost and overgrown for centuries after its sacking in 1431.

During the decades after Mouhot's discovery, archaeologists followed his path to central Cambodia. They cut back the smothering vegetation and found around the Angkor Wat temple the remains of the vast city at the centre of the Khmer kingdom. This was, at times, the most powerful force in Asia—bar the Chinese empire—during the period when Europe was emerging from the Dark Ages. That city was Angkor, the Khmer capital for most of the six centuries after A.D. 800.

The plain of central Cambodia, the country now known as Kampuchea, is a hothouse where life-giving water and the richness of the alluvial soil are counter-balanced by the torrid heat of the wet season, the roaring floods that leave pools to stagnate and rot until the next monsoon and the creatures of all sizes that bite and sting. It was to this fertile hell that the Khmers moved down the great Mekong river from their sandstone mountains in the north when they annexed the declining kingdom of Funan at the end of the eighth century.

The Mekong, forcing its waters deep into a gorge through the mountains, created the Cambodian plain and still controls much of its weather and agriculture. Its massive basin collects the melting mountain snow in spring and swirls the water down to the land it has flattened over the millennia. There on the plain, the Mekong floods its normal banks and reverses the flow of lazy tributaries. One of these, the Tonle Sap, flows vigorously upstream at this season to triple the size of the Great Lakes, which it usually empties. A little later, in May, the monsoon starts its six months of steamy downpour. So floods, rain and heat dominate life for those months and the dry season comes in November as a hard-earned reward for survival.

It was this rhythm of life, especially the violent extremes in the calendar of the Great Lakes, that the Khmer people had to harness for their civilization to flourish. These people, the Khmer, were the same distinct group as the Cambodians today, for they have remained separate for thousands of years despite the constant struggles between the rival nations of South-East Asia. The population of Indo-China was formed many centuries before the birth of Christ from various mixtures of the Caucasian and Negrito people, who inhabited the Pacific islands, too, but mixed with a later wave of Mongolians from China. Since Indo-China is divided by its formidable mountain ranges into a number of obvious regions centred on habitable plains, the people who settled in each isolated part developed individual identities. At the time when the Roman Empire had conquered the Mediterranean, the advanced civilization of India made regular contact with these Indo-Chinese nations through trade and this was to influence the way their cultures developed.

A description of the Khmer people has survived in the thirteenth-century journal of a Chinese envoy who spent a year in Angkor, and his words could be applied just as well to the Cambodians of today. The women are very lovely when young, with full-breasted figures and graceful movements, but lose their looks quickly through overwork and bearing many children. The

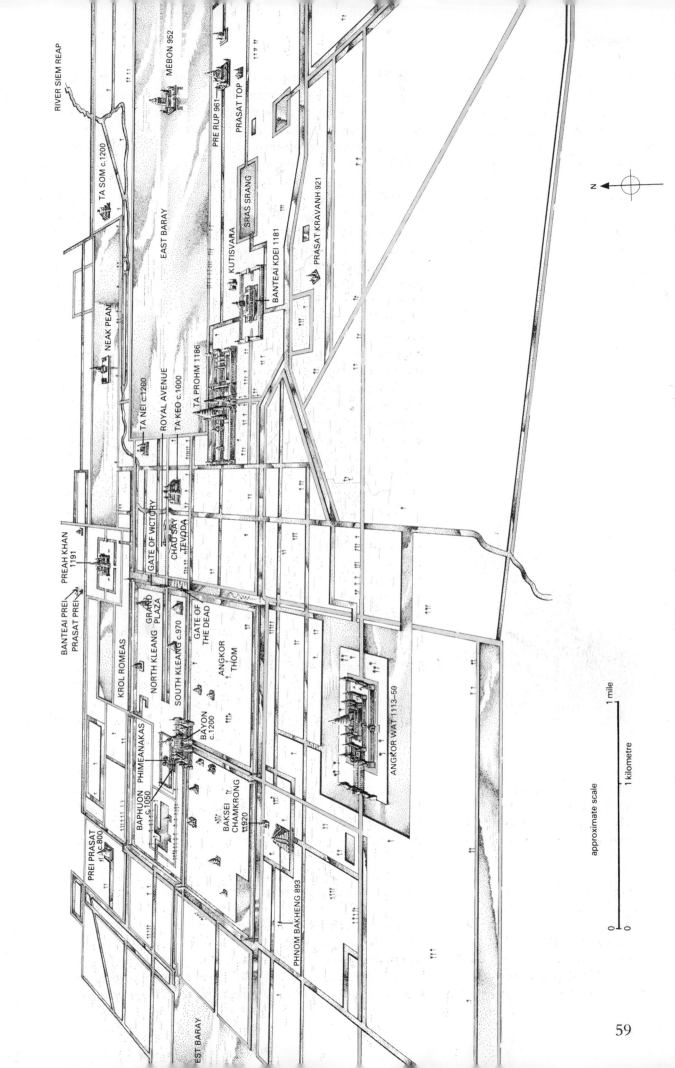

RIVER SIEM REAP

TA SOM c.1200

MÉBON 952

NEAK PEAN

EAST BARAY

PRE RUP 961

PRASAT TOP

SRAS SRANG

KUTISVARA

BANTEAI KDEI 1181

PRASAT KRAVANH 921

TA NEI c.1200

ROYAL AVENUE

TA KEO c.1000

TA PROHM 1186

GATE OF VICTORY

CHAU SAY TEVODA

BANTEAI PREI
PRASAT PREI

PREAH KHAN 1191

KROL ROMEAS

NORTH KLEANG

GRAND PLAZA

SOUTH KLEANG c.970

GATE OF THE DEAD

ANGKOR THOM

PREI PRASAT c.800

BAPHUON c.1050

PHIMEANAKAS

BAYON c.1200

BAKSEI CHAMKRONG c.920

PHNOM BAKHENG 893

ANGKOR WAT 1113–50

EST BARAY

N

approximate scale

1 mile

1 kilometre

0

The exotic robes and stylized movements of these Khmer dancers recall the impressive court life of twelfth-century Cambodia. They are performing in the temple of Angkor Wat, erected by Suryavarman II to the glory of the Hindu god Vishnu.

men are average height for that part of the world, around 1.6 metres (5 feet 5 inches) tall. Both sexes have rather short legs and thick ankles. Their skin is a pale brown, their heads are rounded and their typically Oriental features are strongly moulded. Bernard Groslier, in a perceptive passage in his book *Angkor—Art and Civilization,* has written of their realism combined with sensuality and strong sentiment, and of their preference for concrete thought, rather than abstract. He has observed, too, their liking for the fantastic, their manual skill, obedience to anyone who gains their loyalty, and liability to sudden outbreaks of brutality when stirred to abandon their usual good-natured ways.

These are the descendants of the union between the decadent Funan plains people and the fierce Kambuja from the nearby mountains, who came together first as the small kingdom of Chenla and then, under King Bhavavarman around A.D. 550, extended into the wider kingdom of Khmer. The first 250 years of Khmer rule are confused by civil wars and it was only after A.D. 800 that comparative stability was established. In 790, the exiled Jayavarman II returned from Java. He fought for many years for the kingdom of his ancestors, spurred on by Javanese ideas of a monarch's duty to impose orderly government. By 802 he was victorious and founded his capital and his dynasty in the area around Angkor, to the north of the Cambodian Great Lakes. Over the following four centuries a large city grew up here. The spreading timber dwellings of the ordinary people and their busy thoroughfares have long since vanished beneath the undergrowth. But the ever larger temples which Jayavarman's successors added and their network of canals and huge reservoirs can still be made out.

These large-scale public works to irrigate the land were at the core of Angkor's prosperity, for the Khmers had no strong urge to trade overseas, unlike the earlier Funan people. The Khmer were farmers and, above all, rice farmers. They took the great gift of the Mekong river's annual flood and multiplied its benefits by storing the water in huge reservoirs. As their skills became increasingly refined, they learned the right times to release water along the canals and channels to flood the paddy fields. The annual rice crop was increased to two, three and even four crops a year in this way, enough to feed their growing population. It was the proper duty of each new monarch to put in hand a major enlargement of this system, as well as to build his own temple-mountain.

As with most early civilizations, religion was woven into the everyday consciousness of the Khmer people, rather than forming a separate part of their lives. The Hindu religion and, later, Buddhism were the beliefs which predominated. Both were derived from India, but they were adapted by the Khmers to their own ways. The great Hindu gods Vishnu and Shiva were the favourites in Cambodia. Vishnu is always seen as a benign force, sustainer of the world order acting for the good of mankind. In sculpture or paintings he is usually shown as a finely proportioned young man with four arms. He generally wears a cylindrical head-dress and rides the mythical Garuda, a bird who slays snakes. Sometimes, however, Vishnu himself rides a serpent, in this case the symbol of the primeval waters, and in these works of art the god is in a cosmic sleep often aspired to by the mystics among his adherents. In these works of art, other gods are seen to be awakening Vishnu and urging him to save the world from evil powers.

Shiva was even more important in Cambodia. He is the god of creation-destruction-creation, but the Khmers emphasized his benevolent aspect as the creative male principal. He was usually represented by a phallus or *linga* of stone embedded in a plinth, which represented the earth itself as the female principal. The *linga* was thus in no way obscene, but the symbol of the original creation of the world, of the fertility of the land and of the stable axis around which the earth revolves. When artists depicted Shiva in human form, he was shown as a young man with three eyes and heavy hair gathered behind his head, grasping a thunderbolt or a trident and mounted on a white bull. He is a god of fertile light and heat, of the sun and fire. In Cambodia, Shiva was merged with the personality of the monarch during many reigns, and was worshipped as *Devaraja,* god-king.

The third god of the supreme Hindu triad, Brahma, was unimportant in Cambodia, though those temples which take the Indian three-towered form acknowledged his position. But among the various kinds of Khmer temple, developed from Indian models, it is the temple-mountain that is the most important achievement of Angkor—especially Angkor as it survives today.

In the Khmer culture before the downfall of Funan, single hills or mountains were already the most sacred places. Their importance was this.

Angkor is famed for its many hundred carvings of apsaras *or heavenly dancers. Their freshness and grace are apparent in the flowing skirt, elaborate coiffure and fine headdress of this seductive female. Like the modern Khmer dancers, she wears jewelled earrings, necklaces, armlets, bracelets and anklets.*

Creation myths in many parts of the world tell of the female primeval mound floating on the timeless waters until it is pierced by the shaft of the male principal, fixing it in place and creating order. Hindu cosmology sees the world as a gigantic square surrounded by continuous chains of mountains, with the endless primeval oceans beyond. In the centre of the square of land there rises the lofty Mount Meru, mythical world axis and dwelling place of the gods. It is difficult for Western minds to grasp that the spiritual truth of the model for these people made any apparent differences from it, in the visible world, entirely unimportant. And so for them any mountain could come to represent Mount Meru.

Early Khmer temples—usually of wood and now vanished—were built on selected mountains or hills. When the people moved to the plains, hillocks or man-made mounds came to stand for Mount Meru—the early Phnom Bakheng temple pyramid at Angkor covered the top of a natural hillock—and later the temples themselves were built to represent mountains, rising from previously level ground. These are the temple-mountains of Angkor, and it is useful to remember that their use was not like that of Christian churches; they were built as abodes for Shiva or Vishnu, not as gathering places for the people. To build a temple-mountain was the act of worship that would enable the people to flourish through the presence of the god.

Perhaps the earliest temple-mountain to survive at Angkor is the small Prei Prasat, in the north-west corner of the irregular grid of canals and roads that forms Angkor. It was built on an island site, without encircling walls, surrounded by a backwater of the canal system. Prei Prasat was constructed during the reign of the great Jayavarman II, from A.D. 802 to 850, and already the familiar steep step-pyramid shape can be seen. The building materials were chiefly brick and stucco plaster, with detailing in laterite—a soft stone that hardens after exposure to the air. Architecture and sculpture of this period has been dubbed the style of the Kulens by art historians. It digested influences from the Khmers' Chenla kingdom and from the Java of Jayavarman's exile. The architectural forms, here in Angkor and other Khmer cities, such as Sambor, are vigorous and carved with lively and naturalistic decoration of foliage and people. By the end of the long reign, some of this vivacity of detail had turned into stylized conventions, especially in the carving of the loin cloths and skirts, which are usually the only clothing of the human figures.

During the century after Jayavarman's death, the capital was twice moved to other places, Roluos and Koh Ker on the lakes, for short periods before returning to Angkor with the accession of new kings. This century included the brief but extraordinary rule of one of the major kings of Angkor, Indravarman I. Much of what we know about him comes from the deciphered stone inscriptions on his temples. Between the year 877 and his death in 889, Indravarman organized the digging of a big artificial lake at Roluos to collect the flood water each year, then the spread of a network of irrigation channels to bring it to the rice fields of the town and a wide region around it. Many of the hydraulic techniques of the Khmer had been inherited from the old Funan kingdom. But the Funanese had been concerned to drain the soggy land of the lower Mekong delta, so the problems of irrigating the middle basin of the plain were new. Indravarman's great religious monument, the famous Bakong temple-mountain, is at Roluos, several kilometres south-east of Angkor, but his son Yasovarman brought the royal seat back to the city.

Yasovarman was very much his father's son. He brought the storage tanks of the Khmer irrigation system to the edges of Angkor itself and he built the first of the large temple-mountains in the city as his personal tribute to Shiva and monument to himself. This should not be seen as any sort of vanity, for just as the Inca kings each built a palace that in time became his mausoleum, each Khmer monarch—ruler of Kambuja, as Cambodia was called in the inscriptions from this period onwards—had a duty to build a new temple mountain for the god. On top of the step-pyramid representing the mountain, there was a shrine in which the god dwelt, though there might be a tower above this sanctuary in some architectural types. The god himself, usually Shiva, was represented by a statue or a *linga* in the shrine—this would ensure his actual presence for the benefit of king and people. Furthermore, since the king was a personification of the god, the temple-mountain was the monarch's own monument for ever. When the king died, his body would be cremated and the ashes buried in his temple. Oddly, it has not been established where the ashes were normally placed within the temple, but it seems that they may have been deposited beneath the god's statue.

An inscription on the stele (sculpted stone) known as the Sdok Kak Tmon tells us that Yasovarman founded a royal city 'and led the god-king from Hariharalaya [his father's foundation] to this city. There His Majesty erected the central mountain, and the Lord of Shivasrama placed a holy *linga* in the centre.' That city of Yasovarman was the area between the much later monuments of Angkor Wat and Angkor Thom. The temple-mountain at its centre was Phnom Bakheng, started in A.D. 893 and finished by the time of Yasovarman's death in the year 900. The natural hill on which it was built was probably already a sacred mound of the Khmer and may well have determined the place where the king settled his capital. He carried out large public works around it before he started to build his temple.

The Bakheng was the first of the giant pyramids at Angkor. It rises in five steps from a square base, each side 76 metres (250 feet) long. A stairway runs up each side of the pyramid, oriented exactly north-south-east-west, symbolic of the order of the world established by the original creation when the mound was fixed. On the flat top of the step pyramid, another square platform supports five towers, the first of the 'five-towered sanctuaries' characteristic

The phallic linga *of stone at Phnom Bakheng represents fertility and stability. It is located in the centre of the first great temple-mountain to be built at Angkor.*

of the next three centuries of Angkor temple-mountains. In the central tower of the five was the shrine of Shiva, with the *linga* mentioned in the inscription, though it has now disappeared.

Why five towers for the temple-mountain? Because Mount Meru has always been described as the mountain with five peaks. Apart from this clear symbolism, French scholars have traced much more intricate meanings in the design of the Bakheng—and so in the designs of the many Angkor temples derived from it. Around the base of the pyramid and on its steps, other smaller towers can be seen. They totalled 109—the central axis plus four 27-day phases of the moon. The 60 small towers on the steps apparently correspond to the cycle of the planet Jupiter. The 12 towers on each step represent, in Khmer thought, not 12 months of the sun's year but a time cycle of 12 animals. Most extraordinary of all, anyone arriving at one of the entrances, on the cardinal compass points, would see only 33 towers. This careful arrangement was designed by the architect (a skilled profession in Khmer society) to represent the 33 gods who live on Mount Meru.

The city built by Yasovarman around the Bakheng hill, now thickly wooded on its slopes below the temple ruins, spread for more than 16 square kilometres (6 square miles)—more than the area of the later city of Angkor Thom, whose territory it overlapped. Apart from the stone temple, few of its structures were built of durable materials and traces of two of its moats have been the chief clues about its size. It is likely that only the central area was completely built up, the rest of the enclosed space is believed to have been rice paddies with scattered hamlets. But Yasovarman's greatest work was the system of water channels, with hundreds of local ponds, which were devised to nourish his city and supplied by the colossal reservoir called the East Baray. To build this reservoir close to the city, his men threw up a rectangular enclosure—surveyed with astonishing exactness—nearly 8 kilometres long by over 1.6 kilometres wide (5 miles by 1 mile), four times the size of the reservoir built by the king's father at Roluos. Thus in 11 years Yasovarman created the framework for what could have remained the Khmer capital throughout the kingdom's existence.

It was not to be. The great king's sons were weak monarchs. The small Baksei Chamrong pyramid beside the Bakheng and the Prasat Kravanh, on the eastern side of Angkor, are thought to be their temple-mountains, both dating from the early tenth century. But little else was built and the usurpers that followed took the capital to another site 160 kilometres (100 miles) away on the lakeside. When the throne returned to the old royal family and Angkor became capital again, the wooden buildings had been consumed by the jungle and Rajendravarman II and his successors occupied a different area centred on the group of buildings that later became the heart of the walled city, Angkor Thom.

This was a generally peaceful period for the Khmer in Angkor, yet it was also a time when their kingdom spread very considerably. Rajendravarman conquered the neighbouring Champa nation and went on to annex the territories of modern Laos, Vietnam and Thailand, spilling over into the southern parts of Burma and China during his reign from A.D. 944 to 968. Drawing on the riches of these lands, many temples and other stone buildings were added to Angkor. The Mébon temple on an island in the East Baray reservoir, the Pre Rup temple to the south of the Baray and the delicate masterpiece of Khmer art called the Banteai Srei—32 kilometres (20 miles) into the jungle north-east of Angkor—all date from Rajendravarman's reign. Historians have divided these buildings into three different styles, of which the Banteai Srei temple (one of the first to be built of stone) is rightly

One of the imposing gateways to Angkor Thom, adorned with a giant Buddha-like face smiling on all who entered the city.

recognized as the peak of refined Khmer sculpture, combined with elegant and vivid architectural forms. Pre Rup and the Mébon, on the other hand, are rather ponderous designs, and the last of the big temple-mountains to be built of brick with a plaster covering. Their special interest is that they have long covered halls on the sides of their pyramids, which developed into the great galleries that were to become increasingly important.

The centre of the city of Angkor was defined more clearly during the years following Rajendravarman's death by the building in A.D. 970 of the small and very beautiful temple-mountain, Phimeanakas, the wooden royal palace beside it (now vanished, but imported Sung and Ming porcelain from China has been excavated from its foundations), a walled royal enclosure around palace and temple and a gateway leading to a ceremonial avenue running eastwards towards the Baray reservoir. Spreading on either side of this avenue a large square was built, usually called the Grand Plaza, and this was enriched by the sculptured terraces, such as the Elephant Terrace, over the following centuries. But the gorgeously carved structures known as the North and South Kleangs, which line the avenue on the far side of the Grand Plaza, date from its original laying out in about A.D. 970. At the far end of the avenue, and near the banks of the reservoir, another great five-towered temple-mountain called the Takéo or Ta Keo was built in about A.D. 1000. It emphasized the importance of this east-west axis (reservoir-avenue-plaza-royal palace) as the centre of the city.

By A.D. 1000 the empire ruled by the Khmer king from the royal palace at Angkor consisted of many large provinces or *pramans,* each controlled by a governor appointed by royal order. Each province was administratively sub-divided into a structure of units called *satagrama* (100 villages), *dasagrama* (ten villages) and the *grama* or village itself. The provincial governors at this time were always members of one of the great families of the priest-nobility. This top caste of Khmer society may well have been of Indian origin—its senior member, known as the *vrah guru,* was immensely powerful and conducted all the great ceremonies to maintain the well-being of the land. It seems that the dominance of this caste was ended by Suryavarman I, who ruled from 1011 until 1049 and reformed the whole administrative system.

At lower levels, the Cambodian caste system was not so closely linked to

This carving on the walls of the Bayon in the centre of Angkor Thom illustrates a naval battle between the Khmers and the Chams, a neighbouring people who invaded Cambodia from the east in the late twelfth century, sacked its capital and slew its king. In the centre of the carving, a fallen warrior is being eaten by a crocodile. Scenes along the bottom depict the everyday life of the Khmer peasants.

pallor of skin as are the Indian castes. Beneath the level of the nobles, most Cambodians were free citizens, though the extent of that freedom is difficult to judge from the stone inscriptions, which are the only Khmer records to survive. Below the soldiers, farmers and craftsmen who probably made up these free middle levels of society, there were two kinds of serfs or slaves. The higher grade, known as 'sacred' slaves, were usually prisoners of war pressed into the service of the state, the priests or the city of Angkor. They were treated with some honour and given petty responsibilities. In contrast, there were also many slaves captured from the wild hill tribes to the north of Cambodia—these were allotted the most menial tasks and their lives were held worthless.

During the two centuries after A.D. 1000 the Khmer empire was at its most powerful and the largest buildings to be seen today date from this period. Under the reforming king, Suryavarman I, and his successor, a second vast reservoir, the West Baray, was built in about 1050 to meet the farming needs of the growing populace. Like the East Baray, this ran from east to west roughly along the axis of the royal avenue and had another island temple on its waters, the West Mébon. To the south of the royal palace, the largest temple-mountain yet was built—the Baphuon. This huge mountain of stone is the most ruined of the Angkor temples, for it was built over a hastily constructed man-made mound. The substructure's movements have toppled the towers and even cracked the three main terraces. In Khmer times the Baphuon was one of the central glories of Angkor, described as 'a gold temple on a gold mountain', with galleries at all levels, a complex plan and fine serene sculpture in gilded wood and stone.

This flawed masterwork takes us up to the buildings of the period that have made Angkor world famous and to the reign of the usurping Suryavarman II, the most powerful monarch in southern Asia in his time. His rule, from A.D. 1113 to 1150 followed a period of turmoil and his first years were spent in a series of campaigns to consolidate his empire. He had less success when he tried to extend its boundaries, and so he turned to building. The Thommanon on the royal avenue near the East Baray was built in about 1120, but Suryavarman's supreme work is Angkor Wat, the largest religious building ever built, a tremendous temple-mountain of stone covering the same area as the Great Pyramid of Egypt, and almost every surface is covered with sculpture of renewed vigour and exquisite detail.

Angkor Wat is a monument to Suryavarman himself as god-king and to the great benign god Vishnu, whom this king worshipped in preference to Shiva. During the previous century, Khmer kings had turned more and more to Buddhism for their private religion, while sustaining their overt Hindu obligations as Head of State of a religious kingdom. These obligations included the building of a temple-mountain by each king, but it is noticeable that those built after the Baphuon were comparatively small until the arrival of a ruler who was a personal adherent of one of the Hindu pantheon.

We have seen that the city centre of Angkor had become increasingly focused on the royal avenue between the two great reservoirs. Suryavarman II chose to build his temple-mountain well to the south of this core, several hundred metres beyond even the earlier centre around the Bakheng. Doubtless this was partly to provide room for the vast enclosure, for the long sides of its outer rectangle of moated walls are each 1.6 kilometres (1 mile) long. A decorated causeway crosses the moat from the west and passes through a towered entrance pavilion that echoes the profile of the temple within. Inside the walls, the causeway stretches on above an expansive courtyard, which contains woods and pavilions and square lakes, towards the towering five-

This sentinel stands in a niche of one of the central sanctuaries of Banteai Srei. The temple, whose name means 'Citadel of the Women', stands apart from the city of Angkor and dates from the year 968, a time of relative peace. It is recognized as the high point of refined Khmer sculpture.

The temple-mountain of Angkor Wat has five companion towers on its summit, echoing the five peaks of the mythical Mount Meru, centre of Hindu cosmology. On the walls beneath the soaring pinnacles—fashioned like a bursting lotus bud—dance the figures of bejewelled, half-naked asparas. Angkor Wat is not only the finest monument to Khmer art and craftsmanship; it is also one of the best preserved.

The head of a gigantic naga or snake which guards the entrance to the Bayon. Its long body—hauled by a team of stone giants— forms a balustrade along one side of the causeway.

peaked stone mountain of the temple.

The plan of the building is far more complicated than anything before it. A rectangular outer gallery contains a grid of inner ranges and two large courtyards on the flanks. Within this, the slopes of the square mountain begin to rise—first to a terrace with a square gallery around it, then very steeply in smaller steps with other galleries. On top of the symbolic mountain, the galleries form a square with a cross within it, so that there are four more roughly square courtyards between the five curving pinnacles of silvery-grey stone. The high central tower, over the inner sanctuary of Vishnu-Suryavarman, soars to a height of 65.5 metres (215 feet), but the titanic scale of the design should not be allowed to distract us from the subtlety of the architectural achievement. Long ranges are most satisfyingly punctuated by strong towers, stone masses contrast with spaces punched through the solid forms, areas of florid and large-scale sculpture are set off by others where the stonework is only lightly decorated or even left to show its own fine texture. It is this sculpture that gives many people the most pleasure as they wander along the galleries or through the succession of courtyards.

Angkor Wat is the logical terminal glory of the temple-mountain's development in Angkor over the centuries. But it was not the end of the growth of Khmer art. Suryavarman's death in about 1150 was followed by 30

A pair of apsaras or heavenly dancers adorn one of Angkor Wat's innumerable galleries. Although several thousand such figures adorn the temple walls, none is exactly the same.

Angkor, once a rich city founded on water, is now a ruined city overgrown with jungle. This Buddha at Ta Som wears as a headdress a fig tree whose roots threaten to strangle the fine stone carving.

years of chaos, leading to the fiery sack of Angkor by the Chams from the east. These invaders ruled the kingdom for four years. Then they were driven out by the most remarkable figure in Khmer history, Jayavarman VII.

It was not by chance that the new king took the name of the founder of Angkor, for he too had to wait for many years and fight to gain his kingdom. With the Chams in power, Jayavarman VII came to the throne aged 55 in 1181 and reigned until his death approximately 33 years later. He fought ruthless wars to oust the Chams and to secure, even to extend, the Khmer empire. And he built the great, square walled city of Angkor Thom around the old royal palace.

During Jayavarman's reign, the city of Angkor beyond the walls was enriched by many great temples, some of them the traditional mountains, some of a new type with their towers rising from ground level. Banteai Kdei was built on the eastern side in 1181 and Ta Prohm near it, beside the East Baray, in 1186. To the north, the mighty pile of Preah Khan was started in 1191, and the smaller Ta Som and Ta Nei decorated the northern side of the East Baray at the end of the century.

Preah Khan marks the place where Jayavarman lived while he directed the rebuilding in the 1190s of the city destroyed by the Chams. At Angkor Thom, a 13-kilometre (8-mile) moat enclosed a tall stone wall buttressed from within by a ramp of earth. The four main gates (five with the entrance where the ancient royal avenue crossed the moat) each had a big gatehouse with a tower decorated by stone elephants and huge smiling faces. Inside, Angkor Thom probably had comparatively few dwellings, for most of the people lived beyond the walls. But the ceremonial Grand Plaza beside the palace was embellished by several raised and sculptured walks, such as the Royal or Elephant Terrace. Even today, with the wooden buildings gone and the jungle barely held back from the stone structures, it is possible to imagine the people gathered at this civic centre for the great occasions of the Khmer.

The Bayon, Jayavarman's greatest temple, is not far from the Plaza. The king was a devout Buddhist and here, at the exact centre of the square city of Angkor Thom, he started in A.D. 1200 to erect an unconventional building that was to be the final masterpiece of Khmer architecture. The Bayon is a temple-mountain of sorts, with the main streets of Angkor Thom radiating away from it to the gateways in the cardinal points of the compass. But it was not dedicated to Shiva, or to Vishnu. It is a temple of Buddhist imagery at the inner core of this Hindu religious state.

Much has been written of the decadence of Khmer art by this period, but the impact of the Bayon is tremendous and unique. Bernard Groslier has written that the 'strange and disconcerting edifice, almost exasperating in its confusion, remains undoubtedly the most amazing piece of architecture in existence.' A rectangular base, with an open gallery around it, supports a circular central shrine with 14 radiating chapels. Towers rise above these chapels and above various points over the outer gallery. The result is that the upper part of the building is like a forest of 54 stone towers about the higher-stepped cone of the central tower. Each of the smaller towers has four giant Buddha-like faces smiling from its sides, while on the middle tower these faces rise in tier above tier, the ubiquitous god-king transformed into Bodhisattva (in Buddhism, a spiritual master well-advanced towards *nirvana*).

On a more human level, the Bayon is famous for the stone relief carvings on its walls, which illustrate the clothing and everyday life of the ordinary Khmer people. Here are sculpted scenes of a woman cooking over an open fire, a mother with her children, a market-place, men playing chess, cockfighting, battles, court processions and a woman about to give birth. They are a moving record of the people ruled by the phenomenal Jayavarman.

After that great king's death in about 1215 there was little more building during the remaining two centuries of the Khmer kingdom. During its slow decline, the outward appearance of prosperity and glory at Angkor continued. A written account of the city at this time has survived in the journal of the Chinese envoy, Chou Ta Kuan, who spent a year at the Cambodian capital in 1296–97.

The particular value of Chou's writings is that they tell of life at all the levels he saw it. He describes a great royal procession: '. . . finally the king. He stands erect on an elephant whose tusks are sheathed in gold, and holds the precious sword of state in his hand.' And an audience with the monarch himself: 'two palace-maidens raise the curtain with delicate fingers and the king, sword in hand, appears standing at the window of gold.' Other, more personal sides of the god-king's customs are mentioned. 'Even the king goes bare-footed . . . the soles of his feet and the palms of his hands being dyed red.' And again, 'the king has five wives, one for the principal chamber, and one for each of the four cardinal directions. As for concubines and palace-maidens, I have heard a figure of three to five thousand mentioned.'

At a lower level in Khmer society, Chou was astonished by the active part played by women. They had equal education and could become judges, professors and even royal counsellors. Wives were often married for their skills in commerce or in the barter of the market-place, where money was unknown (for the Khmer never developed a monetary system). He also tells of the deflowering ceremony for girls at about the age of nine, carried out by a priest who then received a fee from the parents. Later, these girls became lascivious to Chou's way of thinking, demanding much love-making from their husbands. He tells how he, with other Chinese visitors, would go off to watch thousands of Khmer men and women of all classes bathing naked in 'the great river outside the town.'

Between the wealthy classes and the mass of Khmer people, Chou noted a huge gap. The ordinary people had thatched houses, while those of the nobles were tiled. The nobles' homes were richly furnished and their meals eaten with silver cutlery, while the poor cooked in clay pots and served food in ladles of coconuts and cups made from large leaves. All this was not simply a matter of wealth; the Khmers lived in a fixed society, where no one would dare to behave in a way improper for his particular station in life.

As a fixed society, the Cambodian kingdom could only stagnate once its impulse to grow ceased. Already in Chou's time there is mention of raids devastating the countryside around Angkor, and of the increase in Theravada or Hinayana Buddhism. Hinayana is the more inward-looking type of Buddhism, which rejected the outward concern for human affairs introduced by the reforming Mahayana movement some considerable time after the Buddha's death. The increasing influence of the older and more ascetic form on the Khmer monarchs, at the cost of the Mahayana ideas, which had attracted earlier kings of Cambodia, contributed to a general apathy about political power. The kingdom shrank gradually and the raids came nearer to the capital. The blossoming Thai kingdom of Siam annexed more land on Cambodia's western boundaries and finally devastated Angkor in A.D. 1431. The god-king fled and his people evacuated the city to follow him. The timber houses and palaces rotted, the water in the reservoirs and canals leaked away, and the creepers grew over the stone temples.

The city remained lost for centuries except for one interlude. In 1585 a Portuguese Capuchin friar, Antonio de Magdalena, wrote an account of the recent discovery of ruined Angkor by a Cambodian king named Satha, who was hunting in that area. This king had striven to restore his ancestors' capital and to some extent succeeded. Magdalena tells of the court there, the ceremonies at the rice harvest, the houses with doors on to the canals, the refuse collection by barges, which went from house to house. But Satha's efforts, too, ended in failure and knowledge of the city faded into myths as the jungle reclaimed it.

Angkor awaited the French naturalist Mouhot. In his book *Voyages dans l'Indo-Chine, Cambodge et Laos,* Mouhot told of the real hardships of travel through the jungle in 1860, unaided by the peasants despite a letter from the Cambodian king to the village chiefs. The country had a terrible disease-ridden climate and the people could scarcely be stirred from their lethargy. When he found Angkor, his questions to local men were answered, 'It is the work of giants' or 'It made itself.' Mouhot worked for weeks in the ruins, cutting away the tendrils and roots of trees growing in the cracks of the buildings, frightened by the noises of tigers and elephants during the night. He worked with a vision in his mind of the book he would write, of the archaeologists and historians who would read it and come to carry on his labours. And his vision became reality. The archaeologists came and they were followed by men with the other skills that were needed to restore the major ruins and let the world know of their splendour.

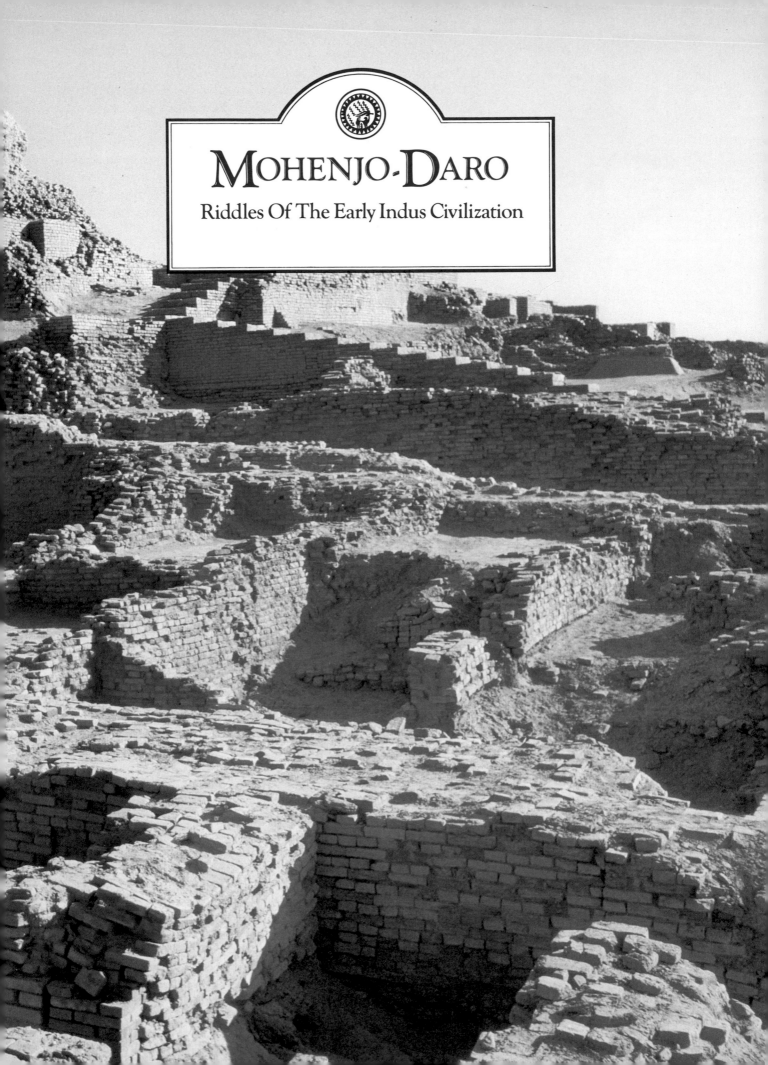

MOHENJO-DARO
Riddles Of The Early Indus Civilization

The famous dancing girl from Mohenjo-Daro, one of the few surviving bronze sculptures of the Indus civilization. She is wearing only a necklace and a plethora of bracelets. Her seductive eyes, sinuous body and tilted head presumably represented the Indus people's ideal of sexual allure.

Previous pages *The austere but imposing aspect of Mohenjo-Daro ('Mound of the Dead') with a later Buddhist stupa (shrine) crowning the citadel above the excavated streets.*
The chapter symbol is a decorated dish of the Indus civilization.

THE SIND DESERT in modern Pakistan, beyond the green border along the lower reaches of the grand Indus river, is an inhospitable place for mankind. The plain is of almost colourless earth, with occasional bushes and stunted trees, blasted by dust storms or by implacable sunlight. Yet here, archaeologists have traced as far back as 5000 B.C. the ancestors of a great civilization which flourished along the Indus, at much the same time as the early Mesopotamian cultures described later in this book.

Although Mohenjo-Daro and Harappa, the two major cities of this period, are now in Pakistan, exploration of their sites started when it was part of India under British occupation. Early discoveries brought the Indus civilization to the attention of the world, but the revelation of its extent and achievements had to await the arrival in India of a celebrated British archaeologist in 1944. Sir Mortimer Wheeler, a man who combined high scholarship with organizational powers and a swashbuckling public manner, was appointed Director of the Indian Archaeological Survey after fighting in World War II. Wheeler swept like a gale into India and, after dealing with other archaeological matters, arrived at Harappa—where some of the ancient objects had been discovered—in May 1944. 'Warned by my anxious colleague that we must start our inspection at 5.30 next morning and finish by 7.30 "after which it would be too hot", we turned in with the dark figure of the *punka-walla* [servant operating a fan] crouched patiently in the entrance and the night air rent by innumerable jackals . . .', he wrote later. 'Next morning, punctually at 5.30, our little procession started out towards the sandy heaps. Within ten minutes I stopped and rubbed my eyes as I gazed upon the tallest mound, scarcely trusting my vision. Six hours later my embarrassed [presumably at the sight of a *sahib* doing manual work] staff and I were still toiling with picks and knives under the blazing sun. . . .'

A few days later, Wheeler travelled 645 kilometres (400 miles) south-west to the Sind desert and Mohenjo-Daro. Wheeler's party slept on the roof of a rest-house (local hotel). 'I recall how the slowly growing light of the pre-dawn dimly showed through the verdure . . . a tall mound crowned, as we discovered, by the considerable wreckage of a Buddhist shrine or *stupa,* perhaps of the second century A.D., raised high upon the heaped remains of an earlier age . . . surely a repetition of the flanking citadel . . . at Harappa.' Wheeler left the Indus then to start recruiting a department of archaeology in India that could tackle the great excavations.

The city of Mohenjo-Daro was built by the descendants of a people whose traces, going back as far as 5000 B.C., have been found in the foothills far to the north. At some time about a thousand years later these people moved down from the hills on to the richer soil of the Indus plain. Corrected radiocarbon dates for the so-called pre-Harappan stage of the Indus culture's settlements go back to 3150 B.C. at smaller towns such as Kalibangan and Kot Diji. Nothing as early as this has yet been found at Mohenjo-Daro, the largest city, but that proves nothing. For the excavations there have revealed only the city at its height in about 2000 B.C.—shafts drilled in the 1960s by UNESCO showed that occupied sites can be found as much as 18 metres (60 feet) below that level!

The civilization of those times covered a large, approximately triangular, area. The triangle runs from an apex 800 kilometres (500 miles) up the Indus river and spreads 960 kilometres (600 miles) along the coastline at its mouth into the Indian Ocean. About a hundred towns have been found.

Among the Indus settlements, Mohenjo-Daro and Harappa were much the largest. On balance, it is likely that they reached their zeniths at about the same time, capitals respectively of the upper and lower stretches of the Indus valley occupied by their people—though no radiocarbon dates from Harappa have yet been published to check this theory. Both were, with Uruk in Sumeria, the world's largest cities in their time—their boundaries were over 5 kilometres (3 miles) in circumference. Many valuable archaeological finds have come from Harappa, but there is little in the way of buildings to be seen there.

Mohenjo-Daro, as rebuilt following a destructive flood before 2000 B.C., is the earliest pre-planned city yet found anywhere in the world. It consists, like most Indus towns, of a large residential area at its lower level overlooked from the west by a higher citadel, a fortified and much smaller area.

Below the citadel, the city was carefully designed for about 40,000 people in a grid pattern apparently of 12 main earth-paved streets, each about 9–13 metres (30–45 feet) wide. This street grid enclosed blocks of fairly even size, each block consisting of hundreds of houses very close together and opening off narrow lanes. The lanes vary in width from about 1.2 to 3 metres (4–10 feet), and are built with frequent right-angle bends—probably as a break against the winds. Most of the houses excavated were quite spacious, with several rooms around a central courtyard, a well and stairs to an upper storey.

It is difficult to visualize more than a vague outline of the people and their lives in these houses, for little sculpture and no paintings have survived. The houses so far excavated seem to tell of a comfortable middle-class way of life for the citizens. Privacy and security were important to them, for there are no windows on to the street. The houses show an obsession with water and cleanliness, but little interest in colour. Their internal walls were often plastered over the brickwork, but the plaster was not decorated. Household pottery was made on the wheel—it was usually pink or buff with a red slip. The pottery decoration varied from lines, checkers and intersecting circles to designs showing roses, leaves, birds and fish.

Meals were probably taken squatting on the ground, in some households from large flat dishes made with slender stems and wide bases. The usual food was fish, chicken, pork and other meats with rice, wheat, barley or millet.

By the time Mohenjo-Daro reached its peak and its decline, the population was highly mixed. There were Mongolians among them and other people with the medium rounded shape of head commonly seen today in the Gujerati of Western India. Most, however, had the long narrow heads typical of ancient inhabitants of the area between the Persian Gulf and the Mediterranean.

They wore clothing of cotton cloth and perhaps of linen and wool too—although neither of those two materials has survived, they grew flax and may have kept sheep. If their homes were very plain and colourless, the figures moving around in them may be imagined as more exotic. The men were bearded, but some at least shaved off their moustaches. Beards and hair were arranged in patterns, the hair drawn back into a bun, and they wore a variety of head-dresses. Male dress was sometimes of patterned cloth—it was made into tunics worn over one shoulder and under the other.

The women wore less—a short skirt was held at the waist by an ornamental belt and that was all. However, they embroidered the cloth with delicate copper needles and they arranged their hair with lively fantasy. They wore much jewellery—necklaces of gold, of faience or of etched carnelian—bracelets and armlets of gold, silver or copper—finger rings of lapis lazuli, agate, shell or steatite paste—pendants, hairpins and mirrors of copper or bronze.

Wandering around the dun brick streets of the excavated part of the city, the contrast between those bright, even gaudy, vanished figures and the harsh mud colour of their background seems extraordinary. Nor can we see into their minds, for their writings survive only on the hundreds of little steatite

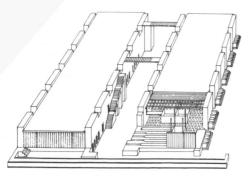

The granaries at Harappa and Mohenjo-Daro are thought to have served the same function as a modern bank or treasury—the amount of grain stored equalled the level of civic wealth. At Harappa (shown here) the granaries were built in two rows of six split by a street. Triangular ventilation shafts line the back of the granaries. Outside there were also 17 round platforms for labourers to pound grain. The Mohenjo-Daro granary had 27 blocks with a recessed unloading bay for the bullock carts.

seals which have been found in the houses, and the script is not yet deciphered. The characters are quite different from those of contemporary Mesopotamia or Egypt and they stir a feeling of wonder at the way in which some societies have devised methods of writing—quite separately from each other—while others, more evolved in some ways, have never done so.

The seals which have preserved almost all the Indus writing are also mystifying. Most of them have a rectangular impression, about 3.1 cm (1½ inches) by 1.9 cm (¾ inches). Judging by their prevalence, every family probably had one, yet the standard of careful carving is very high. It is thought that they were impressed on clay plaques used to seal bales of cotton and their marks are found stamped on pots. Apart from written inscriptions, they show animals, people and in three cases a deity who appears to be predecessor of the symbolism characteristic of Shiva, one of the chief later Indian gods.

There are good reasons for thinking that various facets of Hindu religions may have had origins in the Indus civilization. The Indian archaeologist S. R. Rao goes further than that and sees Mohenjo-Daro and Harappa as giving the world Hinduism, the auger drill, the idea of standardized manufacture, the magnetic compass and yoga. As regards the last of these, the poses of many terracotta figures found in the cities certainly suggest yogic positions. But the religion of these people is by no means proved—in fact, no Indus building has yet been securely identified as a temple of any religion. One possibility is a complex of massive brick structures in the lower town of Mohenjo-Daro, with a wide avenue leading to a central court that was perhaps a shrine.

The most impressive buildings of Mohenjo-Daro, however, lie on the hill of the citadel which rises on the west side of the lower town. Here, as at Harappa, was a formidable fortress, rising nearly 15 metres (50 feet) above the plain. It is a mass of man-made brick platforms in the shape of a parallelogram 365 metres (1200 feet) long and 182 metres (600 feet) wide, aligned north–south. Archaeologists have usually interpreted it as representing the centralized political power which organized the Indus state and drew up the plans which rebuilt the geometrical city below. Yet no royal palace has been found, nor a temple for a god-king such as one finds in most early civilizations.

At the southern end of the citadel mound there is a group of rather complicated structures around the remains of a big almost square hall with sides about 27 metres (90 feet) long. Inside, it seems that it was just the biggest open space the Indus people could build, with a wooden roof (now vanished)

The mysterious Great Bath at Mohenjo-Daro measuring 11 by 7 metres (39 by 23 feet) and 2.4 metres (8 feet) deep. The bath and its flights of steps at either end were waterproofed with asphalt. Although probably put to ritual use, the bath could equally well have been used as a communal swimming pool or some sort of aquatic bordello.

This mysterious 17.7 cm (7 in) stone sculpture (found near a building in the lower town) depicts a god or priest-king in ceremonial robe. It is one of 11 stone sculptures recovered from Mohenjo-Daro, all but two being men or gods. They have in common trimmed beards, shaven upper lips, headbands, low receding foreheads, and hair done up at the back. The eyes are inlaid with shell.

supported by four rows of five fairly massive brick pillars. Absolutely nothing is known about the use of this building. It is usually called the Assembly Hall and may have served that purpose at some stages in the city's development.

The main group of buildings on the Mohenjo-Daro citadel lies at the north end of the hill. On the west, the side away from the city and towards the open countryside, are the ruins of a massive brick structure that puzzled Mortimer Wheeler in 1950 as he watched the Pakistani workmen carting away the sand which covered it. 'The aspect was that of a fortress, towering grim and forbidding above the plain. And yet . . . I wondered.' A few days later the answer came to him as more detail emerged from the debris. Returning from a visit to Karachi, he was met by his assistant. "'Well," I said, almost unthinkingly, "how is the civic granary?" . . . Every detail fell into place. Set prominently amid the royal or municipal buildings of the acropolis, this had been the economic focus of the city.'

What is left of the state granary today is only the ruined base of the building—the wheat and rice would have been stored in a series of high spaces, probably of timber construction, above this podium. But the approach for the carts bringing the grain from the outlying farms, the unloading platform and the system of underfloor air-ducts to keep the grain dry, can all be seen. The

Some of the 1200 seals from Mohenjo-Daro. They usually had a hollow knob on the back for wearing and using. At the top a horned ithyphallic god squats in a yoga position, bangles along his arms. In the middle a three-headed animal is perhaps a prototype Shiva, like the figure above but in the guise of Pasupati, Lord of Beasts. The bottom figure is a rhinoceros.

floor covers an area 45 metres (150 feet) long by 22 metres (75 feet) wide.

The farms which produced the grain for the state granary at Mohenjo-Daro must have spread far north and south along the Indus, for the demands of a city population of 40,000 are considerable. Like many early cultures, the Indus people devised a successful method of irrigation, damming the overflow of the great river when it was in flood and feeding the water out during the dry times across the fields cleared from the jungle.

In these fields they grew wheat, six-row barley and rice as their staples—they may have been the first large-scale growers of rice. Other crops were melons, dates and peas, while sesame and mustard were cultivated for their oils. Cotton was another important product—the Sind area was so identified with cotton by the ancient Greeks that they often called cotton fabric Sindhu a thousand years after the fall of Mohenjo-Daro.

The question of what animals Indus people kept is more difficult. They developed the wheel and their farm carts were pulled by oxen. The hundreds of small seals show many creatures that were presumably present in the thick forests of 3000 B.C. before the field clearances felled the trees—tigers, rhinos, crocodiles, antelopes and elephants appear. Since they used ivory a good deal, it is possible that the elephant was domesticated and perhaps used for heavy labour. Apart from oxen, zebu cattle and possibly pigs and sheep were common on the farms, and cats and dogs around the houses. More mysteriously, a creature like an ox with only one visible horn is often shown on the seals—this may account for the legend of the unicorn.

Some of the Indus civilization's produce was certainly traded in other countries, especially the Mesopotamian cities. It may have been shipped from Indian Ocean ports such as Lothal on the Gulf of Cambay, where a fairly large enclosed dock and models of sailing ships with high prows and deep keels have been found. They exported pottery, seals, ivory carvings, timber of rare types and cotton textiles, receiving precious stones and metal ores in return—for there is no ore in alluvial plains. Tablets of around 2000 B.C. found at Ur list goods from *Meluhha,* thought to be Sumerian for Indus.

Close to the granary on the citadel there is a much better preserved building that has given a rare but puzzling insight into Indus customs. Just as the well and carefully drained bathroom in each house at Mohenjo-Daro shows the importance attached to cleanliness, this civic building—generally known as the Great Bath—indicates that bathing became more than a matter of hygiene to these people.

As it survives now, the Great Bath is a wide platform with the stumps of square brick piers around all four sides. In the middle of the open courtyard a deep tank is sunk into the platform, with flights of steps down into it at both ends. This was the communal bath of Mohenjo-Daro, surrounded by porticoes along the front of ranges of timber buildings where the bathers presumably left their clothes. The tank itself was sealed by gypsum mortar and the steps had treads of wood. A well in one of the buildings supplied the water for the bath and it could be drained through a corbel-arched channel which led to the side of the citadel mound. Above the Great Bath buildings there was either a flat roof or an upper storey.

Looking at the remains of this complicated arrangement today, the imagination gropes for pictures of the way the people could have used the Great Bath. Water plays an important part in the rites and symbolism of many religions, representing the primordial state in some, the powers of healing and grace in others. Ritual bathing is an essential part of the Hindu religion, of which we find many pre-echoes at Mohenjo-Daro, and it may be that people gathered here to attend ceremonies conducted by priests.

There are a number of other buildings in this group on the citadel, but particular importance has been attached to a large edifice between the Great Bath and the towering ruined *stupa* (the Buddhist shrine which dates from another settlement of the site 2000 years after the Indus people). There is another open courtyard here and around it there are many small austere rooms with massive brick walls. Again some of these rooms had staircases to an upper level. It has been identified, without any solid evidence, as a college of priests or perhaps as 'the residence of a very high official'.

Next to this so-called College building, the lower tiers of the platform around the *stupa* start to rise. If the area underneath it is ever excavated, we may learn more about the religious or political life of Mohenjo-Daro. For the basic human sacred monument in most societies, once organized farming has started, is the simple mound—often with a shaft in its centre—re-enacting the creation through the union of male and female symbols. Later the mound often became stepped and took on particular shapes, a pyramid or a hemisphere, for example. The rounded *stupas* found all over India are the result of such development over the millennia. Modern scholars and archaeologists have shown that these were adopted by the Buddhists from earlier religions.

There remains the subject of death at Mohenjo-Daro—death and burial of the people and the death of the civilization. No formal burials have yet been found at Mohenjo-Daro, but a graveyard outside Harappa contained 108 skeletons, most of them laid outstretched with their heads to the north. One of these was in a wooden coffin, another in a brick grave. All had some grave goods—usually a couple of dozen Indus pots and some toilet articles. They seem to have been ordinary people and no 'royal' or 'priestly' tombs are known. What happened to the rest of the dead of a city of 40,000 people which existed for several hundred years? Some pots have been found which have been described as 'post-cremation urns' and this, dubious though the evidence is, may indicate that cremation with little ceremony was usual.

Some time around 1900 B.C. the Indus culture started to decline and it is possible to see some of the reasons for this. No radiocarbon dates later than that have been found and it seems likely that the people had simply exhausted the timber available from the great forests that once had surrounded them. Earlier, Mohenjo-Daro had been flooded at least three times, and each time they had simply rebuilt the city over the mud left by the waters. But their building materials were timber and baked brick, and more timber was needed to fire the huge quantities of bricks used in the city. Without wood at a reasonable distance, repairs and rebuilding were neglected. Later dwellings are jerry-built and the spacious houses of the great period were often divided.

Thus when the Aryan invasion swept into India from the north in about 1700 B.C., the conquerors probably found a demoralized people still inhabiting the grand towns of their ancestors. The Rig Veda, the Sanscrit hymns to the father-figure of the Hindu gods, Indra, are thought to date from this period—they were passed down by word of mouth for thousands of years before being written down. Some of the Vedic hymns seem to tell of the Aryan destruction of the Indus culture. Indra is praised as *puramdara* or fort-destroyer. In one hymn he sacks 90 forts. In another, he 'rends forts as age consumes a garment' and is credited with destroying a hundred old castles. The fact that the Indus people had a hundred fortified towns might be a coincidence, but further evidence of a link was found by archaeologists at Mohenjo-Daro. In one place, nine twisted skeletons were found, including five children. One house contained 13 skeletons of peoples of all ages, some with sword cuts in their skulls. Beside a public well, four men and women lay as if slaughtered and left there. All these were at the last level of occupation.

Another two even more elaborately carved seals. The top one depicts a horned goddess in a fig tree with priestesses or sacred dancers below. The bottom figure is another triple-horned animal.

This terracotta monkey, once a toy in a Mohenjo-Daro tomb, originally had a stick to climb. Most Indus civilization terracotta objects are of plants or animals rather than humans.

PERSEPOLIS

Royal City Of The Persian Empire

Below *The Tomb of Cyrus the Great at Pasargadae. Alexander the Great felt a close affinity with the man who had done for Persia what Alexander and his father had done for Macedonia. Not only did Alexander continue the practice of sacrificing a horse a month by the guardian Magi at Cyrus' tomb, but he also visited it twice. He ordered his architect Aristobulus to restore the tomb when it had been robbed by a Macedonian between his visits.*

Previous pages *The 18-metre (60-foot) columns of Persepolis' Apadana Audience Hall once supported one of the largest enclosed spaces ever built. Construction probably took 30 years. Today only 13 of the 72 columns still stand and no traces remain of its mud brick walls, once over 5.1 metres (17 feet) thick. Behind are the stone door and window frames of Darius' Palace.*
The chapter symbol is Ahura-Mazdah, sole god of the Great Kings.

Right *The extent of Persepolis was dictated by the stone terrace Darius built over a natural rock outcrop. Its nine major buildings filled the terrace over a period of about 60 years.*

W HEN CHRISTOPHER MARLOWE, the Elizabethan dramatist, wrote his tragedy *Tamburlaine the Great,* Persepolis had been lost to the world for nearly two millennia, but its name alone seemed to evoke the ultimate in earthly glory.

> *Is it not passing brave to be a King,*
> *And ride in triumph through Persepolis?*

In our own century two successive Shahs of Persia encouraged its excavation as a symbol for the imperial splendour they wished to recreate. Today, the 1971 Pahlavi celebration of the 2500th anniversary of the Persian Empire seems an act of pride before the fall, yet it was fitting that the death of Cyrus the Great in 529 B.C. should be commemorated at Persepolis. In 30 years Cyrus transformed the Persians from being a subject people of King Astyages of the Medes to the rulers of the largest empire the world had yet seen. Media, the legendary King Croesus' Lydia and mighty Babylon itself succumbed to the military prowess and political shrewdness of the Persian king. He died unexpectedly, fighting on his new eastern frontiers.

At Pasargadae, sacred capital of the Persians, the founder of the Archaemenid dynasty had built himself a simple masonry tomb with a pitched roof. It is still there on one of those stone-covered mounds which are sacred monuments in so many early cultures and, although the great warrior's remains have long disappeared, there are accounts of how he was buried in it. The body was placed in a gold coffin which rested on a ceremonial couch. Beside it, a table was set with fine clothing, swords, precious necklaces and other ornaments of gold and gemstones. Around the monument, grass and trees and water provided an earthly version of the paradise which the hero had entered. Two centuries later one of Alexander the Great's generals recorded the inscription: 'I am Cyrus, who gained the empire for the Persians and was king. Therefore do not grudge me my monument.'

The Persian tribes were Aryans who had descended into what is now the great plateau of Iran from southern Russia. They were of the same long-headed and pale-skinned stock as those who had overrun the Indus people's fortified towns in about 1700 B.C. Persia first appears as Parsua in an Assyrian archive of 836 B.C. The religious beliefs of the people in Iran then are recorded as if they were strange distortions of earlier truths perceived by the Magi, the Persian priests. Demons of all kinds pestered and threatened them, ruled by the Evil Spirit himself, Angra Mainyu, without benign gods to balance their influence. In many tribes, those who reached the age of 70 were starved or strangled. Magi were much occupied with destroying the insects and reptiles which were held to be the physical representatives of the evil spirits. But it must be remembered that these surviving practices were written down by Greeks and Zoroastrians – the rites themselves and their interpretation may have been twisted far from the facts.

It was against this background that Zoroaster or Zarathustra emerged as a religious teacher and prophet before 550 B.C. in Persia. In that year he converted Vishtaspa, one of the Persian chieftains and a relative of Cyrus, to belief in the supreme god Ahura-Mazdah. This deity had been seen as the senior member of the Persian pantheon in some teachings at least a century earlier, but Zoroaster's achievement was to present him convincingly as the *sole* god. Ahura-Mazdah indeed had many attributes recognizable in later monotheistic religions—*Spenta Mainyu* as his Holy Spirit, *Asha* as Righteousness, *Vohu Manah* as Good Thought, *Ameretat* as Immortality, *Khshathra* as his immaterial Holy Kingdom. He was Truth in constant battle with the Lie—which was seen as anti-life and darkness, rather than factual inaccuracy.

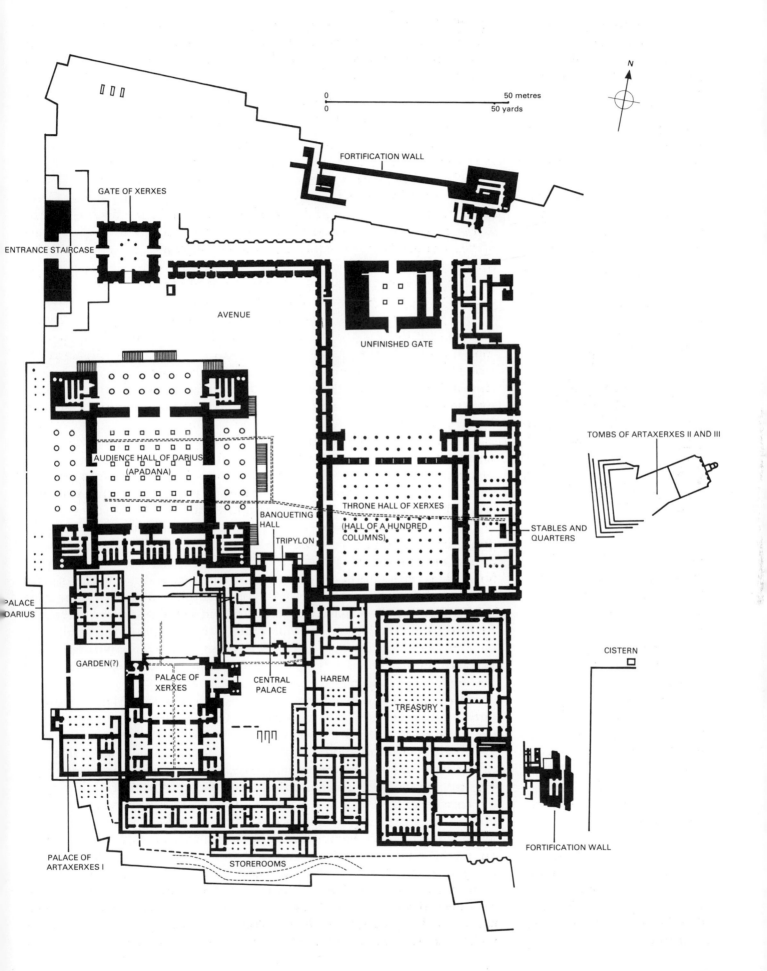

GATE OF XERXES

ENTRANCE STAIRCASE

FORTIFICATION WALL

AVENUE

UNFINISHED GATE

TOMBS OF ARTAXERXES II AND III

AUDIENCE HALL OF DARIUS
(APADANA)

BANQUETING HALL

TRIPYLON

THRONE HALL OF XERXES

(HALL OF A HUNDRED COLUMNS)

STABLES AND QUARTERS

PALACE OF DARIUS

GARDEN(?)

PALACE OF XERXES

CENTRAL PALACE

HAREM

TREASURY

CISTERN

PALACE OF ARTAXERXES I

STOREROOMS

FORTIFICATION WALL

0 ___ 50 metres
0 ___ 50 yards

N

Darius' Palace from the south. On the facade guards flank a central inscription. They in turn are flanked by combats between lion and bull. The staircases are lined with servants bearing food into the palace. The central door of the portico was the main entrance, its sides carved with figures that carried the names of Darius and Xerxes. It is likely that the concave cornices above the doors were carved by 55 Egyptian masons brought to Persepolis. To the left is the western flight of steps. The empty foreground may have been a garden.

Zoroaster condemned earlier superstition and practices such as the sacrifice of oxen to Mithra, another of the Persian pantheon. For the ox was a beast of the sacred occupation of farming.

The conversion of Vishtaspa was to be of unforeseeable importance to the religion of the one god Ahura-Mazdah. For Cyrus appointed Vishtaspa as satrap or governor of one of the provinces of his empire a few years later and he in turn established a college of sorts for Zoroaster. More important still, Vishtaspa's eldest son had been born a year after the conversion. The child was named Daraya-Vohumanah, meaning roughly Bearer of Good Thought. That name was shortened by the outside world and the boy was later known to the Greeks as Darius, greatest of the Persian kings.

Early in 522 B.C. Darius was a royal spearman aged 28, serving in Egypt in the army of King Cambyses, son of Cyrus. Cambyses was a fairly successful ruler and the first Persian to conquer Egypt, but he had murdered his brother for political reasons. One of the Magi claimed to be the murdered brother and in 522, according to Darius' records, deposed the king. Darius hurried back to Persia, arranged a successful conspiracy to assassinate the usurper and, despite his very distant kinship to Cyrus, was enthroned.

Darius the Great ruled for 36 years, until 486 B.C. Many of the 23 territories of the Persian empire, called satrapies, rebelled during his first years. He crushed them, consolidated the empire and went on to extend it greatly by conquering Sind, the north-western part of India. He transferred the political and administrative capital to Susa, on the western side of the Persians' own tribal territories and within easy distance of the river Tigris and the Persian Gulf. Susa became a grand city and Darius spent most of the year there. The religious capital remained at Cyrus' oasis, Pasargadae, on the main north-south road across the plateau of Persia from the Gulf to the Medes' capital Ecbatana. But Darius decided to build a new ceremonial city—or, rather, a palatial citadel—40 kilometres (25 miles) south of Pasargadae. It was to be the king's own centre of the empire, a place of royal grandeur. The Persians called their country Parsa and Pasargadae has been translated as Camp of the Persians. Parsa was the name Darius gave to his new royal city, but the world knows it in the Greek form Persepolis, City of the Persians.

The countryside of the high plateau on which both Pasargadae and Persepolis stand is harsh and mountainous. These mountains shut out all but the winter rains, so that wide deserts and salt lakes are found in much of the plateau. Even in country such as that around Isfahan in the centre of the plain of Shiraz in the south—near which Persepolis stands—the annual rainfall is only 10 centimetres (4 inches). The nights become cold in November, followed by mists and heavy night-time snow on mountain and plain. In January and February the mountain passes are blocked by snow, which melts with sudden uproar in the spring. For a month the country teems with water. Then it is gone, unless it has been stored, and the sun starts its long summer baking of the arid land.

No wonder that the earthly paradise of Cyrus at Pasargadae consisted largely of gardens fed by the priceless water from the annual spate of the Median river, held in tanks and canals. Pasargadae was built on a small plain of its own 1828 metres (6000 ft) above sea level among the rocky hills, its enclosure orientated on the cardinal points of the compass. From there the river cut south-eastwards through a deep gorge to a more extensive plain where it joined a larger stream, the Araxes. At the mouth of the gorge Darius built a fortress where the city of Istakhr later grew up. And farther along the edge of the plain, at the foot of the mountains, he chose a long and isolated outcrop of rock as the foundation for Persepolis.

Work at Persepolis may have started soon after 520 B.C. By 513, an inscription by Darius on the south side of the vast platform records 'in the place where this citadel has been built, no citadel has previously been built. By favour of Ahura-Mazdah, I built this citadel, and Ahura-Mazdah ordered that it should be built . . . and I built it secure and beautiful.' In another part of the same long inscription he says 'I am Darius, the Great King, King of Kings, King of lands numerous. . . . By favour of Ahura-Mazdah, Darius is King.'

Around the natural outcrop at its core, the great stone platform runs for 503 metres (550 yards) almost north-south. It is 302 metres (330 yards) wide and 12 metres (40 ft) high, although the mud-brick walls above the masonry terrace took the height up to a total of 18 metres (60 ft). The big blocks of stone are of irregular size and shape, but they are fitted closely and clamped with iron or lead pins, without mortar.

On top of this great citadel the royal buildings started to rise on smaller platforms of their own in 512 B.C. Tablets and other inscriptions show that work on these continued under Darius for nearly 20 years, with especially fierce activity between 503 and 497 B.C. During this time the big double staircase in the north-west corner of the platform, the only entrance to the citadel, was completed – as was much of the long administrative building at the opposite corner, now called the Treasury. In addition, Darius erected his own palace, looking out over the high west wall. At the very middle of the site, the King of Kings built the comparatively small hall now known as the Central Palace, with the tripylon gateway. One of its carvings shows Darius enthroned, attended by the Crown Prince Xerxes and by ambassadors from 28 countries, evidence that it may have been the original ceremonial centre of Persepolis. If so, this use was only temporary, for north of both this Tripylon building and Darius' palace, a start had been made on the gigantic Apadana, the highest hall of the Persian kings. The tallest columns that still stand at Persepolis are the remains of this great building.

From the relief sculpture, the writings in the stone inscriptions and the accounts of Greek historians such as Herodotus, some picture of the Persian King's life emerges. It is not clear how much of the year the King of Kings spent here—it may have been as little as the days just before and after the New

An Immortal (Persian royal guard, so-named because they were always kept up to a strength of 10,000) from a bas-relief on the northern entrance to the Throne Hall which has five facing rows of five soldiers each beneath the enthroned Great King, Artaxerxes I (reigned 465-424 B.C.). The Immortal stands with his pomegranate spear butt on his foot, presumably the normal parade drill, and grips an oval shield. He wears a long loose Persian tunic with wide flowing sleeves. Hair and beard are plaited in the Persian style. The fluted hat was probably made of leather. In addition to the 2.2-metre (7-foot) spear, a bow and quiver were normally carried.

Year festival. While he was there, Darius presumably stayed in his own palace on the western wall. Many monumental doorways and columns survive of this fairly small palace, with its balconies to catch whatever sun the Persian winter allowed, and it is easy to imagine the King there. We know that he ate most of his meals in royal solitude, though concubines sang and played on lyres to relieve his loneliness. Sometimes the Queen or one of his sons would eat with Darius and after the meal his nobles, who had eaten in an adjoining hall, might be summoned to continue drinking wine with him.

At festivals, and perhaps when legations from the Persepolis satrapies or from foreign countries arrived, Darius would presumably be carried a hundred yards or so eastwards to the Central Palace. There, as we can see in the sculpture, he stood in the big triple portal to receive his visitors. One attendant held a gold parasol above his head, another whisked the flies away from the royal skin.

The new arrivals would, if the wall carvings are to be believed, often be entertained to a royal banquet. Near the Central Palace a stairway leads up to the Banqueting Hall. The sides of the staircase are decorated with rather charming sculpture—servants carry a lamb, a kid, covered dishes, a skin of wine up for the feast. The meal might be prepared in the open for many people, but few would be allowed inside the building with the king. Even those favoured guests would be separated from Darius himself by a linen gauze curtain, so that the King could stay unseen while watching his guests.

Darius died in 486 B.C., four years after the only failure of his reign—the defeat at Marathon of the army he sent to invade Greece. He was buried in an imposing rock-cut tomb which can be seen high on a cliff-face 6 kilometres (4 miles) from Persepolis. His 35-year-old son and successor, Xerxes, was far from the indecisive weakling presented by the Greek historians. Trained as heir and his father's viceroy in Babylon for 12 years, Xerxes carried out the important reforms which enabled his huge empire to embrace nations of many different races and religions in a tolerant and long-lasting regime. He was a convinced evangelist of Ahura-Mazdah, yet did not force his subjects to follow that religion. He extended his eastern empire well beyond what is now Kabul. He reconquered Egypt, whose riches were of incomparably more benefit to Persia than the silver mines and other resources lost when the Greeks were victorious at Salamis, Plataea and Mycale. Xerxes was well aware of his own importance and of his hereditary position. One of his many inscriptions at Persepolis reads, 'Darius also had other sons, but by the will of Ahura-Mazdah, Darius my father made me the greatest after himself.'

If Persepolis was Darius' foundation, its greatest buildings were Xerxes' monument. Work there re-started in 485 B.C., a year after his accession, and continued throughout his reign of 21 years. Many of the building accounts have survived on clay tablets found in the archives section of the Treasury. Thus we know, for example, that in the year 483 there were 313 workmen at one time—underpaid, incidentally, according to the wage rates common in a time of wild inflation of food prices. In 479 B.C., there were 28 stone sculptors at work and a few years later there were 238 labourers working on the Treasury building alone. Rates of pay varied from child assistants and women at one shekel per month, to an overseer goldsmith at 7½ shekels a month. Work accelerated after 470 B.C., when just one work gang on the Treasury numbered over 1300 men.

Although Darius had started the great Audience Hall called the Apadana, most of this supreme work of Persepolis was carried out by Xerxes during the first 15 years of his reign. The other work he put in hand immediately was the construction of a palace for his forceful Queen Amestris. This, the Harem, was on the site now occupied by the museum. It consisted of the Queen's rooms and six apartments, each a small columned hall with tiny individual cells opening off it, for the King's other ladies of various ranks.

Next, Xerxes turned his attention to the ceremonial approach to the royal centre. At the top of Darius' flights of entrance steps in the north-west corner of the citadel, the massive gatehouse still known as the Xerxes Gate was erected. From there, an approach avenue was laid out eastwards almost the width of the citadel. When it reached the far side, this avenue turned sharply southwards at right angles through another gate that led into the courtyard before Xerxes' new Throne Hall, often called the Hall of a Hundred Columns. This tremendous building, covering an even larger area than the Apadana, was started two years before his death in 465 B.C. and was finished by his son Artaxerxes.

South of the Hall of a Hundred Columns lie the extensive foundations of the Treasury, and the greater part of that was added by Xerxes to Darius' early royal storehouse. For it was here at Persepolis, rather than in the political capital Susa, that the Persian kings kept as gold reserves the surplus from the huge tribute of cash or kind paid by the provinces of their empire.

Finally, after finishing the Apadana in 470 B.C., Xerxes decided to move out of his father's palace into a larger one. Again, he could not finish all parts of it before his death, and much of it was built by his son. The remains to be seen at the extreme end of the citadel are more ravaged than those of Darius' Palace nearby.

The Greek historians, who recorded so much of what we know about the Persians, did not apparently know of Persepolis' existence until Alexander the Great found and sacked the royal city 135 years after the death of Xerxes. So neither they, nor the site inscriptions, tell us exactly what the royal centre was used for—apart from the annual festival of the New Year, when delegations came from all over the empire to celebrate and pay homage to the king. The best record of these events, and of whatever other festivities were held there, is contained in the sculptured panels on and between the major buildings.

Visitors arriving at Persepolis during the height of the Persian empire late in Xerxes' reign would see from a distance the great palaces on the citadel, rising above the walls. Arriving at Darius' main entrance steps, they would be challenged for their credentials by sentries of the royal bodyguard. These were from a select thousand of the famous 10,000 Immortals, the élite Persian troops who were the core of the king's standing army. Their bowmen and spearmen can be seen carved on the sides of several flights of steps and especially on the stairways to the Apadana. When Persepolis was excavated their barracks were found within the citadel walls near the Treasury—cramped quarters with appalling sanitation, but a mass of broken wine vessels attested their generous rations of alcohol.

The soldier or attendant who conducted visitors up the broad steps on to the main platform of Persepolis would lead the way into the massive gatehouse of the Gate of Xerxes at the top. There the new arrivals could rest and even wash away the dust of their journey in a great water-filled basin cut into the rock nearby. Little shelter from the sun can be found in the gatehouse today, for only the stone portals carved with big winged bulls and a few columns can be seen within the clearly defined foundations of the building.

From the gatehouse, a visitor might be summoned to either of the two giant reception halls of the royal city. If he was there as an individual supplicant or one of the king's imperial officials, it may be that he would be led through the smaller doorway in the side of the gatehouse and across the stone platform towards the double flight of steps up to the Apadana. For this

A thoughtful conversation between two Median noblemen on the north staircase to the Apadana. They wear the round hat of the Medes with a ribbon at the back and the left hand noble carries a flower. Mede and Persian were given equal prominence at Persepolis to reflect their joint dominance of the empire.

so-called Audience Hall may have been used by the king as a working throne-room, where he listened to petitions and to the counsel of his eunuch advisers before making the decisions involved in the running of an empire.

The stairways rising to the Apadana are lined by panels of relief carvings of both Darius' and Xerxes' time. The earlier carvings are lively and full of humorous touches, though some of the detail is oddly botched. Eight soldiers, presumably Immortals, guard the centre, while rows of splendidly robed courtiers or officials process along either side.

The reliefs of Xerxes' time are generally regarded as the finest of all Persian sculpture. Three bands of sculpture run along the side of the Apadana's base, though the top of the upper tier is missing. The scenes represent the legations from all parts of the empire who came to Persepolis, perhaps for the New Year festival. Soldiers, nobles and slaves in varied clothing mingle with animals of many kinds brought as tribute. Each group is separated from the next by a formalized tree, so that the divisions are clear. Both the design and the detailed execution are immaculate here, without losing a joyous freshness. As with classical Greek sculpture, these works would originally have been painted in brightly realistic colours.

Climbing the stairs on the northern side of this high platform, the visitor would arrive in the Audience Hall itself. The 13 soaring columns that tower over the rest of Persepolis are the survivors of one of the greatest enclosed spaces ever built. The interior of the Apadana was nearly 61 metres (200 ft) square, within giant porticoes on three sides. At each corner the foundations of massive solid towers can be seen—they were of mud brick and have been

Below *Staircase to the Palace of Xerxes, a larger, less well preserved version of Darius' Palace and the highest part of the Persepolis terrace. The staircase reliefs are similar to those of Darius' Palace, guards either side of a central panel in turn flanked by lions savaging bulls. Servants bearing food and drink line the stair rails.*

washed away over the 2500 years since they were built. But within all this was the square hall itself, with solid walls enclosing six rows of six fluted columns, each 18 metres (60 ft) high. It has been calculated than 10,000 people could have been packed into here. It is hard to think of any modern columned space to compare with this. And apart from the spatial effect, the materials and the decoration were of great richness. The columns themselves are of the same fine grey stone—quarried close at hand—that was used for the rest of Persepolis. But the roofs high overhead were of Lebanese cedar, while the brick walls were extensively clad in glazed tiles of white and turquoise, many bearing large inscriptions. Plates and studs of bronze and gold were everywhere, as were rosettes and mythical animals of many rare metals. Much of the woodwork was inlaid with ivory and gold. All this is vanished now, but standing inside the Apadana, the imagination can recreate it.

The architectural style shown in the Apadana, and elsewhere at Persepolis, is a composite achieved by the architects or masons of the Archaemenid dynasty. Its stylistic elements have been traced to the Greek colonies, to Egypt, to Babylon and to other countries which the Persians conquered, so it can be called a truly imperial synthesis.

The other great columned hall of Persepolis, Xerxes' Hall of a Hundred Columns, was probably used for different royal occasions than the Apadana, for its elaborate approach avenue suggests lengthy processions. Starting again at the gatehouse by the entrance to the citadel, the main axis of Xerxes' Gate leads eastwards and then southwards along the avenue to this Throne Hall. Only the bare stones of the buildings flanking the approach are left now, but

Below The Gate of Xerxes has Assyrian-style winged bull sentinels. 'I Xerxes, the Great King, King of Kings' is inscribed above their wings. Beyond one of the gatehouses' four columns is the other, western pair of bulls, which have bull's rather than human heads. All were defaced by Muslim iconoclasts. The wooden door would have been metal plated and 12 metres (40 feet) high.

again it is possible to imagine the impression of magnificence as that corner was turned and the huge portico of the Throne Hall, filled with slender columns and sculpted piers beneath the massive cedar beams of the roof, came into view. Although the sculptured friezes seem to show that the New Year procession took place in the avenue running southwards beside the Apadana to the Tripylon building, at least during Xerxes' early years, it seems probable that his new route and the Throne Hall were devised for this, the main annual event.

It is thought that the Persian new year may have been celebrated at the Spring Equinox, after the great floods from the thawing snow had passed. Each satrapy's delegation set out for Persepolis in time to cover the varying distances from their particular part of the empire. They brought their annual tax payable to the king—whether in gold, goods or livestock herded along the excellent road system which the Persians established through their lands. At the foot of the citadel of Persepolis, the plain grew thick with the tents of these travellers. When the day itself arrived, guards of the Immortals would usher the procession into due order, while another detachment led the representatives of the first satrapies up the entrance steps. Fortunately, Darius' builders had made these steps wide and shallow, so that horsemen and animals could climb them easily—camels, donkeys, oxen, horses and curly-horned sheep are shown among the carvings of the procession and even horse-drawn carts. Each delegation was led by its satrap or another high official. Behind him came rows of men loaded with goods and leading some of the animals they had brought for the king. This procession, doubtless somewhat chaotic in parts, wound through the big gatehouse and along the avenue to the Throne Hall.

We do not know whether Xerxes watched the procession pass or awaited it in the Hall of a Hundred Columns. At any event it seems likely that the animals were left in the court outside the Hall while the men moved on into the wide space inside. None of the hundred columns survive to their full height now, but their stumps are slimmer than those of the Apadana, and so were probably not as tall. Nothing is known about the position of the throne in either of these immense rooms, but the carvings on the doorways show the Great King enthroned there.

Xerxes sits very upright on a seat of gold-plated wood, its legs and back turned in circular rings. His feet rest on a stool. He leans a little forward on a royal gold staff which he holds with one hand, a lotus twirling in the other. His eyebrows are strong, his mouth is set, his eyes protrude fiercely as he watches his subjects. On his head is the cylindrical *cidaris,* the royal head-dress. His hair is carefully frizzed, his long beard is banded horizontally and cut off square at the waist. The robes are evidently of some fine material, pleated where they fall around his back and in the long skirt. Perhaps he addresses the representatives of his empire gathered in the huge hall to celebrate the start of another year. He may tell them of his plans for the future, extend to them his protection in exchange for the taxes they have brought from far away. He may end with an invitation to the royal feast that follows and give them the blessing of Ahura-Mazdah, the sole god of the empire whatever their own religions within it.

For Xerxes and the weaker kings who followed him for over a century—Artaxerxes I, Darius II and III, Artaxerxes II and III—were not god-kings as known in other cultures. They were human kings, placed there by favour of the god. Their palaces were royal, but not holy. Indeed, there are no temples at Persepolis or at other cities of the Archaemenid dynasty's empire. Ahura-Mazdah forbade temples absolutely, as interpreted by Zoroaster. But

Details from two of the 23 tribute groups portrayed on the east staircase to the Apadana. The top group are three of the seven-man Sogdian delegation from the satrapy that was the north-east corner of the Persian Empire between the Oxus and Jaxartes (today Turkestan in the USSR). They bring a length of cloth and a pair of rams. Their lace-up footwear is noteworthy. The bottom group are Lydians of the six-man delegation from Western Asia Minor. They offer bracelets and a two-horse chariot with an axle pin figure that has been identified as the Egyptian god Bes. The figures are 1 metre (3 feet) high and arranged in three rows, moving to the left on the north staircase and to the right on the later and better preserved east staircase.

the Magi who served the one god were important in the empire. A Magus took part in the 'coronation' ceremonies. Magi accompanied the army on campaigns—taking the sacred fire *arta* (law) with them—helped with the education of princes and were in demand as interpreters of dreams. Their position is puzzling for us, for they seem to have been a priestly profession whose services were available to more than one religion.

If there were no temples, there certainly were places of worship. The chief of these appears to have been the fire altar, which often took the form of a high tower. Fires themselves could be acts of worship to Ahura-Mazdah, and Xerxes was particularly active in spreading the idea of the god's *arta*—holy fire representing Righteousness. The great king went so far as to name his son and heir Artaxerxes, combining the god's fire with his own name. But the practice of building great altars for this fire apparently went back earlier, since there is a tall fire tower at Cyrus' Pasargadae and many others at the empire's chief settlements.

Later in the dynasty the kings allowed themselves to be drawn away from the sole worship of Ahura-Mazdah. Thus Artaxerxes III—a savagely cruel king, but the only strong ruler among the later monarchs—encouraged recognition of Mithra, as well as the god of his fathers, during his reign between 359 and 338 B.C. By then, however, much else was changing. In particular, Philip of Macedonia was training an army in northern Greece that was to be the downfall of the decadent Persian empire, which had survived so long largely through the excellence of the administrative system set up by Xerxes.

At the end of 331 B.C. Alexander the Great, son of King Philip, arrived at Persepolis in the course of his long journey of conquest. Alexander had reason to fear ambush and there is a story that he had sworn vengeance for the still-remembered burning of the Athens acropolis by Xerxes in the previous century. Allowing his troops to pillage the rest of the city, Alexander himself took possession of the Royal Treasury. Riches amassed since Darius' time were stored there and Alexander had to summon 3000 camels and great numbers of other pack animals to carry the gold and silver bullion away. It was a hoard nearly three times the size of the one taken at Susa.

The fierce Persian winter came and the conqueror was prevented from leaving Persepolis by snow and rainstorms. Reports reached Alexander that Darius III, the inadequate last Persian king, was waiting for him with a great army to the east. When the spring of 330 B.C. arrived, Alexander prepared his army to leave the winter comforts of the royal citadel at last. Before he left, Persepolis was in flames, though the four Greek historians who tell the story give rather different accounts. In one version the final banquet of the Greeks, before leaving, ended drunkenly with the burning urged by an excitable Athenian lady called Thaïs. In another, Alexander ordered it as a cold act of delayed revenge for the acropolis of Athens. Whatever the reason for this lordly vandalism, the fire spread from the Treasury to the Throne Hall and then probably to the Apadana and the residential palaces. The Persian builders' custom of using cedar beams, rather than stone, for the lintels of many doorways resulted in extra damage to the fabric of the great edifices. The city of Darius and Xerxes was in utter devastation by the next day.

Alexander moved on to find the last Persian king murdered by one of his own satraps. The empire ended there and no later ruler wanted to claim and restore its royal citadel. Persepolis was lost until the Italian traveller Pietro della Valle came upon it in the early seventeenth century and the world gradually realized what these vast ruins had been in their 150 years of splendour under the the Archaemenid Great Kings.

A life-size Darius the Great enthroned with his son Xerxes behind. This central panel of a 6-metre (20-foot) relief is from the rear wall of the Treasury's south portico.

UR

Mesopotamia And The First Cities

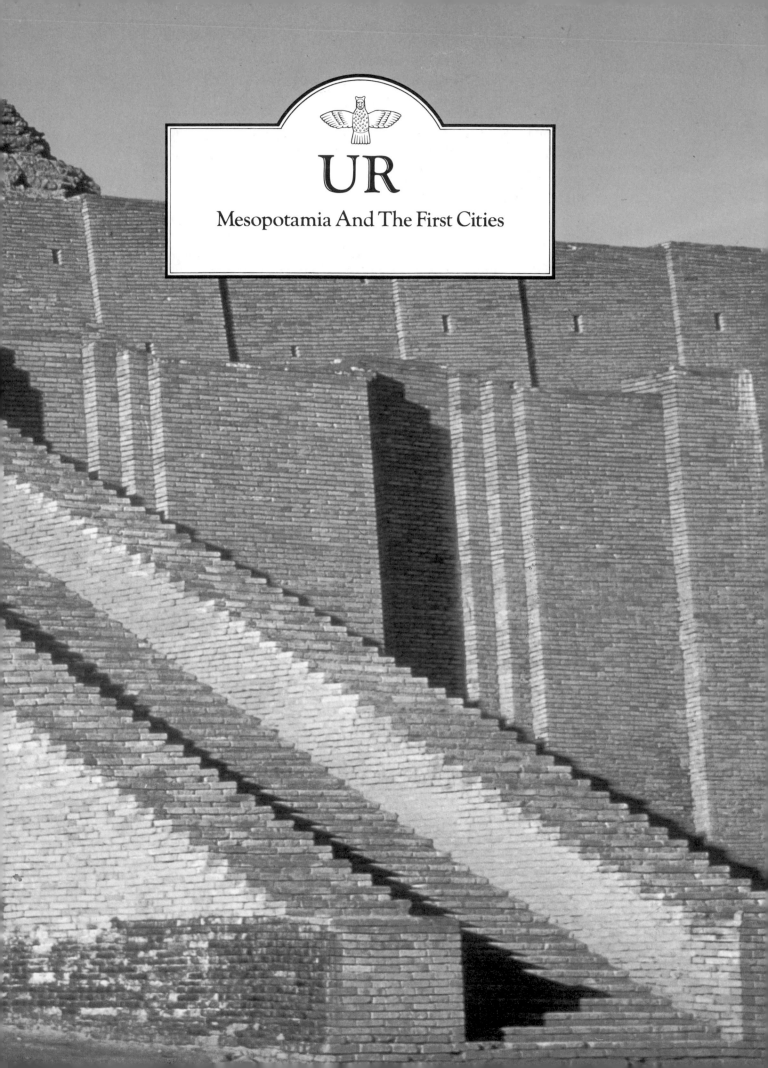

NIMRUD, ERECH, AKKAD, NINEVEH, BABYLON and Abraham's birthplace, Ur, are among the great cities of the early Mesopotamian civilizations which are written of in Genesis in the Old Testament. And one by one in the 1840s and 1850s the first European archaeologists in the area uncovered those names as they dug up the almost featureless hillocks of Iraq.

The leading British figure among these diggers for the past was Sir Henry Layard. He was a rumbustious character, obsessively fond of reading the *Arabian Nights* as a boy and much punished at school for preaching revolution. Layard trained for six years to be a solicitor, then grabbed eagerly at an offered job as a tea planter in Ceylon. In 1839 he set out overland to take up the post. Layard reached Mosul and fell in love with Iraq after seeing some of the big mounds in the desert that covered the Mesopotamian cities of 4000 years ago.

A few years before, German and English scholars had at last started to decipher the writing in cuneiform script (which was used for several languages) found on many ancient stones and clay tablets from that area. After seeing some of these and hearing of the meanings that were starting to emerge, Layard decided to give up the idea of tea-planting.

In 1843 the French consul in Mosul, Paul-Emile Botta, carried out excavations which found the great Assyrian city of Khorsabad, and the public in European countries were thrilled with the carvings of kings, battles and ceremonies that soon appeared in their magazines. Two years later, Layard was given a minor diplomatic post and finance for the expedition that discovered Nimrud and its giant stone winged bulls, now displayed in the British Museum. During the following year, helped by a meagre grant from the British Museum, Layard made extensive digs at Nimrud and later discovered and excavated Nineveh. In 1851 he attempted an excavation at Babylon, but here he made none of the sensational finds of Nimrud and Nineveh.

William Loftus, with the help of the scholar Henry Rawlinson, found and identified the cities of Larsa and Erech (Erech is the biblical name of ancient Uruk, now modern Warka). Then a British vice-consul, J. E. Taylor, found a carved cylinder while digging into a mound called Tell Muquyyar. Rawlinson deciphered the lettering and announced that Ur of the Chaldees, as the Bible calls Abraham's native city, had been found.

The great excavator of Ur was Sir Leonard Woolley, perhaps the most distinguished of all the fine British archaeologists of the early twentieth century. Woolley began work there in 1922 and continued each season for 12 years. He traced the boundaries of the city at its height—from 5000 until 4000 years ago—and found its two harbours off the now-vanished watercourse through which flowed the Euphrates and an offshoot of the other legendary Mesopotamian river, the Tigris. He excavated three areas of ordinary housing, several palaces, a group of royal tombs, the *temenos* (the sacred enclosure at the heart of the city) and the best-preserved of the many Mesopotamian temple-mountain shrines, the Ziggurat.

Woolley's work amounted, quite simply, to the most far-reaching revelation of all about the origins of civilization. For the city of Ur existed, as could be ascertained by its most deeply buried primitive layers, by 4500 B.C. and was inhabited until after 500 B.C. It was not the only great city of that ancient Sumerian culture—Uruk, the largest, and Nippur covered much the same period, while the first layers of Eridu have been traced back five hundred or so years earlier. Later archaeological discoveries have shown that these were not the world's earliest cities, as was thought at the time, for Jericho was a walled town in 7000 B.C., Çatal Hüyük in Turkey goes back to 6500 B.C. and Lepenski Vir in Yugoslavia to 5000 B.C. But early Sumer (as Sumeria is usually

ZIGGURAT

E-DUB-LAL-MAKH GATE

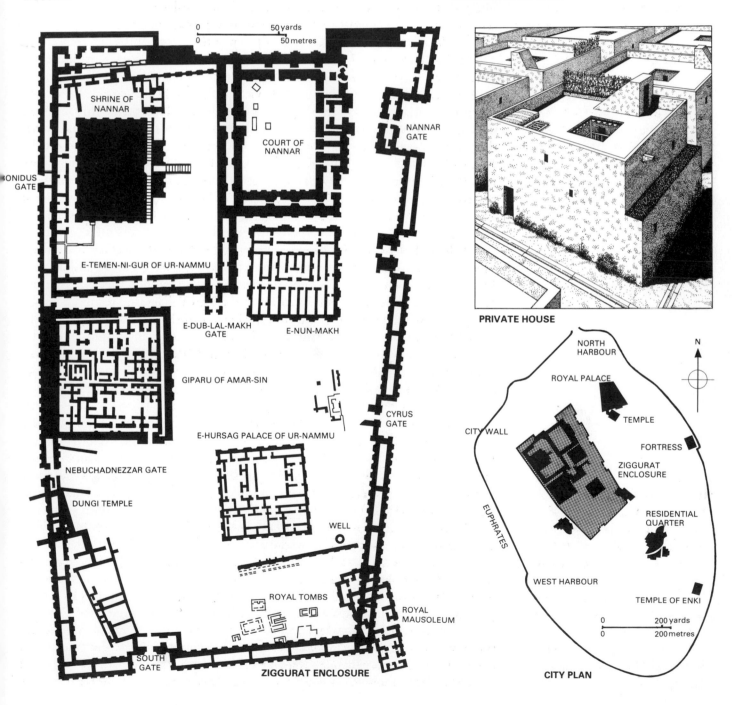

ZIGGURAT ENCLOSURE

0   50 yards
0   50 metres

SHRINE OF NANNAR

COURT OF NANNAR

NIDUS GATE

NANNAR GATE

E-TEMEN-NI-GUR OF UR-NAMMU

E-DUB-LAL-MAKH GATE

E-NUN-MAKH

GIPARU OF AMAR-SIN

CYRUS GATE

E-HURSAG PALACE OF UR-NAMMU

NEBUCHADNEZZAR GATE

DUNGI TEMPLE

WELL

ROYAL TOMBS

ROYAL MAUSOLEUM

SOUTH GATE

PRIVATE HOUSE

CITY PLAN

NORTH HARBOUR

ROYAL PALACE

TEMPLE

CITY WALL

FORTRESS

ZIGGURAT ENCLOSURE

EUPHRATES

RESIDENTIAL QUARTER

WEST HARBOUR

TEMPLE OF ENKI

N

0   200 yards
0   200 metres

A dagger and sheath of pure gold from Ur's Royal Tombs; the finest of many such ceremonial weapons. The filigree sheath has a plain reverse side while the hilt is solid lapis lazuli studded with gold nails. The dagger was excavated in 1926 with its silver-plated leather belt loosely coiled nearby.

Right The 'ram in a thicket', one of a pair from the Death Pit of the Royal Tombs, so named because of its uncanny resemblance to the later Biblical animal found by Abraham after he had left Ur of the Chaldees and was about to sacrifice his son Isaac. Standing 50 cm (19 in) high, the ram (in fact a he-goat) is made of gold, silver, lapis lazuli, shell and red limestone.

called) was a country of 14 great cities which, according to the archives on the surviving clay tablets, passed the position of capital city back and forth between them until Babylon established its ascendancy after 2000 B.C.

The routes of the Tigris and Euphrates have shifted now, leaving Ur without river waters, but the gulf coastline is thought to be unchanged and the climate, too. The summers are hot, very hot, and the winters fairly cold. In late winter, depressions move eastwards from the Mediterranean and bring a little rainfall to a northern strip of Mesopotamia. The rest of the area is fertile only when men irrigate from the rivers. There is some evidence that the wide peninsula of Arabia to the south of Ur became much drier in around 4000 B.C. —this may have driven tribes to move northwards and settle in the delta of the Euphrates, where the marshes were drying up. But the Sumerians themselves were mostly from the north, a first wave from Elam in south-west Iran, then a second—bringing knowledge of working with copper—from somewhere around modern-day Warka (ancient Uruk), also in Iran. Trading routes of great age for caravans of camels, the north-south and the east-west roads, crossed at the upper end of the alluvial plain here, and this may have contributed to the concentration of people in particular places. But the desire to build up large-scale networks of irrigation channels was probably the main reason for the growth of the first cities.

Water was all that was needed to turn the rich soil left by the annual floods of the rivers from desert into crop lands. Barley, which tolerates salt better than other cereals, was their staple grain, though there were small harvests of wheat and millet. Much of the land was given over to sesame, whose seeds produced the oil that was used in every Sumerian household. Figs were another main foodstuff and other fruits that we would associate with hot countries—peaches, figs, pomegranates, grapes and melons. Apples and pears were popular. It is more surprising to find their rich variety of vegetables. Several types of pea were known, onions and leeks were favourites, as were garlic and some spices. Even lettuces and cucumbers were grown and eaten.

The Sumerians were shepherds, too. Many breeds of sheep and some goats were kept for meat and for their milk, which was used to make butter and cheese. They were also valued for their hides and wool. Cattle were highly prized and one of the most appealing works of Sumerian art illustrates the stages in the milking process—long-nosed and rather pop-eyed little men in pleated skirts are shown working around stately cows and their calves. In the first two thousand years of the culture, the people 'fished' the rivers for duck and geese. But hunting died out as herding increased.

At least in the early period, most of the Sumerian farmers lived within the cities. This was not just to make it easier to organize large-scale irrigation projects. It seems clear that there were times of war for the Sumerian citizens, though we do not always know who was the enemy. The cities were all built with high walls around them, of a double thickness of brick. Outside the walls, there would be a series of gardens, then the open fields with scattered houses that multiplied into suburbs later in the civilization. The walls enclosed any river harbours and the group of temples and palaces in each city.

All these buildings and the walls of the characteristic Sumerian city were usually rebuilt many times during their histories. Warfare was not the most frequent reason for this, nor the friability of the unbaked mud brick, which was almost their only building material, for both stone and timber were extremely rare in Mesopotamia. The chief reason for the frequent rebuilding was probably that the rock beneath the alluvial deposits of the Euphrates and Tigris was not stable—it subsided many times during the life of the Sumerian cities, causing floods when the great rivers were next in spate.

Archaeological excavations in Mesopotamia have shown particularly heavy floods in several places at early periods of civilization, but the dates yielded show some conflict. At Uruk and Kish, for example, layers have been found which left a deposit of clay over earlier settlements—this is about 30 centimetres (1 foot) deep and seems to date from 2800 B.C. But at Ur, the layer of new clay was laid at some time in the millennium following 4000 B.C. and averages about 3 metres (10 feet) in depth. It would seem that the Sumerian legends merged several great floods at different places into one catastrophe.

Whatever the complexities of the true story behind the legend of the great flood, it appears that there was one flood which was indeed a turning

A Sumerian version of the Great Flood. This cylindrical seal carving of c. 2200 B.C. comes from Akkad (the Semitic kingdom of central Mesopotamia, which subdued Sumer) and has Utnapishtim as its Noah aboard an ark. Utnapishtim tells Gilgamesh the story of the Flood in the Epic of Gilgamesh *(a Sumerian epic poem retold in Babylonia before 1800 B.C. and translated by the Assyrians in the seventh century). Gilgamesh has been identified as the King of Uruk (Erech) contemporary with Mesannipadda of Ur (Early Dynasty III, c. 2650– 2550B.C.). After excavating the Royal Tombs of Ur, Sir Leonard Woolley dug through a 3-metre (10-foot) layer of mud in 1929 and sent his famous telegram 'We have found the Flood'. The evidence, he decided, was consistent with Genesis' recording of the waters rising to a height of 8 metres (26 feet).*

point in Mesopotamian history. The *Epic of Gilgamesh,* putting into lasting form the oral traditions passed down over thousands of years, lists eight kings (the Sumerian King List records ten) before the flood came. 'After the flood, the kingship came down from heaven.' And so, at some time probably well before 3000 B.C., the confusion after a destructive flood was resolved. The so-called pre-Sargonid era (named after King Sargon of Akkad) began with what archaeologists call the Early Dynastic I period of Ur, somewhere around 3000 B.C.

It is important to bear in mind that Ur, despite its fame and its frequent position as capital, was just one of 14 cities, which grew up at much the same time. It was by no means the largest—it covered about 60 hectares (148 acres) while Uruk spread over 450 hectares (1112 acres). The people of these Sumerian cities, as metalworkers without ore of their own, were unavoidably traders from the start. They traded by land and by sea although the Tigris and Euphrates are not very easily navigable rivers above their lower reaches. Ur's special importance may have been that among the major cities it was the river port nearest to the Persian Gulf. From Ur, river boats could make their way up both rivers towards Nineveh and Babylon in 3000 B.C. thanks to the criss-crossing channels of the delta, and caravans could carry goods from the sea-going ships across the alluvial plain to connect with other overland trade routes. On the north and west sides of Ur, where the main stream of the

The lively style of Sumerian art is seen in this depiction of servants busy with storage jars of milk. It is a detail of a limestone-inlaid relief from the Temple of Ninhursag (goddess of the earth) at Al'Ubaid, 6 kilometres (4 miles) west of Ur and virtually a suburb of the city. See the caption on page 94 for a sculpture from this same temple.

Euphrates flowed beside the town, there were harbours that brought the ships of 2000 B.C. from India and Arabia well inside the high defensive brick walls.

These ships and the desert camels brought all the raw materials of civilization to the Sumerian people. The tablets list copper ore from the Taurus Mountains, gold from Syria, silver from Elam, lead from Anatolia, tin from some unknown mines. Mother-of-pearl came from the towns along the Gulf, soapstone from Iran, rare seashells from India. Timber, including cedar, was brought from the Lebanon, amber from Turkey, and lapis lazuli from Afghanistan. Characteristic seals and perhaps cotton were shipped from Mohenjo-Daro and other cities of the contemporary Indus civilization. In exchange, the main exports were textiles of wool and linen, as well as manufactured objects of all sorts and small works of art.

The kings of Sumer who governed this fluid group of cities and steered it towards prosperity, were responsible for controlling all trade and for initiating the great building works, temples, reservoirs and canals, throughout the country. And the earliest structures known to survive at Ur, where so many older sunbaked brick structures have melted away, were built for kings—the Royal Tombs of about 2550 B.C. discovered by Sir Leonard Woolley.

The Royal Tombs are in the cemetery at the extreme south-east end of Ur's sacred enclosure of temples, only just outside the original walls of this *temenos*. The south-east wall was rebuilt 55 metres (60 yards) farther south in about 550 B.C. (when the *temenos* was enlarged), so the remains of the wall run right across the old cemetery area and over a communal rubbish dump, which apparently grew up above the tombs after a change of dynasty. Woolley's workmen struck the cemetery while he was excavating the dump, which itself provided valuable evidence about the length of habitation in the city. Below a thousand or more graves of ordinary people, Woolley noticed signs of grave robbers of ancient times and he followed their tracks. At the end of the 1926 season he found a magnificent gold dagger, with other gold objects and weapons of copper, at the foot of a deep shaft.

In the next year, deeper still, he found a tomb with two chambers of stone—quite exceptional in that land of mud bricks—though grave robbers had left nothing in the chamber but some small pieces of a broken gold head-dress. Other robbed stone chambers emerged. Then, in 1929, he made one of archaeology's great finds some metres away from these chambers.

On a shallow ramp down into the ground, there were rows of skeletons with fine jewellery. At the bottom of the ramp were several pits or chambers, and two tombs—one of stone. One of the tombs had been found and stripped by robbers—though a seal was found with the name of the dead man—but the other, the tomb of a woman, was untouched. And everywhere in the outer spaces were the skeletons of human attendants and animals, with ornaments and grave goods of gold and other precious materials.

Archaeologists have argued much about the identity of A-bar-ji, the dead man for whom over a hundred people were put to death and buried in the spaces around his tomb. Some have claimed that, since his name is not among those on the Sumerian king lists, he was the chief sacrificial victim among a mass sacrifice to the gods of Ur. But Woolley himself remained confident that this must have been a king, listed or not, and that he died soon after 2550 B.C.

The funeral ceremony probably started with a procession from the royal palace, led by the soldiers bearing the embalmed body of A-bar-ji, perhaps winding through some of the narrow streets of the city and crossing the open spaces around the temples. After the bier came the widow, whose name Shu-bad has been found—Queen Shu-bad, if Woolley was right. She wore a head-dress of gold and gems, and a short outer robe formed by strings of silver

*The gold ceremonial helmet
from the grave of Prince
Meskalemdug, 'Hero of the
Good Land', in one of the last
Royal Tombs of Ur, dated to c.
2500 B.C. Made from a single
piece of 15-carat electrum
(natural alloy of gold and silver)
in the form of a wig with
separate hairs delineated and
done up at the back, it is the
finest surviving example of
Sumerian goldwork. Not only
are the ears left hollow for
hearing but the helmet edges are
also perforated for lacing up the
padded leather skull cap worn
inside. The helmet was found on
the skull of the prince in a
wooden coffin containing a mass
of other treasures.*

*In all 16 royal tombs there were
musical instruments, harps or
lyres. This magnificent bull's
head, with its hair and beard
made of lapis lazuli and wooden
body covered in gold leaf, is a
reconstructed ornament from one
of the four lyres found in the
Death Pit. Such a lyre can be
seen in the 'Royal Standard of
Ur' on page 105.*

and gold beads, lapis lazuli and agate, and other stones.

Nine ladies followed Shu-bad, wearing fine ceremonial head-gear of lapis lazuli and carnelian with long gold earrings and gem-studded gold necklaces. Two of them carried harps, perhaps providing music for the procession. Behind them was a large group of men and women, possibly A-bar-ji's senior attendants, and two wagons pulled by oxen. After that came six more soldiers in double file, with helmets and spears of copper, and two grooms leading donkeys that pulled a highly ornate cart on sledge-runners. This cart was filled with extraordinary objects—a golden saw and chisels, vases of obsidian and alabaster, table dishes of gold and silver, decorated chests and a carved and checkered gaming board about 25 centimetres (10 inches) long, inlaid with lapis and shell.

Towards the tail of the procession were the rest of the royal women, a group of ten wearing bead necklaces and head-dresses of gold with lapis, then a larger group wearing silver headbands and finally ordinary servants.

The destination of the procession was a carefully prepared complex of chambers and pits cut into the ground around the stone tomb of the king. The column moved slowly down a long ramp while the soldiers bore the corpse into its cell. The king's most personal goods were placed around him—though only two model boats were left by the robbers to be found by Woolley—then the soldiers closed off the entrance. The soldiers moved back to line the space outside the chamber, while the procession moved on towards the sealed doorway. The first nine ladies, and perhaps the queen, leaned against the tomb, giving voice to their grief while the priests conducted the funeral rites.

When the ceremony was complete, many of the procession filed into another wide pit to one side of the entrance ramp and Shu-bad was conducted

to a chamber at a higher level than her husband's. There she may have stood beside the bier on which she was to lie and drunk the poison handed to her in a golden cup, which Woolley found at her side. At this, the priests took other vessels of poison, or perhaps a strong sleeping potion, from one to another of the hundred mourners gathered in the pits or on the ramp. Woolley found no trace of any struggle against death.

When the last of the ranks of people below them lost consciousness, the watching priests descended. They placed the harps on two of the women crumpled against the tomb's entrance. The donkeys pulled the sledge of grave-goods forward into the queen's chamber, where she was laid out carefully on her bier. Then that chamber, too, was closed. The priests set about arranging the fallen human beings in neat rows, often with the legs of one rank under the heads of the next. In the largest pit there were six men and 68 women. When their work was done the priests returned to the ground above and watched while the workmen moved in to shovel earth over the bodies.

1 The jewellery of one of King A-bar-ji's court ladies from the Death Pit; golden flowers, leaves, and earrings, necklaces of lapis lazuli, cornelian and pearls. 2 Excavation of the Death Pit, in progress during the 1920s, reveals the honeycomb layout of the Royal Tombs. By paying large sums for finds by his Arab workmen, Leonard Woolley prevented looting of the treasures discovered. 3 An ivory gaming board with pieces for what may have been the earliest form of backgammon.

The Royal Tombs of Ur belong to what archaeologists call the third phase of the Early Dynastic period of Sumer, a phase that lasted from about 2600 to 2350 B.C. During that time it seems that the so-called First Dynasty of Ur was established, and A–bar–ji may have ruled just before that. The small temple at Al'Ubaid, near Ur, has an inscribed foundation tablet saying that it was built by a king of the First Dynasty of Ur, but the evidence about this line of monarchs remains confusing. Even less is known of the Second Dynasty of Ur, and after it several kings seem to emerge as isolated great figures, rather than part of a family sequence. Thus, Luzal–Zaggesi ruled for 25 years from about 2340 B.C. and extended the Sumerian empire as far as the Mediterranean. There followed the tremendous figure of Sargon of Akkad, thought to be legendary until some of his inscriptions and a cemetery of his long reign, starting in 2334 B.C., were found. But the great period of which really extensive remains have survived at Ur is that of the Third Dynasty, founded by the great king Ur–Nammu in about 2112 B.C.

Unlike the geometric street plan of Mohenjo-Daro, as rebuilt around 2000 B.C., Ur was never a planned city. The Euphrates ran past its western side and a man-made moat was built from the river at the north and along its eastern flank. So only the south of the city faced on to dry land. Arriving there 4000 years ago, a visitor would have to gain admission at one of the main gates in the high revetted city mound with brick walls along its top. Inside, he would be faced with narrow main streets that meandered and twisted between the houses towards the temple enclosure in the centre of the city, at the northern end. The streets were not paved but a primitive system of sewage pipes ran under some of them.

The ten or twenty thousand people who jostled in the cramped streets of Ur, and rested in the cool courtyards of its houses, were black-haired, with long heads of Mediterranean type. Their sculpture shows them as thick-set, with protruding and rather bulbous noses. Large luminous eyes seem to have been especially admired. Four out of five men were farmers of the fields around the city. They wore little but a short woollen skirt with a felt cloak, even in winter. Most of them appear to have been clean shaven. However, men of importance in the community had long beards and hair, with skirts of fine wool or linen reaching down to the ankles. Soldiers wore capes, and perhaps other cladding, of leather to act as armour when fighting—only their helmets and weapons were of metal. The women often braided their hair into one long plait, which they wound around their heads. Their normal dress was a full-length unbelted robe, which fell from the left shoulder, leaving the right shoulder bare. Priests and male officials also wore this sort of robe.

Sumerian women wore as much jewellery as they could afford. From 3000 B.C. onwards, their jewellers and goldsmiths were in high demand, for novelty as well as quantity. In response, they experimented imaginatively and mastered almost all the techniques known in later times. On a more practical level, the manufacture of copper objects went back at least to 3500 B.C. and developed rapidly. By the time of Ur–Nammu the smiths were producing the world's first socketed tools, they were soldering with lead, beating out sheet metal, casting and riveting, and even using iron on occasion.

They were equally inventive in their pottery, as one might expect from a clay-based civilization. Sumerian fired pots go back to before the great flood in Ur, and wheel-made manufacture appears soon after it.

All this has been found in the residential areas of Ur, giving us many glimpses of the people's technology and everyday life. To the north of these areas, Woolley also excavated the section between the two harbours, which contained the great palaces and temples. The Third Dynasty of Ur lasted for a

Sumerian picture-writing came to express abstract ideas. A star first meant 'star' then 'god' or 'heaven'; later still 'high'. Cuneiform pictograms first evolved about 3100 B.C. probably first at the Sumerian city of Uruk for the listing of temple estate crops. Ur, 50 kilometres (30 miles) away on the opposite (south) bank of the Euphrates, came next.

full century. Ur-Nammu himself reigned for 18 years, in which he established complete power over Mesopotamia. His son Shulgi ruled for 48 years, then, after two short reigns, the last king of the dynasty, Ibbi-Sin, was on the throne for 25 years.

The king was quite outside the general social structure of Sumer. All other people were theoretically equal and in the south of the country everyone spoke Sumerian, a language that had no family likeness to any other—in northern Mesopotamia, the Semitic language called Akkadian was more widely spoken. Within the general social equality, the principal divisions were those between the temple-cum-palace functionaries and the mass of individual craftsmen and farmers in the rest of the city. The priests themselves were well integrated into the daily life of the people, and there was no warrior class.

By the time of Ur-Nammu's Third Dynasty, there was a system of formal education in schools called 'tablet-houses' for the sons of eminent citizens. Apart from reading and writing, clay tablets show that mathematics, medicine and divination were taught. There were no schoolgirls—indeed, the status of Sumerian women is rather puzzling. The laws included harsh punishments for those women who crushed a man's testicles in a fight, which suggests that they were no gentle doves. But most of them played no part at all in public life. Still, they could become priestesses and a woman sometimes rose to the powerful position of the *En,* the chief priest of the kingdom.

The kings and queens of the early dynasties of Ur probably lived in the very large Royal Palace, partly built by King Nabonidus much later, beside the city's northern harbour, although Ur-Nammu himself built the smaller E-Hursag (or E-Kharsag) palace within the walls of the sacred enclosure that he constructed. Only the lower walls of these complex buildings survive today as ridges of mud brick in the desert around the Ziggurat. But they would have been busy administrative buildings in 2000 B.C., with clerks and

Sumerian heavy infantry in close order, apparently six deep, with large shields and long spears trample their foes underfoot. Armour consists of a leather coat with metal studs. They are led by Eannatum, 'Divine Bailiff' of Lagash who wears a royal helmet with a bun of hair and carries a throwing-stick. This panel of the 'Stele of the Vultures' dates from c.2424–2405 B.C., measures 85 cm (33 in) high and records Lagash's victory over neighbouring Umma. The cities of Sumer had the first organized armies in history. Lagash, 65 kilometres (40 miles) north of Ur and half way between the Tigris and Euphrates, became powerful c.2600 B.C. and was ruled by a dynasty of ensis (stewards or bailiffs who only at Lagash became independent city governors) down to c.2122 with only brief periods of foreign domination.

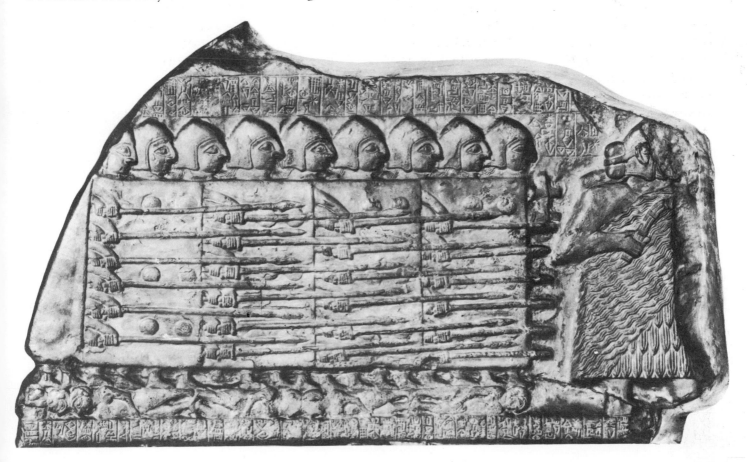

The reconstructed 'Peace' side of the 'Royal Standard of Ur' measures 55 cm (22 in) by 22 cm (9 in). It had triangular ends and was found fastened to the end of a pole on a shoulder of a man thought to be the king's standard bearer. Another theory is that it was the sounding box of a musical instrument because a lyre player is seen at the end of the top panel.

scribes in many of the rooms, apart from the king's apartments and the women's quarters. For the kings, or at least the most able ones, intervened in the economy for the communal benefit. There is evidence in the clay archives that poor harvests of barley or floods brought fairly frequent economic crises to Ur. The royal taxes could then pile up into ruinous debts for the farmers and the king would often have to cancel all except commercial debts.

The building by Ur-Nammu of the *temenos,* or sacred enclosure walls, and the E-Hursag Palace within them, symbolizes the closeness of temple and crown at that stage. The enclosure was a massive affair, with five great gates. The walls of 2000 B.C. were completely rebuilt by the Babylonian King Nebuchadnezzar II in about 550 B.C., but on a similar ground plan with the exception of the south-eastern wall, which was then moved outwards. Entering the sacred enclosure by the south-eastern gate, near the earlier Royal Tombs already described, there was a broad courtyard before the main

buildings were reached. On the right was Ur-Nammu's palace, on the left a number of small structures against the walls, including the little Dungi Temple. Straight ahead, at the north-west end of this first courtyard, was the great bulk of the Giparu of Amar-Sin.

This labyrinthine Giparu temple dates from Ur-Nammu's time, but the king incorporated several earlier shrines in it. His structure was massively fortified and is generally thought to have been the main ground-level or earth temple of Ur, though all trace of its numerous chambers' uses have vanished.

The great triad of Sumerian gods were Anu of the sky, Enlil of the air and Enki of the water, with the older great goddess Ninhursag of the earth. Across their realms moved three other potent gods named Nannar, Utu and Inanna—corresponding to Sin, Shamash and Ishtar of the Assyrian culture farther north in Mesopotamia. Nannar was the moon god, 'lamp of heaven and earth', 'lord of wisdom', 'lord of the months'. Sumerian seals show

The panel of shell figures inlaid on lapis lazuli is set in bitumen on wood. Reading from the bottom as the Sumerians did, we see servants leading wild asses and carrying heavy bundles. The middle row has bullocks, rams, fish (servant in the centre) and perhaps a goat being driven to the feast. The top row portrays the king and his court drinking to the sound of music.

Nannar with a long flowing beard and wearing a crown with a crescent above it. Utu the sun god and Inanna the love goddess were Nannar's children.

The Sumerians saw the universe in a symbolic model slightly different from that of the Hindus. At Ur the earth was seen as a circular disc with the primeval ocean all around it and the hemisphere of heaven overhead. Each part of this universe consisted of the relevant god, and each god had his or her worldly base in one of the Sumerian cities. The god was actually present in his temple statue, which was richly ornamented and in Sumer always had a human appearance. The statue in the temple had his living human counterpart, too, in the king in his palace. The god acted on earth through his king persona. The god's meals were served to the statue, then often eaten by the king.

Ordinary people at Ur could worship Nannar by attendance at daily and, in particular, monthly rites. Continuous worship could be ensured by groups of statues in attitudes of prayer. The peak of the religious calendar was the New Year festival, which occupied several days. Sacrifices and long rites, whose details are little known, were performed by priests and priestesses, musicians and sacred prostitutes. The climax of the festival came when the king celebrated the annual Sacred Marriage. He, as the god, fertilized a priestess, representing a goddess, in a ritual sexual act to ensure the well-being of the people and their lands for the following year.

The Ziggurat of Ur is the best-preserved of many, for each Sumerian city had one at its heart. And it is the best-preserved of all the monuments on the site of Ur. As temple-mountain, its purpose was surely related to that of the mounds, developing into pyramids, which were the primary sacred structures of most early cultures and religions from Egypt to Central America. At Angkor in Cambodia it is clear that, to the Hindu rulers, each temple-mountain represented (and, in a sense, was) Mount Meru, the mythical mountain that was home of the gods and stable centre of the world. It is in this light, as local world centres, that we should see the ziggurats, of which one was the Tower of Babylon or Babel.

At Ur there was a man-made sacred mound, perhaps as old as the city itself, on the site where the great builder-king Ur-Nammu constructed, in about 2100 B.C., the huge Ziggurat that we can see today. Later kings went on repairing and adding to the temple-mountain for 1500 years afterwards.

The remains of the Giparu, the huge ground-level temple of Ur, have already been described. The stepped mountain of the Ziggurat just north of the Giparu may be seen as its sky equivalent—the French archaeologist Jean-Claude Margueron saw ziggurats as expressing 'a will to force a contact with the deity, to remain in touch . . . [or] a sort of ladder inviting the deity to come down among men'. Between the two temples was a gate that seemed to have a special significance. Named E-Dub-Lal-Makh, it was not an imposingly large gatehouse, but it contained a statue of Nannar and according to Seton Lloyd it was still referred to as 'The Great Gate, the Ancient One' hundreds of years later. Some kings even used the gatehouse as a court of judgement. Beside its remains are the ruins of a large building known as E-Nun-Makh, which may have been another temple or an administrative building for the religious enclosure as a whole.

Ur-Nammu also decided to build a new ceremonial route to his enlarged Ziggurat, approaching its frontage almost directly from a special northerly gateway from the city into the *temenos*. True to earlier plans for temples, this approach was along a bending axis, in this case through a series of courtyards. Inside the gate in the northern corner, the route bends slightly to the left across a narrow courtyard to a second gate. This led through an impressive range of buildings into Ur-Nammu's great Court of Nannar, surrounded by other ranges. On the opposite side of this court, but again not quite in line, another gatehouse contained steps that ran up to the higher level of the walled platform, which acted as the broad quadrangle containing the Ziggurat. Emerging here, the main frontage of the great monument itself rose across the yard, though the centre was not directly opposite.

The composition of this frontage of the Ziggurat, which faces the most northerly rising point of the moon, is even today one of the most impressive works of antiquity in the world. Its lower stages have been carefully restored following the reconstruction drawing prepared by Sir Leonard Woolley after his excavations. The massive sloping walls, the powerful buttresses and the three ramps bringing flights of steps up to a meeting point at a ruined gatehouse on the high first terrace can all be seen. The lowest stage of the structure is 64 metres (210 feet) long and 46 metres (150 feet) wide, rising to a height of 12 metres (40 feet).

In its original state, as left by Ur–Nammu, two further terraces—revetted by walls of mud bricks surfaced with fired bricks set in bitumen—rose above the levels now restored. And the central stairway, which today ends at the gatehouse, penetrated through it and swept up to the topmost platform. There, Woolley believed, a small temple to the moon god of Ur, Nannar, surmounted the whole step-pyramid composition and brought it to a height of 20 metres (65 feet). There were also signs that the terraces were planted with trees and gardens, providing an elaborately conceived temple-mountain.

King Ur-Nammu, after uniting Sumer under Ur and carrying out the large-scale building works described here in a fairly short reign, died in about 2094 B.C. He and the rest of his dynasty were buried in the Royal Mausoleum of underground tombs with brick vaults and entrance ramps, which can still be seen near the earlier Royal Tombs excavated by Woolley.

For Ur declined after that. Just before the year 2000 B.C. it was sacked and most of its buildings were destroyed systematically by an army from the city of Elam. Woolley wrote after his excavations: 'Of Ur-Nammu's wall (of the outer city) not a trace remained. We would come on examples of very large bricks specially moulded with the king's name . . . but none of them were *in situ*. Just because the defences of Ur had been so strong, the victorious army had dismantled them with special care.' The Sumerians rebuilt the city in part and it kept its religious and commercial importance—despite subsequent sackings—for a millennium and a half. But it was never a capital city again.

In about 850 B.C. an Assyrian king reconquered Ur from Chaldean tribes who had occupied it—from which comes the name Ur of the Chaldees. Then, after two centuries of neglect and increasing decrepitude, the city was taken under the wing of Nebuchadnezzar II and of Nabonidus, two of the last kings of Babylon. They rebuilt the walls and the temples along the lines established by Ur-Nammu so long before, and Nabonidus rebuilt the Ziggurat with ramps in seven stages that Herodotus described as spiralling around it. This work was done over the earlier structure and added nearly a hundred feet to its height, bringing it to a total of 40 metres (160 feet). But the Babylonian work did not last well, and Woolley stripped away what little was left when he dug out the design of 2100 B.C.

The last ruler to build at Ur was Cyrus, founder of the Persian empire. But the city was decadent beyond recovery and the very last dated tablet is of 317 B.C. It is likely that the Euphrates changed its course soon afterwards. Without the river, the city's function as a port with access to the sea was gone. Worse still, its agriculture depended on irrigation from the Euphrates. In the very year when that shift of river bed occurred and the water simply disappeared, the fields around Ur must have dried up for ever.

EGYPT'S PYRAMIDS

Monuments To The Pharaohs

Previous pages The most famous, most visited and most photographed structures in the world, the Pyramids at Giza. This view is taken from the desert to the south. In the foreground is the 62-metre (204 ft) Pyramid of Mycerinus with its subsidiary trio of one geometric and two step pyramids. None were ever completed and the finding of a woman's bones in the middle subsidiary pyramid is the only firm evidence that the small trio were for Mycerinus' queens or princesses. Behind is Chephren's 136.8 metre (447½ ft) edifice which looks taller than the Great Pyramid of his father Cheops because it stands on higher ground and has steeper sides, but is actually 76 cm (2½ ft) lower (originally 3 metres or 10 ft). Not until the building of Lincoln Cathedral's Central Tower in A.D. 1307 with a 160 metre (525 ft) lead-sheathed wooden spire did the world see a higher building and it has been calculated that the Cathedrals of Florence, Milan and St. Peter in Rome as well as London's Westminster Abbey and St. Paul's would fit in the Great Pyramid's base area. The chapter symbol is the Great Sphinx, enigmatic guardian of Chephren's Pyramid.

As this book has followed the sun westwards around the world, from Central America across Asia to the Eastern Mediterranean, several characteristics have appeared which were shared by very early cultures in far distant parts of the globe. Settled farming—especially of wheat—was the starting point for development, followed much later by trading of implements and ornaments. God-rulers established order. Village settlements grew into towns and often proceeded towards what we have come to call civilization—that is, life centred on a city. Intelligent people studied the heavenly bodies, seeking explanations and benefit for their communities. But perhaps most striking of all for the thoughtful traveller of today, people everywhere built raised mounds of earth or stone, often massive and in many lands developing step pyramid shapes, as their earliest and most potent sacred monuments.

On one level the mound may be seen as the simplest monument to build and its almost worldwide presence explained by that. Yet the stepped temple-mountains of Mexico and Cambodia, the *stupas* of India, the tomb of Cyrus in Persia, the ziggurats of Mesopotamia, all seem to be variations on the same theme, thousands of miles and thousands of years apart. And often they are linked to a myth, a symbolic vision of the world and its creation, with a legendary mountain at its centre. Further variations of this myth and of monumental mounds will be found among the lost cultures of Africa and Europe in the second half of this book, but this is a good point to consider the similarities—for now in Egypt we reach the high point and perhaps come nearer to the source and purpose of this kind of universal monument.

The 20 and more huge step pyramids and true geometrical pyramids of Egypt can themselves hardly be described as lost, for many of them survive in a fairly well-preserved state—these are among the most famous of all human monuments and they have implanted themselves in the collective consciousness of the world. So for what reasons are they included here among the lost cities and cultures of four continents? The answers are clear. Traces of Memphis, their builders' white-walled city, have been rotted to vanishing point by the Nile, and with it it has gone much knowledge of their culture. The intended function of the pyramids themselves is lost, save for a few clues mentioned later. The way in which the mountains of stone were built is lost, though countless theorists and illustrators have displayed their ideas to fascinated readers. Lastly, they appear to be an awesome expression of a lost mystical notion that mankind must, in order to flourish, recreate again and again the universal mountain at the centre of an ordered world, with death and rebirth within it. That notion was lost early in the long millennia of Egyptian civilization, for all the pyramids of Egypt were built, according to their inscriptions, during the Old Kingdom between 2700 and 2200 B.C.—the Middle Kingdom and the New Kingdom, stretching on for over 2000 more years, built very different temples.

The pyramids are among the most ancient of temple-mounds, but they do not seem to be the earliest. Silbury Hill in England was built of great chalk blocks in about 2600 B.C.—at much the same time as the Great Pyramid of Giza. The huge Newgrange chambered mound in Ireland was encased in gleaming white quartz in about 3400 B.C. And the vast Barnenez monument in northern Brittany was built like a step pyramid of stone, elongated to 82 metres (270 feet) in one direction and penetrated by multiple passages, probably as early as 4500 B.C. That five-stepped hill of drystone masonry in France is only a fraction of the bulk of the pyramids of Giza and Sakkara, and its forms are much more irregular. But its similarities of form and its calibrated radiocarbon date, of nearly 2000 years before the first pyram

Egypt, give a clue that the basic *type* of monument did not necessarily originate in the Nile valley. That said, the world has not produced any giant structures more impressive than the Egyptian pyramids in the 4500 years since they were built.

Like many other early cultures, ancient Egypt developed from the fertile ground left by the annual spring inundation of a great river—the gift of the Nile, in the famous words of the Greek historian Herodotus. Until the Nile dams were built in the present century, the floods from the Sudan carried rich dark soil up towards a sharply marked line along the edges of the valley. And up to that mark, for 1200 kilometres (750 miles) down the river on either side from Aswan to the sea, the dense green crops of farmers have flourished since 7000 B.C. Beyond the valley edges, there is nothing but sand and rocks. From July until November or later, the Nile became a broad lake, filling the valley to the edge of the sand with nourishing and navigable water for nearly half the year. If the flooding fell short, thousands or even millions of acres were not fertile that year and famine hovered over the people.

Palaeolithic people inhabited Egypt until perhaps 8000 B.C., while the Nile gradually established its present-day cycle. Much of the Sahara started to dry up as the weather changed and the people, including Neolithic farmers from the north-east, moved into the river valley. Human skeletons of around 6000 B.C. show a fairly tall large-headed people towards the mouth of the Nile (Lower Egypt), and a short people with smaller heads and typically African features higher up the river (Upper Egypt) towards the Sudan.

During the next 3000 years there was a slow maturing of Egyptian society and politics. In this so-called Pre-Dynastic period, the ancient king lists conflict with each other about the extent of the realm, some marking nine or ten monarchs of Lower Egypt only, others showing the double crown of the Upper and Lower parts. The name of the founder of the First Dynasty was Menes. He ruled, the king lists say, for at least 60 years from around 3100 B.C., and he united the separate kingdoms of Lower and Upper Egypt during that time. As far as the later Egyptians were concerned, that unification was the start of human history. According to Herodotus, Menes founded the city of Memphis as his capital.

What is known of the Pharaohs and their ordinary people is largely about death and afterlife, for like many cultures they built lasting monuments for the next world and flexible, even transient, structures for this. But this fact has given a distorted view of the ancient Egyptians as death-obsessed. The evidence is to the contrary. The picture that emerges from the written records and the scenes illustrated on the tomb walls around Memphis is of a joyous and humorous people, very hard-working and rather arrogant about their superiority over other nations.

Hardly anything is recorded of their first capital city itself. Memphis' position near modern Cairo is known, on the west bank of the river—the side later reserved for necropoli. But today, wandering among the palm groves and over the low humps and occasional stone foundations which mark the site, it is hard to believe that 5000 years ago Menes' great citadel stood here. The citadel was surrounded by walls which gave the city its original name, White-Wall. Around this centre, the houses of Memphis spread over an area with a diameter of 33 kilometres (20 miles). As the centuries passed, the mud-brick dwellings crumbled and were replaced with other houses on a higher level, leaving wide mounds many layers deep. In most countries this would offer an ideal site for archaeologists' excavation. But at Memphis digs have shown that the Nile's annual inundation has long seeped into the underground remains, rotting all organic materials and turning the sunbaked

The burial chamber of Mycerinus' Pyramid with the pharaoh's sarcophagus inside. Tragically, this basalt coffin, decorated (unlike the other Giza pyramid coffins) as the façade of a palace, was lost in a shipwreck off Spain while bound for England.

A Victorian print of the entrance to the Great Pyramid of Cheops. This sole entry is on the north side 15 metres (50 ft) from ground level and 7.3 metres (24 ft) east of centre.

Djoser's Step Pyramid at Sakkara, the first of some 80 Egyptian pyramids to be built over a period of 500 years. It was begun as one-stage 8-metre (26-ft) high mastaba *tomb then widened by 4.2 metres (14 ft) on all four sides with a second casing of limestone. The east side was then extended 8.5 metres (28 ft) and again enlarged by 2.9 metres (9½ ft) to be the bottom step of a four-stage pyramid. The north and east sides were now widened while the four steps became six.*

Above right *King Huny's collapsed step pyramid at Meidum with its causeway leading to the Nile valley temple. A seven then eight-stage step pyramid that was filled out with Tura limestone.*

Right *Sneferu's North or Red Pyramid at Dashur. This first true pyramid was only surpassed in size, 105 metres (340 ft) high by 220 metres (721 ft) wide, by its immediate successors—the Giza pyramids.*

building bricks back into undifferentiated mud, the 'black gold' of Egypt.

For the ordinary people who lived in the simple reed-thatched houses of Memphis, family life was not much different from that of the present day. Polygamy was allowed, but extra wives could only be afforded by the rich, so most families consisted simply of mother, father and children.

We cannot say whether most of the mud brick homes had the gaily painted walls shown in those of the wealthy, but we know that wooden furniture was used. There were simple tables and chairs, and low beds for those who did not sleep on plain straw mats. All clothing was of linen. The men wore only a pleated garment like a white kilt, the women a close-fitting white robe which covered the left shoulder and fell to the ankles. Men were clean-shaven and their black hair was cropped like a helmet. Women's hair grew long—they liked to twine it into all sorts of complicated arrangements and they bought and wore as much jewellery as they could afford.

Even in the city, many of the people would be the farmers of the valley fields around. For four or five months of the year, the Nile would flood their lands. During that period, they would take their boats out on to the river's wide lake to fish or hunt wildfowl, or would perform their service to the state by work on one of the Pharaoh's monumental projects. In December or earlier, they would return to their land—or rather the area that the Pharaoh allowed them to farm, for all land belonged ultimately to him—and start to break up the new alluvial soil with wooden hand ploughs or ploughs pulled by oxen. Wheat was the principal crop plant and it had to be kept damp by water from storage tanks which was released along the furrows. Watering and weeding kept the farmers busy until March, when the wheat was harvested with flint sickles. After threshing, each farmer paid his wheat tax to the Pharaoh and the rest of the grain was stored.

The bread made from the wheat was the basis of Egyptian food throughout the dynastic period. With it, they ate meat and cheese from their cattle, goats and sheep, as well as wildfowl and fish. They had a variety of vegetables including lettuce, beans, cucumbers and leeks. They drank a great deal of beer and a certain amount of wine. They were a strongly sociable people and parties with food and dancing seem to have been frequent.

Many of these citizens of Memphis were conscripted into the army when a military expedition was planned. To the north-east, the peoples beyond the narrow Sinai land-bridge were usually preoccupied with their own struggles until the big migrations from Central Asia started in about 2000 B.C. Early expeditions by the Egyptian army seem to have been concerned with finding new supplies of lapis lazuli and other precious materials in Sinai. Later in the Old Kingdom, however, government became more bureaucratic and a middle class emerged as the desert tribes made clear the need for a regular army.

This growth of bureaucracy may have reduced the absolute power of the Pharaoh. For since the beginning of the Old Kingdom, the ruler had been the divine representative on earth and his decrees from the white-walled royal citadel in Memphis were mandatory for every subject. We know nothing of the architecture of that citadel-palace—it was surely an imposing building, for the title Pharaoh itself means Great House. Once seated on his throne there, wearing regalia that included a double crown combining the hollow red circlet and the white cone of the two kingdoms, the sky god Horus entered into the Pharaoh. As the god, the king protected the people of Egypt against their enemies by arms and against famine by irrigation and ritual.

Without the intervention of the Horus-inspired Pharaoh, every Egyptian knew that the land and its people would be devastated or destroyed. It was therefore no hardship at all, whatever the individual's grumblings at the time,

The little that remains of Memphis, once capital of Egypt for 1000 years and greatest city in the world—the ruins of the Temple of Ptah (Memphis' creator god) in the sacred lake. Linked by a ship canal to the Nile, Memphis still had a population of 700,000 and 29 kilometres (18 miles) of walls when Alexander the Great was crowned pharaoh there in 331 B.C.

The Egyptians used measuring cords made of palm or flax to set out the sides of a pyramid. Here a pharaoh with sceptre and cobra-headed (goddess Wadjet) circlet does the task himself.

113

Isis the great mother goddess who was wife and sister of Osiris in Ancient Egypt's most potent legend. Her magic powers were passed on to mankind as skill in healing. She is first mentioned in the Pyramid Texts of Unas' pyramid (c. 2350 B.C.) and, although she was not often dedicated temples or sculpted until the New Kingdom, her cult would survive the coming of Christianity to the Roman Empire and only disappear with the Islamic conquest of Egypt

The Bent Pyramid at Dashur, the southern one of a pair built by Pharaoh Sneferu (reigned c. 2613–2590 B.C.), first king of the fourth dynasty. Also called Blunted, False, or Rhomboidal, it consists of a truncated pyramid with a perfect pyramid on top of it giving a total height of 103 metres (335 ft). The lower stones measure up to 1.4 metres (5 ft) high, those at the top seldom over 60 cm (2 ft).

to be taxed on the wheat harvest and to be pressed into service for public works or for the great monument that each new Pharaoh had to build. For that monument was an absolutely necessary re-assertion of the safety and stability of Egypt as it had emerged from the chaos that went before. The monument served as a tomb after the death of each Pharaoh, and as a memorial to him. But that was incidental.

Three miles north of Memphis at Sakkara, on the edge of the desert, the kings of the first two dynasties built their Lower Egypt temple-tombs. These are all of the type called a *mastaba* (from the Arabic for bench), which is the basic form from which all sacred monuments in Egypt grew. *Mastabas* have a square or oblong plan, and a simple chunky superstructure whose walls slope inwards for strength as they rise. This building above ground is quite low, usually with only a recessed doorway providing relief on its plain sloping sides, and a flat roof. Early *mastabas* were of mud brick, but later they were built of stone. Inside, the early ones contained a number of sealed cells above the ground, and a stairway leading down from a central compartment to underground burial chambers—which became increasingly complex.

Before following the architect Imhotep's ingenious development of the *mastaba* into the step pyramid, a look at the religious ideas behind the building of such monuments is needed. The most famous myth of ancient Egypt, and one which has its equivalent in many lands, is that of Isis and Osiris. The story is that Osiris was the first god-king of Egypt. His wife Isis and his brother Seth were also divine. Under Osiris, the nation flourished, guided by wise laws, fed by ingenious advances in cultivation of the land and informed by a pious understanding of the gods. Then Seth, believing that he could excel Osiris as ruler, killed his brother, cut up his body and scattered it. With Seth on the throne, the divine Isis went into hiding. Secretly she gathered the pieces of her husband's body together and through her powers gave him life again. In doing this, a son was conceived and was born as Horus, god of the sky. But Osiris could not return fully to rule the land of the living. So it was Horus who removed the usurper from the throne and acted as its protector thereafter, while Osiris became king of the dead in the afterworld. Many variations of the story exist but this is its essence.

The power of this tale was so great that, thousands of years after the first Pharaohs, a ruler would still take a 'Horus name' in addition to his own upon ascending the throne and statues were carved with the hawk head of Horus over the enthroned king. In taking the throne, a new Pharaoh re-enacted Horus' triumph over the impious chaos of Seth; in dying, he entered the realm of his sacred forefather Osiris, where he could still benefit his people if they continued to keep contact with him through offerings at his monument.

This potent myth is the source of the immensely complicated system of dualities which evolved in so many different ways in the Egyptian mind. The living and the dead were a pair, both equally real and important. Other dualities flow from that—light and dark, above ground and under, the Nile's west (left) bank for the dead and east (right) bank for the living (perhaps reflecting the sun's course). Beyond that, the kingdom itself was of the Two Lands, upper and lower, and most royal offices had double titles as in 'Overseer of the two chambers of the king's adornment'. In some cases, even royal tombs were built with important apartments in duplicate. The ramifications of the system are inextricable, but as far as the pyramids are concerned, the key duality appears to be the maintenance of life outwardly and the sustenance of the dead inwardly.

Thus the first of the giant pyramids, the Step Pyramid designed by Imhotep for the first king of the third dynasty, Djoser or Zoser, must be seen

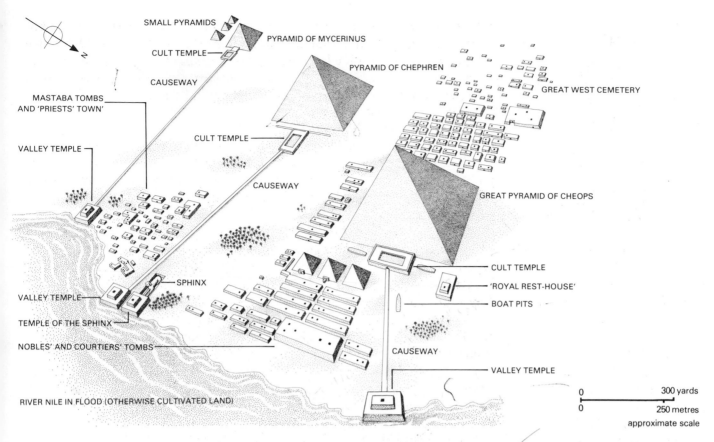

N

SMALL PYRAMIDS

PYRAMID OF MYCERINUS

CULT TEMPLE

PYRAMID OF CHEPHREN

CAUSEWAY

GREAT WEST CEMETERY

MASTABA TOMBS
AND 'PRIESTS' TOWN'

CULT TEMPLE

VALLEY TEMPLE

CAUSEWAY

GREAT PYRAMID OF CHEOPS

CULT TEMPLE

SPHINX

'ROYAL REST-HOUSE'

VALLEY TEMPLE

BOAT PITS

TEMPLE OF THE SPHINX

NOBLES' AND COURTIERS' TOMBS

CAUSEWAY

VALLEY TEMPLE

RIVER NILE IN FLOOD (OTHERWISE CULTIVATED LAND)

0   300 yards
0   250 metres
approximate scale

An artist's impression of the Giza pyramid complex viewed from east-north-east in around 2300 B.C. The causeways from the Nile to the pyramids would have been about 500 metres (550 yards) long.

as rather like the much later temple-mountains of Cambodia. That is to say, its building was a religious act for the benefit of the god-king's people, which became his tomb in due course. Djoser ruled for 28 years, according to one king list—19, according to another—starting in about 2680 B.C. It is recorded in a late inscription that he built the Step Pyramid at Sakkara on the desert edge near Memphis to end a seven-year famine. Djoser consulted his own wise chief administrator Imhotep, and then charged him with the building of the cure that he suggested. Whether Imhotep, later much venerated as magician, astronomer and doctor, was drawing on some older wisdom and practices can only be a matter for speculation. What is certain is that this eminent civil servant developed into the first great architect whose name is recorded.

The experimental nature of the Step Pyramid built by Imhotep is shown by five changes of design during the course of construction, which have been detected by archaeologists. The monument is the earliest important Egyptian edifice of stone and it was to remain the largest step pyramid. It rises in six unequal steps to a height of 62 metres (204 feet) and each side of the base is some 106 metres (350 feet) long, dimensions which were exceeded only when the stepped form was abandoned in favour of the geometrical pyramid shape. Its stone is of a glowing honey-gold colour and the proportions of its six stages, seen by Egyptologists as *mastabas* one on top of each other, seem to have been most carefully calculated, though their significance is elusive. Its sides are oriented north-south-east-west.

The Step Pyramid itself, like the ziggurats of Mesopotamia, towers above an enormous enclosure containing a complex of buildings. The sole entrance through the 10 metre (33 feet) high walls is in the south-east corner, though there are 13 other points along the walls where false gateways seem to offer entry. A colonnaded entry passage leads to a broad courtyard, where the Step Pyramid itself can be seen to the right, while another tomb lies to the left beside the enclosure wall. Moving towards the pyramid, the west or left-hand

Tauert, the hippopotamus goddess of fecundity and the protector of women in childbirth, stands up with the two hieroglyphic symbols meaning 'protection'. One of the oldest and most popular household deities, she was the subject of innumerable amulets and statues.

Thoth, the ibis-headed god of writing, learning and mathematics, was the scribe of the gods. He was associated with the moon (hence the disc).

side of the courtyard is occupied by storerooms, while the right-hand side consists of a quadrangle of 30 or so little shrines around a small court. Beyond that quadrangle, a series of ranges with larger courts run northwards along the side of the pyramid, finally wrapping around the back of it to join on to the Cult Temple. Much of the enclosure, the first monumental complex of Egypt, has not yet been excavated, and restored to the order it deserves.

We know that each pyramid was endowed with a 'Pyramid Estate' to ensure that the dead king could continue to help the living. But we do not know the purpose of the many buildings in this first Sakkara enclosure—for numerous other small enclosures were built by later kings around that of the Step Pyramid during the following centuries—nor do the buildings above ground complete the story. The structures we see in the Step Pyramid enclosure are echoed underground by many chambers and galleries cut out of the solid rock beneath. And under the Step Pyramid itself, which is solidly built of smallish stone blocks, there is a labyrinth of passages and rooms in the rock, culminating in Djoser's own burial chamber. Here, there are relief carvings of the king's life and rows of large vases of rock crystal, alabaster and serpentine.

These subterranean rooms were, we may think, the kingdom of Osiris. As for the pyramid above, it was a temple—not in the sense of a place where religious services were held, but as a structure whose very presence brought divine help and safety to Egypt. One other clue about its significance and its shape exists in the hieroglyphic Pyramid Texts found on the walls of later pyramids. One of many similar passages reads, 'There come to you . . . the gods who are in the sky, and the gods who are on earth. They make support for you upon their arms; may you ascend to the sky and mount up on it in this its name of "Ladder". "The sky is given to you, the earth is given to you", says Aten [the sun-god]. Geb [the earth god] speaks about it, "The Mounds of my realm are the Mounds of Horus and the Mounds of Seth . . ."'. Mounds establishing divine power on earth, ladders to the realm of Horus in the sky—the imagery attached to the functions of the pyramids has many facets.

Three other major step pyramids were erected by Djoser's successors of the third dynasty, apart from small step pyramids in many places. The large ones are far apart from each other along the edge of the desert on the west side of the Nile. None are as big as Djoser's and they can be seen in various stages of ruin. The first was built by Sekhemkhet and its remains can be seen 274 metres (300 yards) south-west of Djoser's enclosure at Sakkara. The next was built several miles farther north, at Zawiyet el-Aryan a little south of Giza, by a Pharaoh whose name is recorded in it as Khaba. The final big Egyptian step pyramid was built by Huny, the last king of the third dynasty, at Meidum—35 kilometres (22 miles) to the south of Memphis and Sakkara. All these step pyramids, and presumably the vanished ones of about nine other third dynasty kings, were built between about 2660 and 2620 B.C.

After that the fourth dynasty began with the reign of the great King Sneferu or Snofru, who married Huny's daughter and took the throne. During his 24-year reign—recorded as one of the most serene and prosperous in Egyptian history—he completed his father-in-law's step pyramid, then started on his own. As if to emphasize that a new dynasty had risen, Sneferu ordered his builders to construct a new type of monument—or rather, monuments. For Sneferu is the only Pharaoh who built two giant pyramids. The so-called Bent Pyramid and the Red Pyramid are close together at Dashur, a few miles south of Memphis. Here we can see Sneferu's architects actually experimenting with and developing the pyramid in its final form. Both pyramids are very large, rising to over 94 metres (310 feet).

In the Bent Pyramid, the sides start to rise very steeply at an angle of 54 degrees from the ground. This probably caused structural problems, so the slope of the upper part was lowered to 42 degrees. For the first time, a high corbelled chamber was built within the masonry bulk of the pyramid's superstructure, as well as the traditional subterranean chamber. This internal plan was repeated when Sneferu ordered the building of the Red Pyramid nearby, with sides sloping at a shallower 43½ degree angle. Here, in another piece of pioneering building, the outer stone blocks have one side angled to give the slope, rather than the whole of each outer block being laid at an angle. And so at last, the true pyramid form was achieved in about 2610 B.C.

No sooner was the form achieved than it found its most complete expression. For Sneferu's successor was Khufu, known to the Greeks and to us as Cheops, builder of the Great Pyramid. The king lists of the Egyptians and the archaeological evidence of today agree that it was built about 2600 B.C. It was the first of a series of three built at Giza, near modern Cairo and farther north of Memphis than all but one of the royal pyramid sites. Internally, the Great Pyramid had a far more complicated series of passages, chambers and ramps than anything that had gone before. Externally, the masonry of its huge blocks of stone and its vast dimensions, 147 metres (481 feet) high and 230 metres (755 feet) along each base, made it one of the Seven Wonders of the Ancient World—the only one to survive to the present.

Many books have been devoted to the methods used to construct the Great Pyramid and to its functions and origins. Imaginary ramps have been raised straight to its peak or coiled upwards around its sides, while slavemasters lashed their teams dragging up the great blocks of stone—indeed, the annals record that Cheops and his successor Chephren were harsh Pharaohs. Other

At the south-east corner of the Great Pyramid (Cheops') stands the reconstructed mastaba tomb of Seshemnefer IV, a minor fifth dynasty king. The monumental entrance, seated statues of Seshemnefer, and little obelisks make it a very special mastaba.

writers have questioned the date, the function as tomb and the human construction of the Great Pyramid. It has been seen as an edifice immensely older than the Pharaoh buried in it, a gift by the gods themselves to humans to mark the centre of the world. Its orientation, as with the Step Pyramid, is almost precisely north–south–east–west. Its sides, rising at an angle of just under 52 degrees to its peak, cast a shadow 81 metres (268 feet) long at midwinter, shrinking to nothing at the spring equinox—making it into a vast sundial.

Whatever else, the Great Pyramid is obviously mysterious in some ways. Its interior contains no fewer than three burial chambers for the king—one cut into the solid rock beneath, the second about 15 metres (50 feet) up into the masonry mass, and the third 41 metres (137 feet) above ground. It was in this high third chamber that Cheops was buried, his mummified body in a great stone sarcophagus. The passages to the chamber were blocked by vast chunks of rock at many points, the last escape shaft of the masons infilled solidly too. But the craft of the tomb-robber in Egypt is as old as the Pharaohs and at least as clever—by the time European antiquaries and archaeologists reached the high chamber, only the empty granite sarcophagus remained there.

Two of Cheops' successors of the fourth dynasty built their pyramids next to his at Giza. His son Djedefre (Radjedef) started his 8 kilometres (5 miles) away at Abu Roash, north-west of Giza, where it can still be seen in the unfinished state it had reached by the end of his eight-year reign. But Cheops' second son Chephren (or Khafre) built his at Giza, close to his father's and—perhaps out of filial respect—very slightly smaller. Beyond it, Mycerinus (Mankaure) constructed the third of the group in about 2550 B.C., with two little step pyramids and one geometrical pyramid beside it (Cheops' pyramid has a similar arrangement). Mycerinus' monument is considerably smaller than the two giants, but he died quite young after 18 years on the throne, before he could add the outer granite casing which would have made it nearer to their size.

The pyramids of Giza are still one of the most imposing sights to be seen anywhere, but in 2500 B.C. the scene must have been overwhelming. For, as with the Step Pyramid at Sakkara, each pyramid was part of a big complex. Crowding groups of nobles' *mastabas* (whose ruins can still be seen) lay to east and west of the Great Pyramid and to the east of Chephren's. Subsidiary pyramids for royal queens stand in rows east and south of Mycerinus' and Cheops' edifices. Ships were buried beside the great king's monument, perhaps for his voyages in Osiris' kingdom. On the east side of each pyramid, towards the Nile, there was the Cult Temple. There, the priests supported by the Pyramid Estate performed the rites to the departed god-king. From the Cult Temple of each pyramid, long sacred causeways ran down the slope to their Valley Temples. From July to December, while the Nile was in flood, the waters lapped against these temples. During this season, people came in boats from Memphis to land at a Valley Temple and walk up the sacred causeway to the Cult Temple beside the pyramid, bringing offerings to sustain the beneficence of the dead Pharaoh and the prosperity of the land. If they came to Chephren's pyramid, whose Valley Temple is the only one now surviving, they would pass the Great Sphinx—Chephren's head with a lion's body carved out of a solid outcrop of rock left from quarrying for the Great Pyramid—on their right as they moved up the causeway.

Apart from Mycerinus' own pyramid at Giza, his mother is buried in a *mastaba* there and his short-lived successor in a *mastaba* at Sakkara. The next major (though comparatively small) pyramid was that of Userkaf built around 2480 B.C. at Sakkara—beside the Step Pyramid and now ruined—and

The cow-horned goddess Hathor (goddess of music, love and dancing; nurse of the Pharaohs) is flanked by the goddess of the hare nome *(Province 15, capital: Hermopolis Magna in Lower Egypt) and King Mycerinus, builder of the last and smallest pyramid at Giza, wearing the white crown of Upper Egypt. This 1-metre (3⅓ ft) black slate statue was one of four found in the king's valley temple. The presence of different* nome *hieroglyphs above the local deities indicates that Mycerinus meant to have these triple statues for all 42 of Egypt's* nomes *(provinces).*

that takes us on to the fifth dynasty of Egypt. During this period, the Pharaohs decided not to compete in sheer size with the monuments of the previous dynasty. Instead they constructed, at Abu Gurab (to the south of Giza) and elsewhere, big temples to the sun god Aten. These consisted of a complex of temples and causeway very like those described at Giza, except that a square platform with a squat obelisk at its centre took over part of the role of the pyramid. The sun god was worshipped at an altar beside the obelisk, and quantities of oxen were sacrificed to him in the area of the platform to the north. Each Pharaoh was bound to build one of these in addition to his pyramid, which may reflect some separation of the functions previously combined in the Giza monuments.

Three of these fifth dynasty Pharaohs built their pyramids between 2470 and 2400 B.C. in a group on the Nile at Abusir, between Giza and Sakkara, and these—though not especially large—are the most refined of all the pyramids in detail. They are the monuments of Sahure, Neferirkare and Niuserre. The second was left unfinished and its causeway was stolen by Niuserre. Sahure's pyramid, however, now gives the best idea of the whole complex leading up from the valley. The temple columns are carved like papyrus stems or datepalm leaves in place of the earlier undecorated pillars. And the walls still have many relief carvings including hunting and military scenes.

Two later kings of the fifth dynasty, Isozi and Unas, again built their relatively small pyramids at Sakkara, though there is hardly anything to be seen of Isozi's. Unas' pyramid of 2350 B.C., however, has fine relief sculpture along its very long causeway and the burial chamber contains the oldest hieroglyphs of the famous Pyramid Texts carved on its walls.

The last pyramids date from the sixth and probably final dynasty of the Old Kingdom. This is marked in social history by the increasing power of the nobles, the development of a bureaucracy and the building of new types of temple. But the duty to build a pyramid still weighed on each Pharaoh. The first king of the sixth dynasty, Teti, built his at Sakkara in about 2320 and it can still be seen to the north-east of Djoser's and Userkaf's. Nearby, he built a little pyramid for his wife Ipwe and a *mastaba* for another wife called Khuye. His successor Pepi I is reported to have ruled for 53 years. Pepi's other name was sometimes given as Men-nfr and he may have built his pyramid (now vanished) very near to Memphis, for the city is said to have been re-named after him. After that, Pepi II started history's longest reign of 94 years, commemorated by a fairly large pyramid south of Sakkara, and finally Queen Nitokerti (in Greek, Nitocris) may have built the last in 2220 B.C.

The Old Kingdom ended with a period of civil wars. Fewer pyramids were built during the Middle Kingdom between 2100 and 1780 B.C., only one in the New Kingdom which, after the Asian invasions, was established in about 1570 B.C. At that time, the capital of Egypt was moved 480 kilometres (300 miles) up the Nile from Memphis to Thebes. No more is known of the New Kingdom's capital than of the old, for modern Luxor stands on the site. Thebes was on the east side of the river, the side of the living, and vast temples for the living grew up around it. These temples of Karnak and Luxor are among the greatest works of Egypt. But the religion and its monuments were different in many ways from those of the Old Kingdom. The local god of Thebes, Amun, became the predominant god of the Pharaohs and the temples were his. Instead of building a pyramid, each ruler added to the edifices at Karnak, Luxor or other places, as his renewal of the kingdom. And instead of being buried in their own monuments, the rulers carved splendid tombs for themselves on the other side of the river from Thebes, the side of the dead, in the Valley of the Kings and the Valley of the Queens.

A false door to the causeway of Unas' Pyramid covered in hieroglyphs. The king's name cartouche can be seen on the outer frame. False doors allowed the spirit of the dead man to leave and return at will.

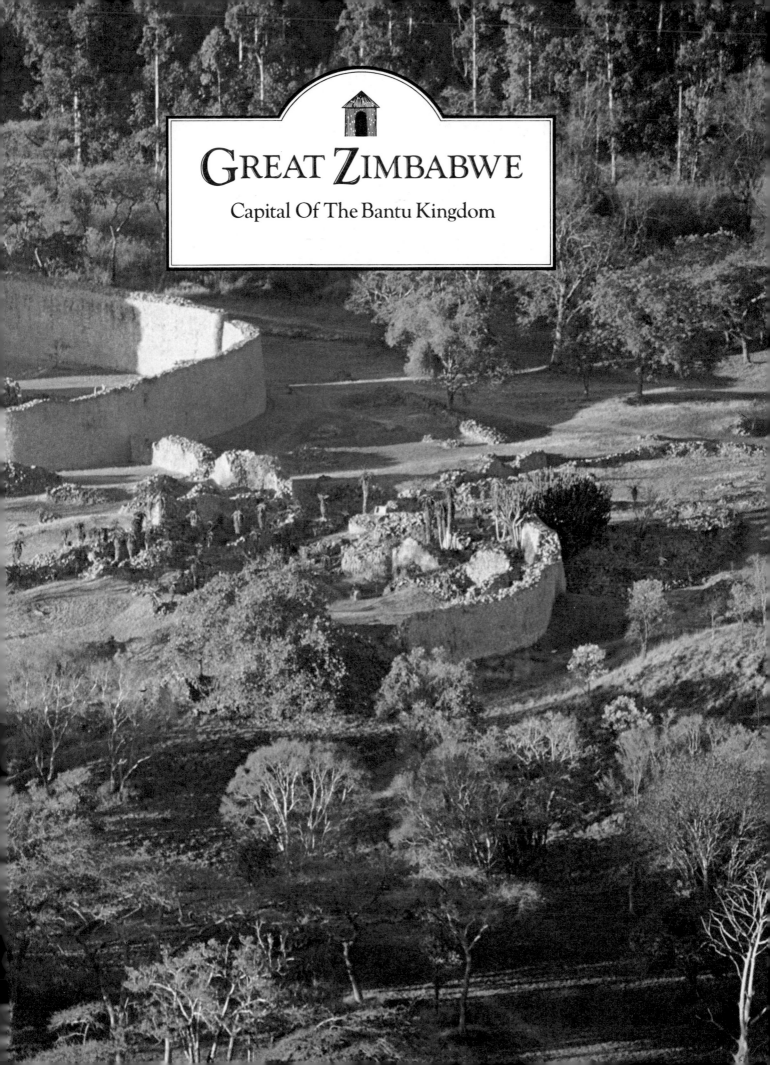

GREAT ZIMBABWE

Capital Of The Bantu Kingdom

THE LEGEND OF the Queen of Sheba and King Solomon's Mines has long haunted the minds of Arabs and Europeans alike. The story is vague, flowing into many versions. All of them tell of the wise son of David, who ruled from about 970 to 930 B.C. and was the builder of the great temple of Jerusalem. The legend tells of Solomon meeting the lovely ruler of a rich kingdom somewhere to the south of Egypt. After that meeting, the story develops in many different ways—in some she returns to her kingdom, in others a political alliance is formed, and in many she becomes his serene queen Balquis. Their wealth stems from mysterious gold mines somewhere far into the interior of the African continent.

These lost gold mines seemed very real to the Arab traders who pushed southwards down the east coast of Africa while other Muslims were ruling much of Spain and the Mediterranean. The southernmost of the Arab trading settlements in Africa, established at the end of the tenth century A.D., was called Sofala, on the coast between the mouths of the Zambezi and the Limpopo rivers. When the first Europeans under the Portuguese navigator, Vasco da Gama, reached Sofala in 1505 they found that Arab merchants were trading profitably with the Bantu kingdom inland, in what later became Portuguese Mozambique and British Rhodesia. The Arabs told of exchanging their beads and textiles for large amounts of gold, which some of them believed was mined by the Bantu-speaking peoples from the legendary mines of Solomon.

The Portuguese planted a colony at Sofala to exploit this trade and over the next century a series of reports of the Bantu kingdom came back to Europe. A despatch of 1506 to the King of Portugal explains that the Bantu ruler's title was Mwene Mutapa (which means Master Ravager) and that in 'Zunbanhy', the royal capital, 'the houses of the king . . . were of stone and clay, very large and on one level.' A few years later, the Portuguese explorer, Antonio Fernandes, actually visited a place in which 'a fortress of the king of Menomotapa (Mwene Mutapa) is now made of stone'—this structure seemed quite a marvel compared with the usual African villages of clay and branches. Such visits by Europeans, however, were extremely rare, for the Bantu rightly suspected that travellers came only to rob them of their wealth.

The next known mention of Great Zimbabwe dates from 1552, when the Portuguese historian João de Barros, published his book about the Portuguese explorations, which contains an evocative passage that re-lit the old stories of King Solomon's Mines:

> These mines are the most ancient known in the country. They are all in the plain, in the midst of which there is a square fortress, masonry inside and outside, built of stones of marvellous size. And there appears to be no mortar binding them. The wall is more than 25 spans [about 6 metres/19 feet] in thickness, while the height is not so great considering the thickness. Above the door of this structure is an inscription. . . . This structure is almost surrounded by hills, upon which are others resembling it in the use of the stones and the absence of mortar. One of the structures is a tower more than 12 fathoms [about 22 metres/72 feet] high. The natives of the country call all these edifices Symbaoe, which according to their language signifies court, for every place where the Menomotapa [Mwene Mutapa] may be is so called. . . . There are always some of Menomotapa's wives therein. . . . When and by whom these structures were raised, there is no record as the people of the land do not know the art of writing.

This fascinating, though frustratingly sparse, report of Zimbabwe enclosures continues with an intriguing reference to the Solomon's Mines legend. 'It

Previous pages *Zimbabwe's Great Enclosure viewed from the Hill Ruin to the north. In the site's heyday during the fourteenth and fifteenth centuries there were probably fewer trees and the hills beyond provided granite building blocks; some 15,000 tons worth were needed for the Great Enclosure.*
Zimbabwe is the anglicized form of the Shona word dzimbahwe meaning 'stone houses'. Over 100 similar ruins have been found on the southern African plateau that straddles modern Zimbabwe, parts of Botswana and South Africa.
The chapter symbol is an African hut typical of those built in Great Zimbabwe's enclosures.

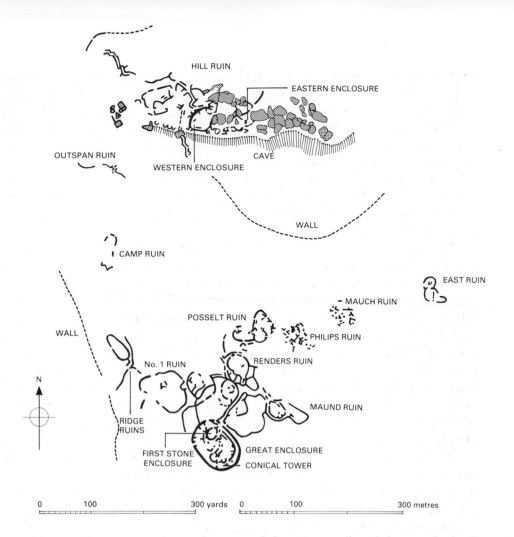

HILL RUIN

EASTERN ENCLOSURE

OUTSPAN RUIN

WESTERN ENCLOSURE

CAVE

WALL

CAMP RUIN

EAST RUIN

MAUCH RUIN

POSSELT RUIN

WALL

PHILIPS RUIN

No. 1 RUIN

RENDERS RUIN

N

MAUND RUIN

RIDGE
RUINS

FIRST STONE
ENCLOSURE

GREAT ENCLOSURE

CONICAL TOWER

0   100   300 yards   0   100   300 metres

would seem that some prince who owned the mines ordered them to be built as a sign of his possession . . . as these structures are very similar to some found in the land of Prester John, at a place called Acaxumo, which was a municipal city of the Queen of Sheba, which Ptolemy calls Axuma.' A later account, dating from 1609, is even clearer about the legendary link—though the author, a Portuguese missionary, João dos Santos, was writing about one of the many much smaller enclosures also called *zimbabwe* in various parts of the country (formerly called Rhodesia) now known itself as Zimbabwe. He writes of the tradition 'that these houses were anciently a factory of the Queen of Sheba, and that from this place a great quantity of gold was brought to her down the Cuama rivers to the Indian Ocean. . . . Others say that these are the ruins of the factory of Solomon, where he had his factors who procured gold from these lands.'

On closer examination of these stories, it seems that most of the mentions of Solomon and the Queen of Sheba originated with Arab traders who lived there, for both of these monarchs were important figures in Muslim folk traditions. But it is not surprising that Europeans associated the place with particular passages in the First Book of Kings in the Old Testament: 'And King Solomon made a navy of ships. . . . And they came to Ophir, and fetched from thence gold, four hundred and twenty talents, and brought it to King Solomon. . . . And all King Solomon's drinking vessels were of gold. . . . Once in three years came the navy of Tarshish, bringing gold, and silver, ivory, and apes and peacocks. So King Solomon exceeded all the kings of the earth for riches and wisdom.'

During the next centuries, unsuccessful expeditions to find the legendary gold mines of Ophir were mounted by the Dutch, the Portuguese and by South African Boers. Finally, in 1871, a young German geologist called Carl

Zimbabwe spread over 24 hectares (60 acres) according to the dictates of trade and ceremonial and not as a systematic capital. For many years the ruins were thought to be too advanced to be the work of African builders. Cecil Rhodes, founder of Rhodesia (modern Zimbabwe), was convinced they were built by the Phoenicians.

The finest section of the outer wall on the south side of the Great Enclosure. Successive courses were set back from each other to produce the sloping effect. Monolithic standing stones, many restored, crown the chevron-patterned top of the wall. The rich yellow colour was caused by lichen growth.

Mauch—fired by a German missionary's account of a journey to find Solomon's Ophir at Great Zimbabwe—set off across country and met a local German trader named Adam Render, who simply led him straight to the ruins.

When Mauch published his discovery in Europe, he noted particularly that the great enclosure was known locally as Mumbahuru, 'the House of the Great Woman.' And he found lintels of a local hardwood which he thought was cedar. His conclusion was almost inevitable. 'Salomo [Solomon] used a lot of cedar-wood for the building of the temple and of his palaces: further: including here the visit of the Queen of Seba (*sic*) and considering Zimbabwe or Zimbaoe or Simbaoe written in Arabic (of Hebrew I know nothing), one gets as a result that the great woman who built the *rondeau* could have been none other than the Queen of Seba.' This triumphant conclusion, rather sadly, was wrong. For modern archaeology has shown that Great Zimbabwe was built by the black ruler of an African empire, probably at the end of the fourteenth century A.D.

Today the ruins of Great Zimbabwe lie 27 kilometres (17 miles) south-east of the small town of Fort Victoria. The great plain of southern Africa, stretches on and on and is dotted with trees, mostly feathery acacias, which

The walls of the Western Enclosure built on and among the natural stones of the Hill Ruin rise to 9 metres (30 feet). Great Zimbabwe's only surviving doorway pierces it, a very narrow entrance with stone lintels to bear the wall above. It gives access to the so-called secret passage.

gather into woods here and there. Waves of soft hills and steeper mountains surround most of the horizon, and the smooth surface of the plain is often punctured by a *kopje*, the strange type of small hill formed by rocky outcrops that looks almost man-made.

The oldest site at Great Zimbabwe is on top of one of these *kopjes*, a large cluster of irregular dry-stone wall enclosures around a group of massive boulders projecting from the bedrock. In a valley below the thickly forested southern slope of the *kopje*, the outlines of many small stone buildings can be made out—the ruined survivors of a large settlement of huts, most of which were clay-walled. And beyond the valley, on a gentle eminence with the foundations of many more stone edifices around it, rises the Great Enclosure—elliptical in shape, with huge dry-stone walls surrounding a handful of trees grown up among its strange internal structures—the 'House of the Great Woman'. That is all there is at Great Zimbabwe—around the ruins, fields and tree-covered hills gently unfold towards the skyline.

Six hundred years ago, however, it must have been very different, with the servants and soldiers of the Shona king filling the town huts between what was probably the chief religious sanctuary on top of the hill and the royal residence in the Great Enclosure. It was the centre of an extensive kingdom ruling many tribes in an area of over 1126 kilometres (700 miles) by 1609 kilometres (1000 miles), from the Limpopo river in the south to near the northern end of Lake Nyasa.

Until the third century A.D. most of southern Africa was inhabited only by fairly light-skinned people, the ancestors of the Hottentots, who now inhabit the arid south-west, and perhaps the Pygmies of the central African forests. It is generally thought that Negro peoples moved southwards from the Sudan and its surroundings at about the time of the birth of Christ. From Ethiopia they penetrated along the great Rift Valley, through the dense tropical forests and emerged on the southern plain before A.D. 300. Excavated timbers at Great Zimbabwe have shown radiocarbon dates of that period, but these are followed by a gap of two or three centuries before the next dates yielded by the lowest layers of another part of the ruins, under the Great Enclosure.

The hilltop sacred enclosure was in use by A.D. 1100, and it was probably in the decades before that that a new wave of black settlers arrived from the north, bringing an advanced metal-working culture (including iron) with them. And we can reckon that their leader at some stage was King Mbire who, African oral traditions say, was the founder of the Great Zimbabwe kingdom. His people were the Shona, and there is archaeological evidence that they were indigenous to central-east Africa, emerging as an élite among the many Bantu-speaking tribes in that part of the continent.

Mbire's people (who often used his name to describe themselves collectively) brought to Great Zimbabwe the worship of a supreme god called Mwari and, under him, of powerful spirits representing ancestral rulers. There seems little doubt that the hilltop sanctuary—often called the Acropolis or the Hill Ruin by European visitors—was the centre of ritual ceremonies, for archaeologists have found many cult objects in the ground beneath its enclosures. The early walls there, as in the rest of Great Zimbabwe, were doubtless of *daga*.

Daga is still the most common building material of rural Africa. It is made by watering and mixing clay soils with an aggregate of very fine gravel. When it is carefully prepared, it can be of great durability, especially if the freshly built surfaces are patted patiently while wet, for this brings the finest particles to the surface and the *daga* then dries hard, with a slightly polished appearance. *Daga* structures last for many decades, but it is only the stone walls that have survived the centuries above ground at Great Zimbabwe. It is not yet possible to say exactly when some of the clay structures were replaced by stone walls, but it was in the period between 1300 and a little after 1400, when Great Zimbabwe was at its height as capital of the kingdom.

In the hilltop sanctuary, the stone walls form a bewildering tangle and it is necessary to look at a plan to get any idea of how the complex of enclosures developed. The big outcropping rocks were probably sacred in themselves long before anything was built there—particular rock outcrops had religious importance in many early cultures. An ancient staircase follows a tortuous course from the valley up to the rocks, much of it squeezing between high boulders that leave room for only one person to pass. Then one is among the jumble of rocks and spaces between them that formed the original sanctuary. We cannot know what gods or spirits lurked among these stones for the earliest inhabitants, but we may well imagine the central western boulders, or the space beside them to the north, as a setting for the high god Mwari, and the maze around as the dwellings of the ancestral spirits.

Around these natural rocks there are several towers and a few long standing stones (there were many of these originally). Stone walls run from boulder to boulder, uphill and down, weaving a network of small enclosures and looping out into larger ones. There are three identifiable styles of stonework at Great Zimbabwe. The earliest of these has stone courses that undulate erratically and are thought to date from between A.D. 1250 and 1380. Most of the hilltop structure is of this period, including the tall walls, over 9 metres (30 feet) high, which surround the largest man-made court. This is the so-called Western Enclosure, lying just to the west of the imposing boulder group just mentioned. The enclosure is thought to have contained 14 huts of *daga*—perhaps for the sanctuary's attendants—and it was paved with the same material.

Sixty-one metres (200 feet) away, on the other side of the same group of boulders and beyond many mysterious walls among the rocks, lies the Eastern Enclosure. This was certainly a very sacred place indeed and, to judge from the level courses of the stonework in the walls around it, was last re-built in about A.D. 1400. Today, the ground inside the enclosure slopes steeply and is strewn with rocks—as built in 1400, the slope of the court was terraced into many small circular platforms, each holding slender standing stones. Some of the

Four of the seven strange solid conical turrets still stand on the western wall of the Western Enclosure. Among them is a stick-like granite monolith. It is assumed that they had a ritual purpose.

stones had carved stone birds at their tops, thought to represent particular
ancestral spirits. Eight of these splendid birds were found during excavations,
but most of them are now in museums in South Africa.

Beside the Eastern Enclosure are two other features that probably played a
part in the rites enacted there. A few metres downhill, a low cave opens out
just over the cliff that falls to the valley below. Many pieces of iron ore and
some gold, with tools for working gold, were found on the floor of this cave
and human voices calling in it are projected out so that they can be heard eerily
in the valley. At the top of the slope of the Eastern Enclosure, a slender passage
leads up between vast rocks on to a broad flat-topped boulder—this is the
highest point of the Great Zimbabwe ruins and its carefully walled platform,
dubbed the Balcony, by European visitors, overlooks both the sacred enclosure and the valley beyond.

It is difficult to reconstruct the ceremonies that took place in this complex
of rocky outcrops and walled enclosures to worship Mwari and the ancestral
spirits of kings. The forms—with tortuous natural gaps between the boulders
made more maze-like by projecting walls that made it difficult to slip
past—suggest trials of fortitude and persistence, perhaps ritual passages in the
dark to gain blessing and recognition. Strange objects of iron have been
excavated from the ruins here, gongs and ladles and items resembling hoes,
but their purposes in the sanctuary are unknown.

The only rites of which there are records are those told to Mauch in 1871
by the son of the reputed last head priest of Great Zimbabwe. Every two to
four years, on some unknown rota, the head priest summoned the
Rozwi—descendants of the original rulers—to come to the sacred place. The
Rozwi drove their cattle—or, apparently, goats if a rain-making ceremony
was involved—to the bottom of the Great Zimbabwe hill. Some animals were
taken up to the most sacred shrine, the Eastern Enclosure, and sacrificed on the
circular platforms there to the god Mwari. The rest of the beasts were

Another of the carved soapstone birds. This one from the Philips Ruin is the most elaborate with a crocodile climbing its shaft and a decorative base.

slaughtered in the valley and, when the secret rites on the hill were finished, a general feast was held in the Great Enclosure in the valley before the Rozwi left Great Zimbabwe for their homes again.

In the valley below the hill sanctuary, archaeologists have found traces of circular and other dwellings of *daga* and masonry of all stages in Great Zimbabwe's growth between A.D. 1100 and 1400. Most of the walls to be seen now were enclosures for groups of huts. For example, the so-called Maund Ruin was 1254 square metres (1500 square yards) in area and contained 10 huts. In Shona villages today, each couple occupies three or four huts and historical reports suggest the same average. So it has been estimated that, at its height, the stone enclosures of Great Zimbabwe housed between 100–200 adults, while the *daga* huts known to have existed around brought the total up to perhaps one or two thousand.

Little is known of the lives of the people who lived here, but they left huge quantities of rubbish, especially broken pottery. The pots were not wheel-turned, but were built up with coils of coarse clay and turned in front of burning wood to fire them. Rounded pots with wide necks were the most common vessels, holding about 500 millilitres (1 Imperial pint or 1.25 US pints), and they used these for both cooking and drinking. They probably ate with their hands directly from such pots, for no wide bowls for eating have been found. The other containers often found were storage pots for liquids and grain that held about 4.5 litres (1 Imperial gallon or 1.25 US gallons).

The ordinary people wore little but aprons of animal skins or cloth made from the bark of trees. A wealthier group wore woven cotton cloth and many metal ornaments—rings, bangles and bracelets made from copper or bronze, and occasionally iron. A number of gold beads have been found, but despite the near-by gold mines, whose ancient workings are exhausted, this metal

The completely solid 5.4-metre thick (18-foot) conical tower of the Great Enclosure that has become the symbol of Great Zimbabwe.

seems to have been rather unusual among the Shona themselves. Theirs was a civilization based on iron—furnaces have been found in many of the enclosures and their weapons (spears, knives and arrows) and tools (chiefly hand-ploughs and axes) were of that metal. According to an early seventeenth-century Portuguese report, every man had a string of small pierced wooden discs, which may have been used as 'divining dice'. That is almost all that can be said about the people who lived in the huts in the valley of Great Zimbabwe, and not much more is known about the kings who lived in the Great Enclosure.

The Great Enclosure—also known by Europeans inaccurately as the Temple or, prosaically, as the Elliptical Building—rides on a slight spur above the lower walls of the valley dwellings. Its entrance faces across the valley northwards towards the steep cliff rising to the hilltop sanctuary. Its outer wall is by far the biggest ancient structure in Africa south of the Sahara Desert. This was the last of a series of ever-larger enclosures built by the Shona kings, probably to shelter their daily lives and court ritual from the eyes of their subjects, for the gateways were not well designed for defence.

It is curious that, among the kings whose names have come down to us in the oral traditions of the Shona, those of the rulers who actually built the huge structures at Great Zimbabwe during the century after 1300 are not known. Between the uncertain date well before 1300, when Mbire founded his dynasty, and the accession of King Nyatsimba Mutota, who ruled from before 1440 until 1480, no king's name has survived.

Inside the huge outer walls of the Great Enclosure, there is a roughly circular stone structure, 21 metres (70 feet) in diameter, and another much bigger enclosure—filling most of the southern half of the area within the outer walls. The walls of these two stone courts are quite low and their stonework

129

shows that they are much earlier than the outer ramparts. The inner courts may date from some time shortly after 1300, and they were probably the first stone enclosures for the king.

By the middle of the fourteenth century Great Zimbabwe had become the wealthiest town in southern Africa. The wealth was based on both commercial and political importance and the gold mines near-by embarked on a steady ore production, which was sought by the Arab traders settled on the coast. The Shona kings possessed these mines and Great Zimbabwe, already established as a religious centre, was in the best geographical position to control the route to Sofala and the world beyond. Archaeological evidence shows that at this time the culture in the Great Zimbabwe settlement flowered. Countless new craft techniques appeared, some self-generated, some imported. Metalworking, jewellery, pottery and masonry took on new refinements. And trade expanded, too.

Just down the slope outside the main north entrance to the Great Enclosure, there lies another fairly large enclosure with low walls, which is generally called the Renders Ruin. Archaeologists' finds in two separate places in this ruin suggest that it may have been a trading centre, as well as a residential area. The finds show that during the fourteenth century, Great Zimbabwe traded its gold for stoneware and celadon (green glazed) dishes from China, painted and glazed bowls from Persia, coloured glass from somewhere in the Near East, huge numbers of glass beads from Arabia and metal tools and ornaments that may have come from other parts of Africa.

The Renders Ruin is very near the Great Enclosure and this suggests royal control of all trading. Doubtless the king, or his womenfolk and attendants, were among the chief users of imported luxuries, though there is little evidence to support this for the rulers presumably took away such possessions when Great Zimbabwe ceased to be the capital. Indeed, the only clues we have about the lives and powers of these kings come from Portuguese accounts gathered at secondhand after the rulers moved northwards about 1440 to less monumental settlements.

In about 1350 the king at Great Zimbabwe exercised loose control over a widespread federation of chiefdoms spreading from the Kalahari Desert and the gold mines to the Indian Ocean, excluding the tribes on the coastal strip itself. In the old inner enclosure at Great Zimbabwe (for this was before the great outer wall was built) the king and his wives probably lived in the *daga* huts protected from view by the circular walls at the northern end, while his courtiers had dwellings in the broader enclosed space to the south of it.

On formal or ritual occasions, these courtiers would gather at the appropriate place in the larger enclosure—possibly around the two circular platforms of *daga* that can still be seen. They would be an impressive group, wearing richly-coloured skirts and cloaks of gold-embroidered silk or cotton, which set off the dark brown of their faces and arms. Most of those arms were encircled by row after row of bracelets made of iron or copper, or woven from gold wire.

When he appeared among these grandly clad attendants, the king would be dressed with contrasting simplicity. For he was a religious leader as much as a political one. His robe would be of plain cotton grown on his own land. It was perhaps the king himself who conducted the ceremonies of sacrifice in the religious enclosure on the hill above, then presided over the great banquet of beef for his subjects gathered in the Great Enclosure after the rites were finished.

By 1380, the wealth of Great Zimbabwe was so great that the king decided to make his Great Enclosure still more monumental. It was at this time that part of the old outer wall was broken so that a circular stepped platform of stone could be inserted in it, leading to a doorway. And beyond that doorway, on the outside of the old wall, the Shona built a round tower of solid stonework 9 metres (30 feet) high. Most walls at Great Zimbabwe have stonework that slopes inwards as it rises, for durability. In this tower the sloping effect is exaggerated and this accounts for the name by which it is usually known today, the Conical Tower. It stands among high trees in the parallel passage between the older and the later walls of the Great Enclosure. Was it a watch tower or religious symbol? No clue has been found.

During the same period, the famous outer wall was started. Over the 20 or so years of its construction the craftsmanship of the masonry advanced considerably. Starting at the north–west side, in about 1380, the stones were laid in courses almost as irregular as the earlier structures—here the wall is only half as thick and high as its later sections. As the team of builders moved along southwards before curving around towards the east past the Conical Tower, the wall was made bigger and bigger. Finally, in the eastern stretch that runs outside the narrow parallel passage and completes the 246-metre (800-foot) long perimeter of the enclosure, the wall reaches the tremendous dimensions of 9.8 metres (32 feet) in height and 5 metres (17 feet) in thickness. And in this stretch the builders of about 1400 added new refinements. The courses of stone are level and smoother, a double row of stones forming zigzag patterns is inserted into the surface at three courses below the top, and thin standing stones like sentries are ranged along the flat top of the wall. This section is beyond question the high point of African masons' craft south of the Sahara.

Many theories have been put forward and disputed about the Great Enclosure's use as temple as well as palace, about the purpose of the Conical Tower and about the possibility that Great Zimbabwe's architecture was influenced by outsiders. One of the most appealing of these theories refers back to the legend of the Queen of Sheba, for the plan of the Haram Bilqis palace in the Yemen, attributed to the great queen in Arab tradition, has a huge elliptical enclosure with its wall pierced by a very formal palace. But such arguments are not convincing. It seems that the building techniques and styles of Great Zimbabwe were developed locally by Shona craftsmen over the fourteenth century.

Little was added to Great Zimbabwe after that date. The oral legends of the Shona tell of a critical shortage of salt in the kingdom during the 1430s. Salt was an essential item of diet and extensively traded. The shortage became so serious that the king of the time, still of the Mbire dynasty, sent scouts far away to find a new source of supply. One of these scouts found salt-mines in the Dande area in the middle Zambezi valley. Hearing this, the king who was called Nyatsimba Mutota, considered the matter. After conferring with his advisers and, presumably, seeking the guidance of the supreme god Mwari, the king gathered an army and his people together. Leaving one of his courtiers in charge of a small group (including some royal wives) at Great Zimbabwe, Mutota led the rest northwards in 1440 to conquer Dande and the surrounding lands and to settle there. The king awarded himself the title of Mwene Mutapa, or Master Ravager, by which his successors too were known. He continued to build up the extensive empire known by reputation to the first Portuguese settlers, though they arrived 25 years after its founder's death in 1480. Great Zimbabwe was no longer a political capital by then, though its importance as a religious centre, visited by the king of the Shona, continued for centuries. The last ceremony known to have taken place there was a great sacrifice of goats to bring rain in 1904.

A female fertility figure carved from soapstone. This unique 40 cm (16 in) sculpture was acquired by the British Museum in 1923 and said to be from Great Zimbabwe.

131

BENIN

Bronze Heads Of West Africa

THE PORTUGUESE, who discovered the sea route to Benin in the 1470s, were looking for an Atlantic landing point to reach the Sudan and the Christian kingdom of Ethiopia, for Islamic navies were making trade through the Mediterranean dangerous. They also hoped to find a way to the country of the legendary Christian king, Prester John, whose elusive kingdom was said to be of untold wealth, though it sometimes became confused with the legend of King Solomon's Mines. In 1474, Fernão da Gomez was exploring and charting the Nigerian coast—as undertaken in his trading contract with the King of Portugal—when one of his ships chanced on the mouth of the Niger river. Sailing up a channel busy with canoes, the ship reached the riverside town of Guatun. From there, later traders found a broad earth road running 64 kilometres (40 miles) inland across continuous mangrove swamps to Benin City, capital of the Edo (Bini) people, who were part of the great Yoruba empire.

Modern Benin is now part of western Nigeria and lies on an open plain of red sandy soil north of a wide band of swamps running between the plain and the ocean and spreading along the coast from the delta of the immense Niger river. To the north of the city there are mountains and the start of the Niger basin's tropical jungle that runs on eastwards to the Congo.

From the innumerable courtyards of the palace in Benin, the king, or Oba, ruled an empire that included most of modern Nigeria west of the Niger river and spread beyond its present western boundary to Cotonou in the present-day Republic of Benin (formerly Dahomey). In the fifteenth century, the Oba was overlord of kings and chiefs of several tribes, most of whom were culturally interlinked with his Yoruba ancestry. The origins of these people are disputed. Some scholars believe that Negro peoples developed in Nigeria, others that the physical type first appeared in the area around the Sudan, far to the east. In support of the first theory, the oldest Negro skeleton yet identified, radiocarbon dated to 9000 B.C., was found at Iwo Eleru in Nigeria.

Ife, in south-western Nigeria, was the first Yoruba capital and has remained a spiritual centre right up to the present. It was here and at Igbo–Ukwu, deep in the tropical rain forest to the east of the Niger river, that the school of art, which later produced the famous Benin bronzes, was developed from about A.D. 900 onwards. The city of Benin was at the height of its power when the Portuguese arrived and it produced an extraordinary amount of the bold sculpture that astonished the Europeans. And so the world has attached the name of Benin to all Nigerian work of this kind, which is now among the most highly prized of all relatively primitive works of art.

Some of the earliest examples of West African sculpture are the terracotta statues found at Nok in northern Nigeria, dating from 400 B.C. Metal sculpture did not appear for another thousand years or more, but Yoruba legends suggest that people from the north first brought techniques for working in iron to the south of the country at some time well before A.D. 1000. These metalworking people were probably integrated into those already in the Benin area, for the languages of the Yoruba and Edo peoples bear no resemblance to the Hausa and other tongues of the north.

The so-called 'bronzes' (most of which are in fact made of brass) were intricately involved with the roles and authority of the rulers of the Nigerian kingdoms—the Oni of Ife, the Oba of Benin and the Alafin of Oyo, a separate kingdom established some time in the thirteenth century. These rulers were god-kings to their people, like the monarchs of many other early cultures, and they derived their power from the creators of their worlds. To the Yoruba of Ife, the supreme god (sometimes said to be a goddess) was Olorun, who lowered his or her son Oduduwa to the world when it was nothing but ocean.

Previous pages A magnificent Benin bronze of a javelin-armed horseman (late seventeenth to early eighteenth century) faces a relief of the annual cow sacrifice. This was performed by the Oba (king) at his father's altar. Both items were spoils of the British capture of Benin in 1897.

The chapter symbol is a Benin bronze of a hunter carrying an antelope.

The leopard was a sacred beast of Benin. This is one of an ivory pair sculpted in the nineteenth century and studded with copper spots. An African fable tells how the leopard got his spots—from his friend the Fire.

Oduduwa carried some earth and a palm seed and put earth on the waters and planted the seed. It grew up at Ife into a palm tree, whose branches became the chiefdoms of Yorubaland.

At Benin, the Edo people have a slightly different creation myth. For them, too, the world was originally nothing but water. Olorun (Olokun), their supreme god, sent down his sons to inhabit earth. Each son brought something he thought would be useful, but the youngest, Osanabua, brought a snail's shell full of earth. The older sons were nonplussed when they found nothing except water, but the youngest tipped out his earth and the land of Benin was formed. He became god-king, awarding his brothers territories for their chiefdoms. The making of land on the primeval waters appears in creation myths all over the world, as does the tree. In both these Nigerian versions a wise bird plays a key role in advising the deity who brought the earth and, as among other peoples (including those of Zimbabwe and Easter Island), birds became important images of divine rule.

Olokun and Osanabua remained as the controlling gods of the waters and of the land respectively. Rivers were (and still are) sacred to Olokun, who also controlled the path to the afterworld, the world of the spirits, which lay across the ocean. Osanabua included in his domain not only the land but the living people and creatures in it. Thus, for the Benin people, there was a basic duality between land and sea, life and after-life. The gods and ancestral spirits could pass from one dimension to another when they wished, and they reserved particular hills, rocks and small woods as their habitations on earth. At certain times of the year, and especially at the great annual festival for the renewal of the divine powers of the king, they would become present in the bodies of priests and would make their wishes known. The Oba of Benin had very important functions to fulfil at such times; indeed, apart from his political role, he had to lead over 200 lengthy rites in the course of each year for the benefit of

his kingdom. So heavy was his full regalia that the Oba needed arm-bearers.

The finds from a royal burial pit dating from the ninth century A.D. at Igbo-Ukwu include vases, bowls, staffs, model conch shells, pendant elephants' heads, bracelets of coiled snakes, openwork objects thought to be 'altar stands', and other items—all of bronze or brass and all of the most complex decorated workmanship. The technique often used to produce these items was lost wax casting, a method thought to have been introduced at this time by traders from the Mediterranean.

In lost wax casting, a rough outline of the head or other object was made in clay, then the detailed sculpture was formed over it in a thick layer of wax. This in turn was coated in skins of clay with a hole left in the top. The cast was turned upside down and baked, so that the molten wax ran out. The space left by the wax was filled with liquid brass or bronze and after cooling, the clay was broken to reveal the cast metal. The Benin heads rarely compare with those of Ife for refinement, but they have a majestic ferocity of their own.

The great series of heads of brass (or bronze), terracotta and sometimes ivory, begin with those of the holy city of Ife. Ife, also called Ile-Ife, lies east of Ibadan and 161 kilometres (100 miles) north–west of Benin city. It is still a holy place and over 400 different sects are said to flourish there. Recent excavations have shown that the city was inhabited by A.D. 600 by a people who farmed oil palms and yams. Archaeologists believe their religion had the same aim as that of early farming communities everywhere in the world—ensuring harmony between themselves, their land and the seen or unseen forces around them. West of the Niger, among the Ibo people, defended villages were rare, but east of the river, the Edo and Yoruba tribes found it necessary to live in towns behind strong defensive earthworks. It is not yet known whether the threat came from population growth leading to rivalry between neighbouring towns, or from slave raids from the north. The second explanation would provide a reason for the emergence of kings to organize the defence and all the better if the kings had divine guidance, such as a farming priesthood was already known to receive.

Ife emerged as the dominant city probably a little after A.D. 1000, and seems to have kept this position until the rise of Benin in about 1450. Not only was Ife the seat of the sacred figure, the Oni, but it occupied a key position on the trading routes of West Africa. The Yoruba area wanted salt, copper and brass in rods, textiles, weapons and horses. In exchange, Ife supplied large quantities of kola (a tree crop) and later—if the evidence including many Ife bronzes depicting tied and gagged human beings is anything to go by—the prosperity of the god-king Oni's city may have depended on the export of slaves to North Africa.

At the centre of Ife stood the big walled enclosure of the Afin, the Oni's extended palace. As the city grew, the surrounding area was defended by a series of walls built out in great loops. Ife is still a prosperous city with later buildings over these early levels. Parts of the Afin area have been excavated, revealing floors of terracotta and many potsherds, and a museum now stands there, but little detail has been gleaned about the form of the medieval palace.

The museum does, however, contain many of the bronzes and terracottas of Ife's high period. These were brought to the attention of the outside world after a major find in 1910–11 by that rather outrageous individual, the German ethnographer Leo Frobenius. In a grove sacred to the god Olokun outside the city, Frobenius was shown a crowned bronze head of great beauty and particular importance to the Yoruba. He was told that it was left buried in the ground there all year except for the period of the great annual festival, when it was brought out for the ceremonies. The head was almost life–size, its serene

This wooden mask represents Eshu, anti-god of the Yoruba and thus the opponent of Ifa the good god. Like the evil principle in many African religions, Eshu, the spirit of unpredictability, plays tricks—as, for instance, when he persuaded the sun and moon to change places in the heavens.

Left *Royal messengers from Ife have their faces marked with typical scarifications.*

Negro features most delicately rendered and the skin decorated by the lightly striated lines commonly found in Ife sculpture. The bronze crown was intricate, with a stepped cone feature in front and something like a spear-head rising above.

Further digging revealed several more heads. These were of terracotta and Frobenius took seven back to Germany with him. To his fury, he was forbidden to take the crowned bronze. Forty years later it was found that the head he left at Olokun's grove was a forgery, made recently by a method different from the lost wax technique. The original head has never been traced, but an ancient one almost identical to the forgery was later found in a compound just outside the Afin palace.

When Frobenius got back to Germany, he exhibited the seven lovely terracotta heads and announced that he had found Atlantis! In this sculpture, he said, there is 'a delicacy of form directly reminiscent of ancient Greece.' This proved, in his view, that another race 'far superior in strain to the Negro' had lived there once and made these works of art. This, he concluded, must have been a Greek colony that lost contact with Greece itself after about 800 B.C., and the creator sea-god Olokun was therefore Poseidon.

After the initial sensation, Frobenius's Atlantis theory was forgotten, but his find did focus people's interest on Ife. Over the following decades, more bronzes came to light. In 1937 the then Oni of Ife himself published photographs of an ancient smooth copper mask in his possession, said to be a portrait of the third Oni, Obulafon. This work is exceptional among the Ife heads in that it has no rear part. The slits under its eyes indicate that it was intended for use in ceremonies, when the Oni would presumably take on the persona of his ancestor for a time.

In the following two years, 17 more bronzes, heads made of copper or brass, were found in the grounds just outside the Afin palace. Most of these were striated, though some were smooth, and they confirmed that a school of sculpture had existed in Ife, which achieved results of startlingly high quality. The naturalism and grace of the 30 or so metal heads found so far (apart from many more in terracotta) were particularly puzzling to art historians, used only to the stylization and savage power of the Benin bronzes. But most of the latter were probably made rather later than the Ife pieces, during Benin's ascendancy in the fifteenth century.

Benin is today an important city on the site of the fifteenth century buildings, so what we know of it is derived from a few archaeological excavations and some descriptions and drawings by early travellers. It was thought at one time that the city was encircled by an inner and two outer walls, but excavations have now shown that the outer structures divided it into a dozen or more districts. These divisions may have been areas of municipal government, but it is more likely that new parts were walled as the city grew. The walls were built of clay blocks and were up to 6 metres (20 feet) high. Eight guarded gateways entered the city and an early trader has left his impressions of the scene within. From the main gateway a 'great broad street' ran straight across the city, which seemed very large to him. After walking for a quarter of an hour, a visitor would see 'a big tree in front of him as far as the eye can reach' and even from that tree the other side of the town was not to be seen. Around this and a few other wide streets, the city was a web of small roads and narrow lanes, their sides crowded with closely built houses on platforms. The houses were red walled, for they were built of the clay from the Benin plain, moulded into building blocks about 60 centimetres (2 feet) square. The roofs were thatched with thick layers of broad leaves on a frame of palm branches, and these overhung the walls in deep eaves.

A crowned brass head from Ife of the twelfth to fourteenth centuries. It is 24 cm (9½ in) high, slightly less than life size, and was found among 13 similar heads in 1938 inside the Wunmonije compound behind the afin (palace) of Ife.

In the centre of the city, on a site only abandoned by the rulers as late as 1897, was the palace of the Oba, a descendant of the royal family of Ife. The first Oba was established in Benin in about 1300. This king, Eweka, may have been sent there to reduce the power of the Edo chiefs in this eastern province of the Yoruba empire. Eweka married a daughter of one of the Edo chiefs and gradually appointed their children to the key chiefdoms. When his son Ewedo duly became Oba, he was forced to fight a battle against the administrator of Benin City itself to establish his authority. According to Edo tradition, it was Ewedo who named the country Ubini or Benin, and it was his son Oguola who brought in the custom of casting the royal history in brass.

To rule the Edo and its chiefs needed much strength, as can be seen from the bloody stories of many reigns. One Oba, Ohen, became partly paralysed. To hide this, he always had himself carried into the throne room before anyone arrived and remained on the throne until everyone, barring a few trusted servants, had left. Ohen's chief minister stumbled on the secret and the Oba immediately had him executed to stop him from revealing it. The people of Benin, who thought the chief minister a good deal more acceptable than his master, rioted when they heard of the execution and Ohen was killed by their stones.

When the European traders came in the 1480s, the kingdom had recently been enlarged to the Niger river by one of the most successful Obas, Ewuare the Great. During his long reign he installed an efficient centralized system of government and trained a large and fierce army to extend his territories. The core of Ewuare's army was apparently stationed at Benin itself. This permanent force was not more than a few thousand men, but each of the numerous regional chiefs kept a small force of soldiers, too. These could be summoned by the Oba at any time and other men could be called up quickly from their ordinary work. At the height of the kingdom, the Oba claimed that he could field an army of 80,000 within a week.

The soldiers of Benin can be seen, armed and carrying shields, on many of the plaque bronzes. When gathered for the Oba's service, the army would prepare for battle with extensive rites of chanting and dance, enlisting the help of the gods. Ewuare's tactics were to make his men as frightening as possible. All would have their bodies painted brightly and they would carry various sorts of implements to make an uproar—some had trumpets or horns, others carried drums, rattles and gongs. The noise from these was increased by the soldiers' bellowed threats and chants as their ranks advanced on the enemy. When the range was right, they would release wave after wave of poisoned arrows from their short bows, then follow up with a charge, using their spears or swords and daggers. Military campaigns by Benin were rare, however, for the Oba's political power was firm after 1450. Most of the lives of those ferocious soldiers were spent in peaceful occupations in the Edo towns and villages, or in the city itself.

The Edo still exist today and are a fine, tall people with very black skin. During the time of the Benin kingdom, most of the men wore tribal marks on their faces—a row of three short vertical lines above each eyebrow. Ordinary men and women wore skirts of dyed cotton, gathered at the waist and falling to the ankles; the men's hair was cut straight across the forehead, while the women's was often dressed in countless thin plaits. Both sexes wore as many ornaments as they could—necklaces, bracelets and anklets of copper or brass, and beads of glass or stone.

Their houses tended to be quite large, for they lived in extended families of several generations, including quite distant relatives. These houses would be altered as generation followed generation, but the normal plan was of thatched

A 27 cm (10¾ in) head of an Oba (king) of Benin from the late seventeenth century in the cruder, more massive later style. The head has three coral clusters with more coral pendants on the forehead. These hollow bronzes were designed to support carved elephant tusks at ancestor altars.

Three of Benin's seventeenth century courtiers immortalized on a bronze plaque measuring 48.5 cm (19 in) by 38 cm (15 in). They hold calabash rattles, the African equivalent of castanets. The different head-dresses, number of neck rings and the middle courtier's chain surely all indicated status at court.

covered areas around open courtyards. When the weather was dry, much household life took place in these courtyards. During the wet season, the family would retreat under the thatch and the drains would be cleared to make sure that the torrential rains could run away.

Most of the work in the houses—including cooking, cleaning and carrying water—was done by the women, often with babies on their backs. The women also made the simple household pottery and textiles, and they were usually in charge of business transactions and marketing, too. In most West African countries, to this day, women are held to be better at business than men. But the head of each household was normally a man who exercised quite wide powers. Men were also responsible for the heavy labour of farming and hunting.

Hunting was carried out by bands of men in the great rain forests to the north of Benin. Their primary weapon, as with the soldiers, was the bow and poisoned arrow, with covered pit-traps to catch larger animals. They sought almost any creature for its meat and many for their skins. The meat they brought back supplied much of the people's protein, together with fish and the

Perhaps the most striking of all the many thousand Benin works of art, this 23 cm (9 in) ivory mask came from the Oba Ovonramwen's bedchamber when the British sacked Benin in 1897. It has been dated to the sixteenth century and the row of copper-encircled heads at the top are ten bearded Portuguese victims of the Oba's power. The two forehead slits were made to hold iron strip tattoo markings and the eyelets above and below the ears were presumably for suspending pendants. The mask has a coral bead collar and was probably worn on the chest not the face.

The proud head of a Queen Mother from Benin, fifteenth to sixteenth centuries. Height 40 cm (15¾ in).

goats and chickens kept by most households. Organized farming of the fertile land supplied the staple foods—yam prepared in many different ways, plantains, beans and cassava. But there were many other vegetables and fruits, and a beer fermented from the sap of palm trees.

Apart from this way of life typical of most of the population in Benin, there was a wealthy élite—usually the officials of the Oba. Such people, chiefs or functionaries of the increasingly centralized government, lived in large houses of many courtyards leading through to the kitchen courtyard of the slaves. Important men and women dressed with great finery, again shown in some of the bronzes. Their skirts fell in complicated drapes, their head-dresses were fantastic, and their necks, arms and ankles were encircled by layer upon layer of ornaments (many of the bronzes show neck-rings pushing up to and over the chin). If favoured by the Oba, these people were allowed to wear coral, a material otherwise reserved for the king and his court.

The Oba's own palace, the central building of Benin, is recorded in some early engravings, though we cannot be sure how accurate these are, for early travel pictures were often drawn incorrectly from verbal accounts. Within a great enclosure wall, there was an apparently endless series of courtyards and buildings, many of them topped by towers or spires with great copper birds on their pinnacles. One early traveller described how he looked through the entrance and saw gateway after gateway within, receding into the distance. Another was allowed into the palace and wrote of pillars covered with copper 'engravings' showing the battles of the Obas. A third reported a gleaming snake of copper winding its way down the length of a pillar 12 metres (40 feet) high.

The Oba was hidden from his people for most of the time, for he was divine and spent his time secluded with his many wives in his own part of the palace, while the rest of the big enclosure hummed with the business of a large kingdom. It was rumoured that he did not need food or drink or sleep. But priests attended him constantly with potions to enhance the spiritual powers that he exercised in a year-long sequence of rites for the benefit of his people.

Most of the greatest Benin bronzes and ivories were made for use in these rites, though the details of their significance are not known. The palace had large numbers of works of art, some on display, some kept in shrines or in store-houses except at festivals when they played an important part. Some of the most famous depict individuals and scenes illustrating the achievements and lives of the Obas. Here, the sculpture is in relief against the plain background of a panel, and these are usually called plaques. Much of our knowledge of the appearance of Benin courtiers and others during the great period of the kingdom is derived from these plaques—many of which were removed by the British punitive expedition of 1897 and are now in England and the USA.

The most important bronzes, however, are the heads. To the followers of the religion of Olokun and Osanabua, the heads of both live and dead kings were the essence of their sacred powers. Thus, one of the key ceremonies of the year involved the worship of the current Oba's head, while the sculpted heads of bronze or brass maintained the beneficence of dead rulers. During their lives, in most cases, the metal heads were therefore made to preserve their influence for future generations.

The most important religious event of the year was the festival of renewal. On that occasion a long procession left the palace to wind its way through the streets of Benin. The column was headed by marshals who cleared the way with sticks. Then came a group of servants handing out, in an act symbolic of the Oba's role, large quantities of food. After that, bearers and priests carried the king's sacred objects, including the ancestral bronze heads, to be seen by the people. For this occasion, the Oba wore his full regalia—a weighty robe of pierced coral pieces sewn into a fabric, a plump stiffened skirt down to his ankles, boots of the coral fabric, ivory ornaments, bronze rings around his neck and a winged or horned head-dress. He came as the climax of the procession, borne high by servants, and surrounded by musicians and captive wild animals.

This annual ceremony was a happy re-enactment of the Oba's role as protector of his people. Other occasions had a much less festive twist to them. The rites of worship of the living Oba's head have already been mentioned and this was a bloody affair. After priests had collected materials for a potion to sustain the king for the next year, a very young virgin pounded these into a paste. Then various sacrifices of animals (and, at some periods, of humans) were made and the blood was mixed with the paste to form a stiff substance. The Oba himself then carried out long rites in which he danced around the compound in his heavy robes as he and his wives had the sacrificial blood poured over them. Other festivals included ones devoted to the rain, the blessing of the royal coral, and the yam. Early in November, when the yam harvest was ready, elaborate earth and fertility rites would be held.

The kingdom of Benin was the last part of Nigeria to come under British rule in the nineteenth century. And it was British trading ambitions, combined with horror at that tradition of human sacrifice, that brought about its downfall from independence. The story is a macabre one. In 1892 the vice-consul visited Benin and the Oba signed a treaty placing the kingdom under British protection—Benin was to have certain trading rights guaranteed, and in exchange was to give up slavery and human sacrifice. To abandon slavery would have been an economic loss, which could be compensated, but the British completely misunderstood the importance that human sacrifice had by then taken on for the Edo people—the gods had to be propitiated by frequent sacrifices or the country would perish. The Oba's signature of the treaty was only playing for time and the rites of slaughter continued. Hearing about this, the British administration decided to take further action. Early in 1897 the acting consul, General Phillips, sent a message to the Oba that he was on the way to visit Benin.

The Oba was genuinely distressed by the message, for a festival was just starting during which he was forbidden to see anyone who was not an Edo. Despite his fear of the British, he decided that he feared the gods more. He sent a large party to meet the acting consul and tell him to turn back. Both sides became enraged during the meeting. Shooting began and General Phillips, six of his nine British companions and most of his escort of 200 troops were killed.

Within six weeks a large British expedition was on its way to Benin. The Oba heard of it and started on a terrible series of human sacrifices to avert the destruction he foresaw. But Olokun and Osanabua did not come to his assistance. The British fell on the city and burned it, including the ancient palace. The great copper birds on the pinnacles fell to the ground as the flames licked at the towers and toppled them. The Oba fled from his capital, but his attendants gave him up after six months. He was tried and sentenced to confinement for life in the town of Calabar on the coast. The British protectorate government took over the trading control of Benin and brought more than 2000 of its sacred and ancient bronzes back to Europe. Benin City was built anew on the same site and another Oba was installed as spiritual leader in a new palace, without political power and without his ancestral sculpture.

The art of Benin was not confined to human subjects or events. This lively seventeenth century plaque depicts a crocodile eating a fish and is inlaid with an elaborate tracery.

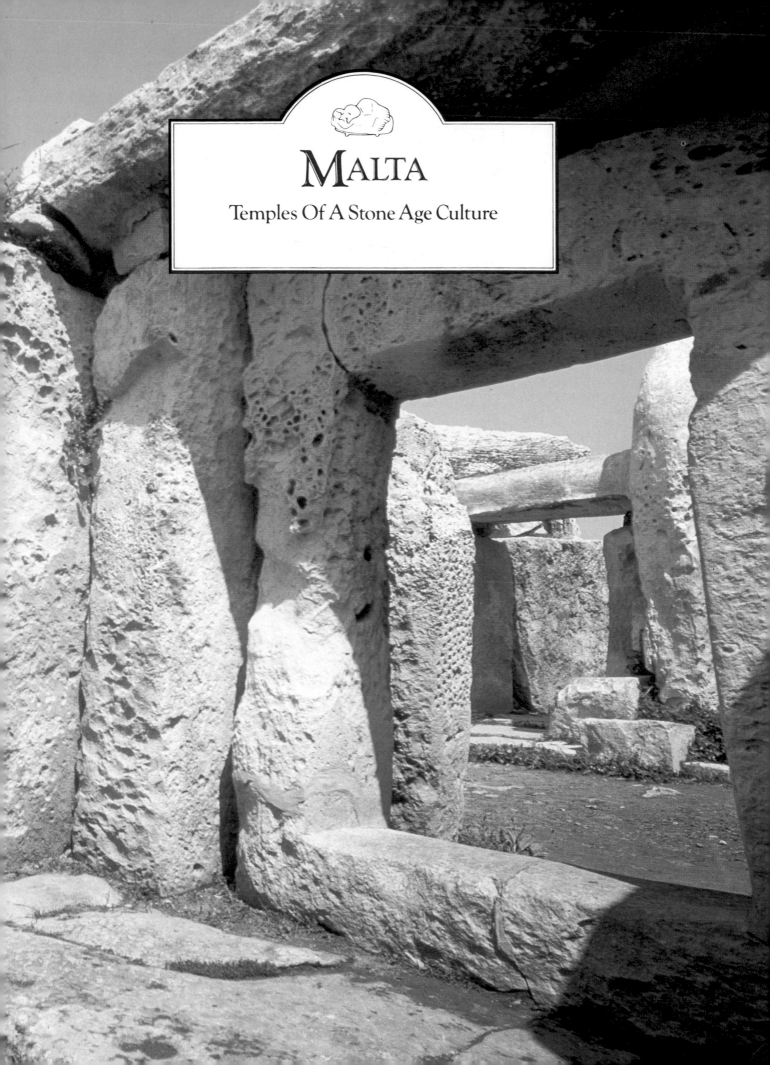

MALTA

Temples Of A Stone Age Culture

LONG BEFORE MEMPHIS became the great city of Egypt—indeed before the Great Pyramid was built at Giza and before Egypt even emerged into its recorded historical period—an extraordinary Stone Age culture grew up and built massive stone temples on a tiny island in the middle of the Mediterranean. Here, on Malta, people developed a religion of some complexity by about 3500 B.C., erected megalithic temples to house a priestly caste, and then, a thousand years later, simply disappeared.

Malta really consists of two main islands, Gozo and Malta itself, with two smaller islands and a few other rocks. It is a land of a special sort of beauty, the beauty of stone. The fields are grudgingly fertile, but so firmly enclosed by high walls to protect them from the Mediterranean gales that one sees little except honey–coloured stone on all sides when crossing the islands. The rock is always close to the surface and it is still the natural building material. The Maltese have been constructing huge, domed Baroque churches of stone all over the island since the seventeenth century. It has been said that building in stone on Malta is only a matter of re-arranging rock that is already there.

It took a thousand years or more for mankind to realize the possibilities of this stone. The first known inhabitants were farmers who settled on the island in about 5000 B.C., according to recent radiocarbon dates from Skorba, in the north of the main island. These people brought seeds with them and were soon cultivating barley, two kinds of early wheat, and lentils. They also brought cattle, pigs, sheep and goats. According to archaeological investigation, all this was new to the island, so they must have had sizeable boats. They made pottery of a kind found in many early settlements on the Mediterranean coasts, and it has been suggested that they were part of a general emigration by farmers from the eastern end of that sea. We know that these people kept in contact with Sicily, 112 kilometres away (70 miles), for the natural volcanic glass called obsidian has been found among their remains, and Malta is not volcanic.

Some time after 4000 B.C., the Maltese farmers started to use natural caves or to cut chambers in solid rock for the burial of their dead. It is possible that this custom evolved locally, but it is more likely that newcomers imported the custom, for rock-cut tombs of this period are found along the northern Mediterranean coast from Sicily to Spain. And a new type of pottery was made in Malta from this time, of a kind similar to contemporary Sicilian designs. Anyway, the Maltese soon started to develop both pottery and stone working in their own way, for it was the descendants of these people who began to build the big temples in about 3500 B.C. Nothing like them is known.

Although the massive stone walls of several of the temple ruins had not passed unnoticed over the centuries, it was the discovery of the underground temple of Hal Saflieni that brought the island most strongly to the attention of archaeologists and a wider public. In 1902 some houses were being built at Paola, a small town adjoining the capital, Valletta. As the workmen were cutting into the usual solid rock of Malta to make water cisterns, they broke through the top of a great cavern. Climbing down, they found a series of chambers with countless bones. The contractor, frightened of delays for his job, told no one of the find until the houses were finished. A Jesuit priest, Father Magri, was put in charge of the investigation which the authorities then ordered. Magri had the main chambers cleared without making any record of where the objects were lying, then left the task abruptly to become a missionary in the Far East.

After that the site was scientifically explored by Sir Themistocles Zammit in 1905–9, and when the neighbouring above-ground temple of Tarxien (pronounced Tarshen) was found in 1914, Zammit again conducted the

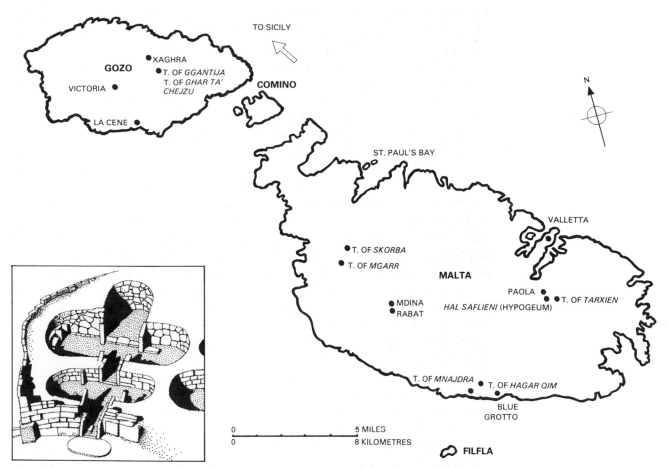

excavation. Numerous delicate carvings and figurines were unearthed at both places, and at Tarxien the lower half of a large statue, apparently of a goddess, was found in the south temple. What was this extraordinary culture, people wondered? Was it part of some wide cult? And of what date was it? The guesses, based on the pottery or on the refined Tarxien carving, were wild—500 B.C., 1000 B.C. Most archaeologists would then have laughed at the idea that the real dates, as recently shown by calibrated radiocarbon tests, were before 3000 B.C., a date which in fact agrees with the findings of Zammit himself, who classified them as Neolithic. Even now, however, the accuracy of the calibrated dates, given here, awaits confirmation.

One of the strangest things about the Maltese temples is that the most titanic of all is among the first built. This huge work, worthily called Ggantija (as spoken, Jeguntiya), was built about 3500 B.C. and now stands on the outskirts of Xaghra, a town on the northern island, Gozo. Like all the big Maltese temples, it was one of a neighbouring pair, (not necessarily of the same date), though little but a single underground chamber remains of its companion, Ghar ta' Chejzu, a few hundred metres to the west.

This immediately raises the whole matter of pairing and dualities in ancient Malta. The temples are found in pairs, their ground plans consist of pairs of lobed chambers, the carved spiral patterns usually run in double rows or simply reflect each other in couples, and everywhere there are double holes bored into the walls or floors which meet each other inside the solid stone. After visiting several of the temples, one is driven to the conclusion that this duality was an important symbol of something in these people's religion— whether it was a matter of a goddess and her young god, or dark and light, or earth and sky, or death and rebirth. Thus at Xaghra, Ghar ta' Chejzu may have been an earth temple while Ggantija was related to the sky in some way.

Like the statues of Easter Island, the spread out but usually paired Malta temples may have been built by competing clans or tribes in their respective territories. Over 30 megalithic temples have been found on the islands, this map marks the most important (italicized names) where substantial remains still stand. Malta was probably first settled by farmers from Sicily 112 kilometres (70 miles) away about 5000 B.C. The settlers could have come by raft, landing on Gozo first.

The inset drawing is of a temple model ground plan showing the distinctive trefoil pattern.

The Mnajdra temples stand 500 metres from their 'twin' at Hagar Qim and in a hollow separated by a terrace from a 100 metre (100 yard) slope to the sea. This detail is of the lower or south temple which has three pillar niches behind the coralline limestone.

Ggantija itself consists of two large temples within one mass of masonry, both entrances facing roughly south-east across a broad man-made terrace which overlooks a spacious valley. As with early megalithic chambered mounds all over western Europe, this orientation of entrance and central aisle means that the sun rising at midwinter would shine straight through the temple and illuminate the apse at the far end.

Another parallel with European mounds is the concave megalithic frontage to each temple, which may have been the focus for ceremonies involving large gatherings of people in the forecourt. For the Maltese buildings are indeed megalithic—the word megalith simply means 'great stone'—and can to some extent be read as the Maltese equivalent in stone of the huge earth barrows, such as Newgrange in Ireland, which were being built at almost exactly the same time. At Ggantija there are enormous stones all around the temple at ground level, with large-scale or cyclopean drystone walls towering above. The main doorways have no lintels now, but, as with the other temples, these entrances were originally trilithons—two large upright stones with a third placed across the top.

The southern of the two Ggantija temples is the larger, the better preserved and—by perhaps a hundred years or so—the older. Both have plans of two twinned lobes, with a central apse at the far end. The inner walls and those around the outside of the two temples are of stone, but the walls inside do not by any means follow the lines of the exterior, and the gaps between are filled in with rubble. The floors are paved with slabs or with a cement (called *torba*) made by crushing the local limestone to powder and then watering it, an exceptional technique for such an early period. It seems that the temples were originally roofed with great beams or tree-trunks, to judge from a contemporary clay model found in one of them, although no roofs have survived. This speaks of the presence of tall-growing species of trees on Malta that have since disappeared.

All this fits in well enough with the idea that the temples shared their source with the big European mounds or passage graves, though, as with many of those monuments, they were not primarily burial places. The detail inside seems to show a unique development of religious rites. At Ggantija the first lobed apse on the right and the second on the left have surviving ranges of 'altars', formed of upright stones with slabs laid across them, and other furnishings for unknown purposes. The walls were originally covered with a deep red plaster of which traces can still be seen, and some of the altars have weathered spiral carvings on their sides, similar to those better preserved at Tarxien. There are several of the double holes, carved in and out as it were, into the stone. These may have been receptacles for libations, rather than the widely held idea that they were tether-holds for sacrificial animals or made to hold wooden doors. One altar has a circular hearth in front of it, with stones still marked by fires that burned almost 5000 years ago.

The deity served in this and other Maltese megalithic buildings was almost certainly the Great Goddess represented by the bulging female figure seen in many statues found there. This Great Goddess has been traced in early settlements from Spain to India and scholars have tracked down her many aspects. She is the essence of the planet Earth, the female principle, bringer of healing sleep, mother and wife, the mystery of dark places, taking fertilization from the male but outlasting his thrusting energy with her implacable stillness. She is seen as a fat, even gross, shape in carvings of stone or clay from many lands, and she is present in the *oculi,* or eyes, of double spiral patterns and in motifs like a pair of eyebrows. The bull has been seen as her servant and the annual sun god as her dependant until he emerged to establish his dominance for men. She is awesome, mysterious, sinister in her power over darkness and death, but she is the source of life, food and tenderness, too. Her temples often face the point of midwinter sunrise and let its light stream into their core each year, for that is when the sun is reborn after its annual waning.

Who were the Maltese people who built these mound-like temples to the Great Goddess? Hardly anything is known about them, for not a single domestic dwelling of the temple period has been found. At Skorba the caves or mud huts of the very early villages were apparently abandoned by the time the surviving temple there was built in about 3500 B.C. We do know, from the remains found at Hal Saflieni and in the rock-cut shaft and chamber tombs of the temple phase, that they were a long-headed people of a racial type still common in the central Mediterranean, but different from the round-headed Maltese people of today. Their food was presumably similar to that found at Skorba—beef, mutton and goat with bread from their barley and wheat crops. Female attire can be guessed from the clay figurines of the Goddess, which show her in dresses with pleated skirts, both knee- and ankle-length. These dresses, apparently of fabric, usually cover her top and her voluminous breasts, some having long, leg-of-mutton sleeves, others sleeveless in a décolleté manner rather reminiscent of modern evening dress. From a figure scratched on one potsherd, we may imagine that massive breasts and buttocks were admired in more than just the Goddess herself. None of the figurines have been positively identified as male, so nothing can be said of men's dress.

The building techniques seen in the temples were impressive, but we know nothing of the houses in which the people lived. If they were of timber, from the woods which must have been common enough on Malta at the time, they have been built over or rotted away and their postholes have vanished with the eroded topsoil. If they were houses of clay or plastered stone walls, they have been washed away over the centuries.

The manual workers had tools only of stone and bone, but there is evidence that a ruling priestly caste lived among them and produced the ideas and designs expressed in the temples. For, with the help of present-day anatomists, it has been shown that some of the skeletons found in Malta were those of a light-muscled people who were free of physical toil and whose teeth bit only food that was free from tough fibres and grit. The archaeologist Colin Renfrew has combined this information with that given by the geographical position of the temples. He has pointed out that each pair of major temples is fairly central to a territory that could have supported between 1000 and 2000 people. Gozo would be one territory centred on Ggantija, while the mainland of Malta would be divided up into five territories, each with its temple pair. From this, Renfrew puts forward the theory that the islands were made up of six 'chiefdoms', each ruled by a family or caste which had special scientific or spiritual knowledge. He demonstrates that such systems operate today among primitive societies and may or may not evolve into wider political unions.

Of the five temple pairs on mainland Malta, two are of exceptional fascination. On the southern coast, the high temple of Hagar Qim is paired with the lower Mnajdra on a steep hillside that falls to the sea opposite the tiny island of Filfla. It is the most beautiful setting of any of the temples, and Hagar Qim (pronounced roughly Hajar Im) is the most evocative of the ancient buildings. It stands in a broad levelled court on the end of a ridge, with the sea below it. Because of its unusually lofty position, it seems to be addressing itself to the hemisphere of the sky above it, while the Mnajdra (spoken as Mnydra) temple complex, a few hundred metres away down a steep stone path, seems tucked into the earth.

The outer walls of Hagar Qim, though they do not now rise above the bottom row of giant stones, are of considerable splendour. The main entrance is a grand trilithon and the slightly concave frontage around it is formed by finely dressed and fitted megaliths. At the left-hand end of this frontage, four even taller stones overlooking the sea have been deeply eroded by the salt. Within, Hagar Qim has a unique plan among all the Maltese temples. Instead of two pairs of lobed chambers and an apse at the far end, the central passage runs straight through the building and out again. Near the rear entrance there is the largest single standing stone in Malta, slightly detached from the wall. In the second right-hand chamber, a large oval hole—an 'oracle' hole—connects with an external shrine in the outer wall.

Hagar Qim was probably built to a conventional five-lobed plan in about 3400 B.C., but was enlarged one or two hundred years later. But instead of adding a second temple, as was done at the other sites, the Hagar Qim priestesses decided to open a rear doorway on the central axis and also to break through the wall of the second left-hand apse into a series of new chambers. One may imagine the temple darkly roofed, with statues of the Goddess against the deep-red walls lit up by fires. The effect of passing this series of altars and chambers, along a passage that constantly changed direction, must have been awe-inspiring. In fact, the passage almost completely doubles back on itself, ending in a chamber near to the main entrance, but cut off from it by a solid stone wall. There, in this final chamber, there is a mysterious stubby column-altar and a dark cell, almost hidden in one wall—perhaps the inner sanctum of the chief priestess.

Down the hill, the Mnajdra temple—or rather temples, for there are three adjoining buildings of successive centuries—gives the best available idea of how all these Maltese sanctuaries looked in their original state. The furnishings of the two larger temples are very complex, with many altars and oracle holes between the main chambers and hidden cells within the walls. The plans of all three enclosures are typical of their particular stage and their grouping around the big forecourt, with the sea and Filfla Island beyond the other side of it, is memorable. All the Maltese temples had these wide forecourts and it is likely that they were the setting for ceremonial gatherings of ordinary people, to watch and perhaps to join in the celebrations and dances.

The other major geographical pair of temples on Malta is made up of the two whose discovery was described earlier, Tarxien and Hal Saflieni. Today, in the outskirts of Valletta, Tarxien is found amid modern housing blocks and surrounded by high walls with barbed wire to defend its treasures from vandals and thieves. For when it was uncovered by archaeologists earlier this

The Ggantija ('Work of the Giants') Temples stand up to 8 metres (26 ft) high on the edge of the Xaghra plateau, Gozo Island (Malta's smaller sister). The group, built nearly 5500 years ago, is the earliest free-standing building in Europe and consists of two temples side by side with a total of five enclosures. Visible on the right is the beginning of a terrace wall extension that was added later, presumably for some kind of forecourt ceremonial.

Above *A 48 cm (19 in)
limestone female figure found at
Hagar Qim. Originally painted
red, the sculpture has a single
folded arm characteristic of Maltese
statues.*

Right *Entrance to the inner
rooms of Hagar Qim flanked by
two unique mushroom-shaped
altars. It is the only temple made
of globigerina limestone.*

century it was found to contain the finest stone carvings of all the Maltese
temples. And, of course, they had been wonderfully preserved by 4000 years
under the soil. So it is for beauty of detail that Tarxien is notable, despite the
ugliness of its surroundings. There are four temples there, arranged in a
curiously higgledy-piggledy way. The smallest and oldest is of about the same
period as Ggantija, 3500 B.C. The famous south temple, where the great
truncated statue of the Goddess and the finest carved panels can be seen in
replica—the originals are in the Valletta National Museum—was added 200
years later. Then the other two temples followed, the last in about 3000 B.C.,
the latest date for any in Malta. The carving in the south temple is mostly of

A main hall of Hal Saflieni, the Hypogeum series of catacombs. Traces of red paint decoration are visible and the burial recesses are framed by stone blocks reminiscent of Malta's surface temples. Hypogeum's third and lowest level is 9 metres (30 ft) below the rock surface. Unfortunately, green mould is now taking hold.

spirals in formal patterns, but there are also panels of realistic relief sculpture showing sheep, pigs and especially bulls. One highly carved altar has a stone drawer in its centre, in which the excavators found a flint knife and the horn of a goat. Animal sacrifice undoubtedly played a part in some of their ceremonies.

Hal Saflieni—often known by the Greek word for an underground chamber, Hypogeum—is a short walk from Tarxien through the streets of modern Paola. It is an exaggerated underground counterpart of Tarxien's series of rather disorderly lobed chambers. The original entrance was destroyed by the workmen who discovered it in 1902 and the modern way is through a house and down a deep flight of spiral steps. It is an unpleasant but impressive place to visit. At the bottom, one emerges into a series of over 20 natural and man-made caverns. Most of these are of the familiar oval or lobed shape, and they intersect and flow into each other at so many different angles and levels that one soon loses all sense of direction. In reality, however, there is a north-south sequence of rather large chambers, with the so-called oracle room opening off one side and the carefully carved 'Holy of Holies' at the southern end. Off this series of large spaces, there are many small side chambers and it was in these that most of the human bones were found. When the bones were removed, they were found to be the remains of more than 6000 human beings and tests have dated them between 3500 and 3000 B.C. This, it is

believed, shows the approximate dates when Hal Saflieni was built and when it fell into disuse. The underground temple's function as a collective tomb is therefore well established. Whether it was used for other ceremonies as well, since there seem to have been few bones in the central spaces, is not known. If that first Jesuit investigator had recorded exactly what he found there, we might well have learned much about the functions of the pairs of high and low temples. It is certain, however, that Hal Saflieni was not the only Hypogeum in Malta and that archaeologists or more careful workmen may find another intact that is safe enough to excavate.

Oracles, priestesses to the goddess of fertility and darkness, animal sacrifice, ceremonies of death and rebirth, crowds gathering for seasonal ceremonies—hints of all these are found in Malta, but no proof. The end of the culture is just as uncertain. The building of the temples had ended by 3000 B.C. and all traces of the culture vanished 500 years later. Revolt against the priestesses or priests, drought, plague, famine, invasion—all have been suggested as the cause. As with Mohenjo-Daro in the Indus valley, it is evident that the sparsely forested countryside of Malta today would not have produced the timber needed for the buildings of 3500 B.C., so again, the possibility of men destroying their own resources must be recognized. In any event, when a Bronze Age people, who buried their dead in upright stone dolmens, arrived in Malta in about 2000 B.C., they seem to have found a deserted land.

The first or South Temple of Tarxien which is followed by two more with six enclosures curving off to the right in a total area of 8 hectares (20 acres). In the foreground is the altar with spiral decoration (perhaps signifying the eyes of the Great Goddess) where a flint knife blade and animal bones were found. On the left is a stone bowl decorated with drilled holes.

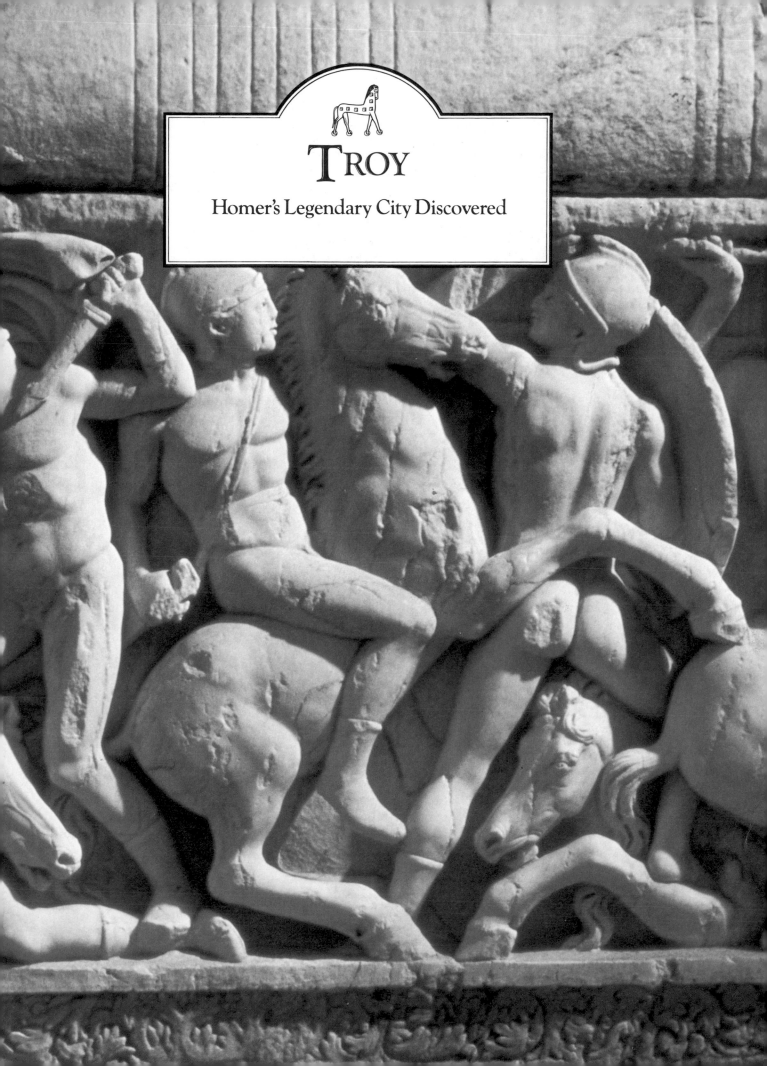

TROY

Homer's Legendary City Discovered

T ODAY, STANDING ON the ravaged hump called Hissarlik in north-west Turkey where Troy stood, most visitors feel disappointed. There is no group of grand ruined buildings to be visited, no special splendour to the landscape, no collection of fine works of art from the excavations. Deep trenches slice up the dusty ground, revealing stone foundations here and there but leaving the site a jumble of mounds and platforms on different levels among the scrubby bushes. For archaeologists, there is much fascination in the strata revealed by the excavators' cuts through the many levels of the city and this was, after all, one of the first sites where digging partly confirmed a splendid legend. For other people, the real fascination of the place only exists in the mind, through the greatest of early epic poems. For the *Iliad*—probably derived from stories told by Greek minstrels present at the siege of Troy, composed into the vast and brilliant work by the great poet or poets known as Homer, preserved by the oral tradition and then written down several centuries later—is set in and around Troy, otherwise known as Ilion or Ilium.

However disrupted the place as a whole, there are many points on the site which the visitor can link with incidents in the *Iliad*. If it happened at all, this was the city to which Paris, son of King Priam of Troy, brought the lovely Queen Helen after abducting her from her royal husband in Sparta. The coast beyond the plain around Hissarlik is where the poet's thousand Greek ships landed to retrieve her, and the plain itself where the Achaean Greek soldiers led by King Agamemnon of Mycenae made their camps for the siege which, the *Iliad* tells, lasted for ten years. There are still stretches of the walls around which the terrible hero Achilles pursued Priam's magnificent eldest son Hector and slew him. And one of the surviving gates may even be that through which the Trojan Horse was pulled by the citizens—a wooden statue with Greek warriors in its belly, who crept out at night to open the gates for the army that destroyed the city and slaughtered its people. The echoes of the great story can still be heard at many places on the hill of Troy when the sun is not too blinding or the famous wind too biting.

After the Achaeans destroyed Troy and sailed back to Greece in about 1260 B.C., the site was built up again and several later periods of habitation were to follow until the place was finally abandoned at the time of the Roman Empire. During the following 2000 years, all knowledge of its location was lost. By the nineteenth century, most classical scholars believed that the city and the story of the *Iliad* had been imagined by Homer and his predecessors.

The credit for discovering the correct site must go to a Scottish journalist and amateur archaeologist, Charles Maclaren. In his book *The Plain of Troy Described,* published in 1863, Maclaren concluded that the Hissarlik hillock on the Troad, the plain of Troy, fitted the descriptions best and must contain the remains of Priam's city. Little notice was taken of Maclaren's book, but five years later Heinrich Schliemann came to Troy for the first time.

Schliemann had been born in 1822, the son of a poor German clergyman who introduced him to the classical literature of ancient Greece and Rome. Schliemann said that he was still a boy when he became determined to find Troy. The family's poverty forced him to start work at 14, first in a German grocer's shop, then, after being shipwrecked as a cabin boy, in Amsterdam. There, he started to learn the first of his 13 languages, using his new knowledge both to study Homer and to start his own business, trading in dyestuffs and other goods. Schliemann was piratical by nature and happy to include smuggling tea into Russia among his enterprises. He was so successful that he retired a millionaire at the age of 36 and travelled all over the world. Then, after two years studying archaeology in Paris, Schliemann settled down in Greece in 1868. He immediately started to look for the sites of Homer—the

Previous pages *Combat between Greeks and Trojans. This superb relief forms one side of a Hellenistic marble sarcophagus, dated to the third century B.C. and entirely decorated with scenes from the Siege of Troy. Though found at Tyre in the Lebanon (then part of the Seleucid Empire, one of the successor states to emerge from Alexander the Great's conquests), it is likely to have been imported from Greece. The chapter symbol is one of the innumerable depictions of the Trojan Horse drawn over the last 3000 years.*

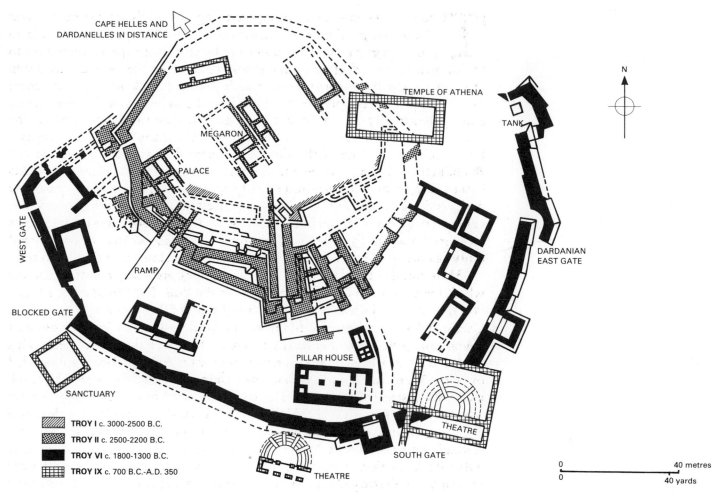

CAPE HELLES AND
DARDANELLES IN DISTANCE

TEMPLE OF ATHENA

TANK

MEGARON

PALACE

N

WEST GATE

RAMP

DARDANIAN
EAST GATE

BLOCKED GATE

PILLAR HOUSE

SANCTUARY

THEATRE

◨ **TROY I** c. 3000-2500 B.C.

▨ **TROY II** c. 2500-2200 B.C.

■ **TROY VI** c. 1800-1300 B.C.

▦ **TROY IX** c. 700 B.C.-A.D. 350

SOUTH GATE

THEATRE

0   40 metres
0   40 yards

Ithaca of Odysseus (Ulysses), the Mycenae of Agamemnon and the Troy of Priam all fascinated him.

It is not certain that Schliemann knew Maclaren's book, though it is likely that he did. When the wealthy German arrived at the Troad, he inspected some other possible sites and then decided that Hissarlik was the place. In 1870 he began the massive excavations which went on over a period of 20 years. As early as 1873, the huge trench which Schliemann's gang of a hundred workmen cut into the depths right across the mound had produced evidence which led him to announce that he had found Homer's Troy. For, at a low level among the nine layers, he discovered caches of gold and bronze objects and signs of destruction by a great fire. Elated, Schliemann and his wife worked alone to dig out 'Priam's treasure'; she hid the precious pieces in her red shawl so that neither workmen nor Turkish officials could seize the jewellery and gold.

The excavations had been directed by Schliemann himself and by Sophia, the clever young Greek he had married when he was 47 and she 17. 'I will not say anything about our way of life in this solitude,' he wrote. 'Where everything is wanting and where we have to take four grains of quinine every morning as a precaution against malaria.' A dispute he then had with the Turkish government stopped work at Troy for a few years. Later, the Schliemanns returned to Troy with Wilhelm Dörpfeld, who continued the work there after the great man's death in 1890. Before he died, Schliemann had the satisfaction of seeing his work generally vindicated by a visiting team of professional archaeologists—for his amateur status and destruction of archaeological evidence had brought dismissive comments from many academics. The task was continued by Professor Dörpfeld in 1893–4 and by

The nine cities of Troy make for a site of extraordinary complexity. The most visible parts are the theatres of the much later and larger Greco-Roman city of the first century B.C. onwards. However, the different layers can be simplified into Troy I and II (the latter had three sub-stages), Troy VI (the Homeric city) and Troy IX (Greco-Roman).

the American Professor Carl Blegen in seven years of work during the 1930s.

The site of Troy on the Hissarlik mound is on the western end of a low ridge 32 kilometres (20 miles) south-west of Çanakkale. Across the plain to the north and west of the site, the Aegean Sea is 6 kilometres (4 miles) away, the waters of the Dardanelles a little closer. That is a good position for a city in primitive warlike times—close enough to the sea to control the trade routes, yet far enough inland to have warning of raiding ships. Schliemann and Dörpfeld's nine major cities, one above the other, were broken down further by Blegen into 46 strata of settlements, dating from 3000 B.C. until Roman times. The numbering of these levels and the dates attached to them have been endlessly debated, and for the sake of clarity it is best to keep to Dörpfeld's numbers I to IX and to Blegen's dates.

The first settlers at Troy still had stone implements, but they were among the early users of metal, mostly bronze. They built humble houses, which have been traced on the bedrock at the western end of the city, though they had many other small villages scattered over the plain of the Troad. But during the centuries after 3000 B.C. the importance of the centre grew, for it stood at a strategic point on the emerging sea and land trade routes. Military control of these routes and the wealth from taxes levied on the traders were enviable and probably much fought for. Rubble walls surrounded the early town, but it was destroyed in about 2500 B.C.

The first major citadel and culture of Troy was built up after that destruction and flourished for the following three centuries—still during the early part of the age of bronze. This was the level, generally known as Troy II, whose high culture and ultimate burning misled Schliemann into calling it Priam's Troy.

It is difficult to know whether to describe Troy II as a city or as a royal fortress. The foundations of many of its structures can still be seen. It was not large—its very roughly circular plan was about 109 metres (120 yards) from side to side. Entering the walls through the main south-eastern gate, which had inner and outer doors in a complex stone gatehouse, one found a cobbled courtyard some 12 metres (40 feet) wide. Across this yard could be seen another wall and, near the centre, a smaller gatehouse with double wooden doors about 1.8 metres (6 feet) wide. Those doors led into the inner court of the citadel, which was paved with pebbles.

Facing the doors across the inner court, there was a row of five imposing buildings, the royal ceremonial buildings of Troy II. The largest of these, the great *megaron* (a hall with a plan of a kind that became typical of pre-Hellenic Greek architecture), was around 30 metres (100 feet) long. It consisted of a deep portico the full width of the building, with a door leading into the big hall itself.

The ceremonial hall within the royal *megaron* was a big space, perhaps 18 metres (60 feet) long and 9 metres (30 feet) wide. Archaeologists have looked in vain for traces of wooden columns to support a roof of such size. Near the centre of the room was a low circular platform about 4 metres (13 feet) wide, which was a symbolic royal hearth of the kind found at Mycenae and Tiryns in early Greek buildings of state.

The other four buildings in the row beside the great *megaron* were of similar design, but smaller. Dörpfeld and Blegen believed that these were the residences of what amounted to a royal palace complex, but others have argued that they were all public buildings.

Numerous small houses of the later part of this period have been found within the outer walls of the citadel, and it seems that the walled area originally reserved as a royal fortress became more of a city after 2300 B.C. These little

Below *'Priam's treasure' as Schliemann misnamed his first great find in a recess of the city wall. It contained 8700 gold beads, 3 vessels (including a double sauceboat), 2 diadems, 4 basket-shaped ear ornaments, 56 coil hair-fasteners (?), 6 bracelets, 1 electrum goblet, 6 tongue-shaped bars, 4 tankards, 2 saucers, 1 shallow bowl, 2 bottle-like silver vessels and a small silver lid. In copper or bronze there were 3 large vessels, 20 dagger or spear blades, 3 chisels, a knife, 14 flat hatchet blades, and a damaged saw blade. Schliemann's Trojan finds were exhibited in Berlin until 1945 when much of the material was destroyed or taken to the USSR.*

Left *Hector, stripped of armour, being dragged round the walls of Troy by the victorious Achilles. The Trojan prince was drawn behind the victor's chariot with leather straps. This relief forms one end of the sarcophagus also illustrated on pages 156–157.*

The walls of Troy, easily the most impressive feature of an otherwise multi-layered and confusing site. This stretch is part of the eastern wall of Troy VI (1800–1300 B.C.) with its great tower; the fortifications of the Iliad. *The view is taken from the approach to the angled Dardanian Gate. This narrow entrance, like other gates, makes a left turn thus exposing an attacker's shieldless side to the weapons of the defenders. In the far distance across the Plain of Troy (the Troad) can be seen the mountainous Gallipoli Peninsula, the opposite shore of the Dardanelles.*

houses were irregular in shape and huddled closely together in the restricted space. At this period walls encircled the city to a height of at least 3 metres (10 feet), punctuated by small projecting towers every 9 metres (30 feet) or so.

We know hardly anything of the people who lived in Troy II. The only representation of a human figure is a crude picture scratched on to a piece of broken pottery. It shows a warrior holding a banner on a staff in one hand, the other arm raised as if to hurl a spear. A broad band or sash over his right shoulder runs diagonally down his chest and a club or quiver is suspended from it. On his head is a crested helmet. The face is so primitively drawn that one can tell nothing about the features.

Rather more is known of the population and way of life of Troy II. Their clothing was mainly of wool from their large flocks of sheep and goats, though it cannot be proved whether they grew cotton or flax as well. Terracotta spindle whorls and traces of looms have been found in such numbers that the manufacture of textiles was probably an advanced craft.

How the Trojans wore the cloth they made is not known, but much gold jewellery for women has been found. Hair-bands, delicate ear-ornaments, pins and hair-fasteners, bracelets, beads and magnificent necklaces of gold were worn by women of the wealthier classes. The men seem to have collected ornaments for their implements and weapons, rather than body jewellery—sword-heads of rock-crystal, battle-axes of green nephrite, crystal lion-heads for the top of staffs. The tools and swords themselves were of fine bronze, but many household silver dishes were found by Schliemann.

Such household goods were surely restricted to royal or noble families.

The people who lived in most of the houses of Troy II, rough brick structures with clay plastering, used implements of plain copper—much less tough than bronze—and dishes of simple pottery. Wheel-made pottery appeared for the first time in Troy in about 2300 B.C.—from then on both the new method and the old hand technique were used to produce a vast range of pots and dishes, many of which were exported. It is handsome and practical ware, but little decorated. Indeed the homes of Troy II show little desire for decoration at all—no sign of sculpture or wall painting has been found.

The food the Trojans ate was largely produced on their farms, on the plain of the Troad spreading below the city. There they grew wheat, which they ground with heavy millstones for their bread. They ate a great deal of shellfish and meat from the wild animals they hunted, as well as their own mutton and goat, grilled on spits over the fire. Their vegetables included beans and lentils which were cooked, like most of their food, in pots set on open fires or braziers.

Few of the archaeologists' finds give much information about religion in Troy. Like Mohenjo-Daro, early Troy is unusual in having no buildings which could be called temples. We have no idea whether the rulers took on any sort of god-king status—if so, perhaps the great *megaron* was sacred as well as royal. The evidence suggests that religion was a private matter for most Trojans—hundreds of 'idols' (vaguely humanoid in form) of marble and other materials, some large but many pocket-sized, were found in the houses.

So Troy II was a community that was culturally advanced in some ways, yet curiously primitive in others. Certainly its position on the trade routes

The paved limestone ramp leading up to the south-west gate into the city of Troy II (c. 2500–2200 B.C.). Although Schliemann, a millennium out in any case, thought it was specially built for the Trojan Horse, its 1:4 gradient would have been too steep for wheeled traffic and originally it had stone side walls, probably chest high.

meant political importance and its rulers were very wealthy. It seems that they exported large quantities of woven textiles, pottery, livestock and timber. In exchange they received precious metals and valuable stones for their craftsmen, some foreign ornaments, the marble idols and finer pottery than their own. They did not use money, but Blegen believed that they had a highly organized form of barter before 2000 B.C.

Troy II, like its predecessor, ended with a great fire and the following three cities on the site did not reach the importance of the second settlement. Then, in about 1800 B.C., another great culture grew up there in the middle period of the Bronze Age. Troy VI was initiated by a new wave of settlers, probably from Asia, and the evidence suggests that they were of the same stock as those who settled at Mycenae, Tiryns and Pylos. They took up the same earlier native architectural types and developed them over the centuries. They brought the same sort of pottery, called Grey Minyan Ware. They arrived on

Homer's Iliad *was as much an inspiration to Classical art as the Bible would be to that of Christianity. Here Achilles and Hector fight it out on a Black Attic vase of the fifth century B.C.*

the opposite sides of the Aegean Sea at the same time and always kept contact with each other. Both peoples introduced the horse to these territories for the first time. All this considered, it is hard to doubt Blegen's argument that these early Greeks and the Trojans were of the same background and language, and that they were in 1800 B.C. the first wave of the Hellenic people to arrive in Greece and Asia Minor. And Troy VI, often called Troy VIIa after most of its houses had been rebuilt following an earthquake in 1300, was the Troy of Priam which the mainland Greeks destroyed 40 years later.

Troy VI was about twice as large a city as Troy II, and much more mightily walled. Even then it was no more than 182 metres (200 yards) from end to end. But the famous walls have been excavated for two-thirds of their length and can be seen today—their northern stretch was demolished in Roman times, when the whole top of the hillock was removed to give level space for a wide court around a temple. Sadly, the Roman builders shaved off

An engraving of Schliemann's excavation of Troy from the archaeologist's Troy and Its Ruins *(1875). Turkish labourers deepen the great trench dug into the Temple of Athena. A born publicist, Schliemann wrote three books on his successive excavations at Troy.*

the Troy VI level of the royal enclosure on the peak of the hill during the same site clearance work. So we do not know what Priam's palace was like, nor whether a temple stood on or near the hilltop—the *Iliad* suggests a palace and two temples here, which is quite likely. The part of that Troy whose foundations can still be seen all stood downhill from the walls of Troy II.

The foundations of Troy VI buildings that have survived consist of 17 rather grand houses on the lowest terrace of the city near the southern perimeter walls, eight of which are complete enough to give a good picture of the structures that stood there. A detailed study of these was carried out by Professor Dörpfeld in 1893–4 and showed that they were considerably larger than anything but the royal *megara* of the earlier Troys. They are free-standing houses of one large room, often with one or more smaller rooms opening off them. Above their stone foundations, the walls were sometimes of plastered brick, more often of small stone blocks. Architecturally, they are similar to the *megaron* type of Mycenaean Greece and earlier Troy.

The most remarkable of these Troy VI buildings was only discovered during the excavations of the 1930s. This is generally called the Pillar House or Hall, and it can be seen near the major south gate in the city walls. The building was 24 metres (80 feet) long and nearly 12 metres (40 feet) wide, with massively thick stone walls. Inside, a door through one long side led into a large hall whose roof was supported by two square stone pillars. At the eastern end of the building a small room runs across the entire width, while at the west there are three little cells opening off the main hall—almost like chapels off a modern church. The design of the Pillar House is puzzling and the finds in it do not show its original purpose.

The great works of Troy VI, however, are the fine city walls. The surviving ranges (of various heights now) run 347 metres (380 yards), swinging from the north-west to the south and then around to the north-east corner. In that distance there are four gates of various sizes, including the major south gateway. The style of masonry and architectural detail varied a good deal, and it is evident that they were built and improved over a long period between 1800 and perhaps 1280 B.C., just before the army led by Agamemnon arrived. The best stretches are 4.5 metres (15 feet) thick and 4 metres (13 feet) tall, of big limestone blocks smoothly surfaced and aligned so that they were very difficult to climb—the height was probably even greater, for there are signs of brick parapets above the stone. The outer surfaces are not vertical, but slope for strength, with regular buttresses and occasional towers.

At the smaller gates, the walls overlap each other so that attackers who smashed the doors would still have to penetrate a narrow passage manned on both sides above their heads. At the great south gate, a high tower rose above one side of the entrance and anyone forcing their way through the doors would find themselves in a restricted inner court, gated on all sides and overlooked by many high platforms for defenders.

By the time that the Greek invaders of the *Iliad* arrived, the inside of the city was very different from the heyday of Troy VI. In about 1300 B.C. an earthquake toppled most of the buildings inside the city and some stretches of the walls. New houses were built and the damaged sections of the wall had to be repaired.

There is evidence that all this was done in great haste and it may be that an invasion from Greece, because of trading disputes, was feared long before the kidnapping of Helen the beautiful gave a more poetic excuse. Three of the big houses known to us today, including the Pillar House, show signs of repair and re-use at this time. The rest of the surviving area of Troy VI within the walls contains a crowded jumble of small houses built during the short period known as Troy VIIa. One building appears to have been fitted up as an eating-house, others were crammed in a continuous row backing against the inner side of the city walls. Every house examined by the archaeologists had big storage jars for food and drink let into the solid clay beneath—stone lids above each jar enabled their tops to be treated as if they were just part of the floor. The only open space of any size left in the city was paved around a deep well.

If ever archaeological finds pointed to a long siege, those at Troy do. There is little to be seen today of the crowded city quarters in which the Trojans and their allies were crammed and one cannot place the events inside Troy which are recounted in the *Iliad*. But the southern side of the stone walls of Troy VI, which have been described, are those from which King Priam looked over the plain where the Achaean army camped and later watched as his son Hector was chased by the divinely protected Achilles. And the big southern gateway is perhaps the very entrance through which the Trojans pulled Odysseus' giant model of a horse, leading to the downfall of their city.

We shall never know how many of these Greek and Trojan heroes and their deeds were invented or elaborated by the poets, but the outline of the story is confirmed by archaeology. 'Homer,' Schliemann once wrote, 'writes with poetical licence, not with the minute accuracy of a geographer.' Certainly, the Troy described in the *Iliad* has a splendid royal palace, wide streets, temples to Athena and to Apollo, and room for perhaps 50,000 people within its frowning walls studded with towers. Poetical licence indeed, but hardly surprising after the lapse of some centuries. For Homer could not go to Troy to check its size and description. After the Greeks had burned it, the city was re-inhabited by the few survivors until the arrival of new invaders. By 1100 B.C. it was deserted and remained so for centuries until Greek settlers built a colony on its mound and called it Ilion. Here came Alexander the Great in 334 B.C. to sacrifice at the tomb of his hero and supposed ancestor—Achilles—on the eve of the conquest of the world. Ilion passed into Roman hands before the birth of Christ and became Ilium. Finally, the Christian Emperor Constantine visited the area in A.D. 326 on his journey to found Constantinople farther to the north. With the growth of that city, the town on Troy hill was gradually deserted until the very site was forgotten.

Heinrich Schliemann (1822–90) as photographed about 1870 before the discovery that was to make him the most famous and colourful figure in archaeology.

Sophia Schliemann wears what her husband once thought was the personal gold jewellery of Helen of Troy. The diadem measures 90 cm (35 in) with 90 chains of two different lengths all with a small leaf suspended. Eight 38 cm (15 in) chains hang to her shoulders, each with an idol-shaped pendant decorated by rows of dots and bosses. The 74 chains of her necklace are 10 cm (4 in) long with two-pointed leaf attachments. The chains consist of interlocking rings beaten out of four-sided wire.

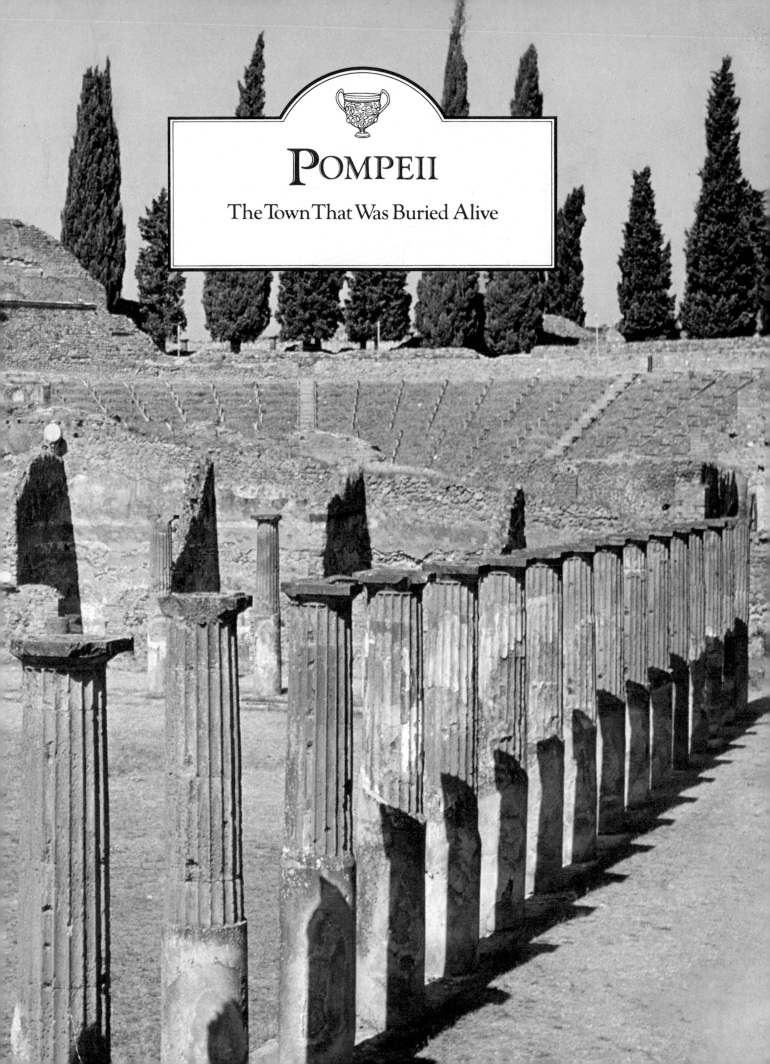

POMPEII

The Town That Was Buried Alive

Previous pages The colonnade of the Gladiator's Barracks at Pompeii. It was originally the portico of the large theatre beyond until converted in the final decades of the city's existence (reign of Nero A.D. 54–68). The gladiators' monastic-style cells are visible backing on to the rear wall of the stage. The theatre was built in tufa stone c. 200–150 B.C. into the natural hollow of a hill. The addition of an upper gallery in Roman times still only gave it a capacity of 5000.
The chapter symbol is a silver drinking cup typical of the dinner services belonging to wealthy Pompeians.

Right Pompeii's buildings included 4 baths, 10 temples, 2 theatres, an amphitheatre, 5 inns, 20 wine-shops, 118 bars and 25 brothels behind 3.2 kilometres (2 miles) of fifth to fourth century B.C. walls. These had 12 three-storey towers added c. 100 B.C. Only 60 per cent of the city's 64 hectares (158 acres) have been excavated so far.

AT ABOUT NOON on 24 August A.D. 79, after some days of rumbling and slight earth tremors, Mount Vesuvius erupted. There was no flow of lava rivers from its peak to give warning, for during its centuries of dormancy a thick crust had built up over all outlets from the depths of the earth. The buildup of pressure, which caused a severe earthquake in the Bay of Naples area 17 years earlier, at last fractured that crust and was released. A huge cloud of ash and volcanic fragments rose into the sky, so thick that the hot August sun was obliterated and the land around fell into darkness. The heat caused a freak precipitation from the summer clouds and torrential rain fell on the slopes. Any vine growers on the sides of the mountain who had not been killed by the explosion were drowned in a flood of volcanic mud. Most of the inhabitants of the fishing town of Herculaneum, between Vesuvius and the sea, had already fled from their homes when the mud engulfed it.

Farther round the Bay of Naples, the famous Roman writer Pliny the Younger, then aged about 17, was staying at his uncle's villa on the coast at Misenum. His uncle, Pliny the Elder, who was in command of the imperial fleet at Misenum, had been sunbathing when he was called to look across the bay at a strange cloud the shape of 'an umbrella pine tree, with wisps on the top like branches'. The cloud kept changing colour, white at some moments, then dark and blotched. Pliny the Elder ordered a small ship to be prepared so that he could go and look more closely. His nephew refused the invitation to go, saying that he had much studying to do, which was as well for him, since few aboard the ship survived.

Pliny the Elder, realizing what the disaster was and ordering his warships to be launched as well, had sailed to rescue some friends only to be trapped in their villa for the night by a contrary wind. They dined, pretending to ignore the blazing mountain overhead. Then, driven out of the villa by an increasing hail of pumice rocks from the sky, the members of the party stumbled around in the darkness with pillows on their heads. Most of them reached the ship, but a strong wind still blew off the sea. They lay down to wait, but the sulphurous fumes intensified and flames appeared near them. The party scattered, and two days later Pliny the Elder was found dead, a victim of the poisonous fumes.

Meanwhile Pliny the Younger and his mother were getting on little better at the villa. During the night a series of violent earthquakes awoke them. The building seemed likely to fall and he took her out on to the terrace between the house and the sea. There he read to her from the works of Livy by torchlight, as if nothing extraordinary was happening, while the tremors continued. At dawn, the heaving ground prevented their escape in the carriages summoned. Looking across the bay, the cloud over Vesuvius was spreading towards them, opened up occasionally by long flames like huge lightning flashes. Along the coast, the sea seemed to have been sucked down so that 'many sea creatures were captured on dry land.'

Pliny and his mother eventually set out on foot. Soon ashes fell on them lightly, then more heavily as the great cloud overtook them and the land became totally dark. The darkness was filled with the cries of children, the screams of women and the shouts of men, 'some praying to the gods, but most of them saying that the gods themselves were dead and that the final night had fallen on the world.' The Plinys struggled on and survived, for they were quite distant from Vesuvius. But at the town of Pompeii, nestling in the shadow of the volcano, the northerly wind which had pinned Pliny the Elder's ship to the coast carried the bulk of the falling ash and pumice on to the town and its surrounding countryside. Pompeii was completely buried by the rain of death and lay lost to the world.

POMPEII

H. – HOUSE
T. – TEMPLE
V. – VILLA

0   100   200 yards
0   100   200 metres

SARNUS GATE

AMPHITHEATRE

VIA DELL' ABBONDANZA

V. OF JULIA FELIX

GREAT PALESTRA

TOMBS

NOLA GATE

H. OF VENUS MARINA

NUCERIA GATE

H. OF MORALIST

H. OF LOREIUS

VIA DI NOLA

H. OF JULIUS POLYBIUS

H. OF ORCHARD

CAPUA GATE

H. OF GLADIATORS

H. OF FABIUS AMANDO
H. OF P. PROCULUS
H. OF EPHEBE
H. OF MENANDER
H. OF LOVERS

H. OF LUCRETIUS FRONTO

H. OF CENTENARY

H. OF CRYPTOPORTICUS

H. OF CASCA LONGUS

VERECUNDUS' FULLFRY

STEPHANUS' FULLERY

STABIAE GATE

H. OF CITHARIST

H. OF SILVER WEDDING

CENTRAL BATHS

H. OF M. LUCRETIUS

ASELLINA'S INN

T. OF JUPITER MILICHIUS

ODEON

H. OF C. JUCUNDUS

VIA DI STABIA

H. OF CORNELIUS RUFUS

T. OF ISIS

GLADIATOR BARRACKS

STABIAN BATHS

SMALL PALESTRA

LARGE THEATRE

ESUVIUS GATE

H. OF GOLDEN CUPIDS

H. OF ORPHEUS

H. OF VESONIUS PRIMUS

H. OF SPURIUS MESOR

H. OF GAVIUS RUFUS

H. OF BEAR

SITTIUS' HOTEL

TRIANGULAR FORUM

T. OF HERACLES/ PALLAS ATHENE

H. OF VETTII

MODESTUS' BAKERY

BROTHEL

H. OF LABYRINTH

H. OF FAUN

T. OF FORTUNA AUGUSTA

H. OF ANCHOR

MACELLUM

T. OF LARES

T. OF VESPASIAN

EUMACHIA BUILDING

HALL OF AEDILES

VIA DI MERCURIO

HS. OF FOUNTAINS

VIA DEL FORO

ARCH OF 'CALIGULA'

TOWN COUNCIL

H. OF TRAGIC POET

FORUM BATHS

T. OF JUPITER

FORUM

H. OF PANSA

T. OF APOLLO

BASILICA

HALL OF DUOVIRI

H. OF SALLUST

H. OF VESTALS

H. OF SURGEON

T. OF VENUS

MYSTERIES

MUSEUM

V. OF SEA GATE

V. OF 'CICERO'

HERCULANEUM GATE

SEA GATE

TOMBS

DIOMEDE

171

Below left *The House of the Great Fountain in the Via di Mercurio (street of Mercury) dedicated to the Nymphs. The steps behind the bronze boy carrying a dolphin lead up to the still-functioning fountain-head below a magnificent mosaic portrait of Oceanus. But the water which once gushed from the great tragic mask heads flanking the arch mosaic has long ceased to flow. This type of* nymphaeum *with its shell and mosaic decorations was a feature of many Pompeian gardens.*

Below right *The front hall* (atrium) *of the Samnite House, a second century B.C. house of Pompeii's preserved neighbouring town of Herculaneum. A sky light illuminates the hall and allows the* impluvium *to collect rain water.*

Exactly 1630 years later, in the year 1709, an Austrian prince of the Habsburg empire, Prince d'Elboeuf, bought an estate at Portici on the Bay of Naples. The prince was a connoisseur of the ancient Roman remains that had been unearthed from time to time in the countryside around Mount Vesuvius and he decided to dig for classical statues on his land. His team of workmen dug tunnels down into the relatively soft volcanic tufa and by chance one of these bored straight into the theatre of Roman Herculaneum, a town that had lain unknown under the deep layer of volcanic mud which had flowed down from Vesuvius.

D'Elboeuf took only works of art from the underground chambers found by his men. The estate passed into other hands after a few years, when the Kingdom of Naples came under Spanish rule, and the King of Spain appointed an engineer colonel to continue the digging in 1738. This man, Rocco Alcubierre, also did some desultory excavations at other easier sites and in 1748 he stumbled on a wall painting at a place identified 15 years later as Pompeii.

Alcubierre's discoveries at Pompeii caused a sensation among antiquarians and architects all over Europe, especially after the grandfather of modern art history, the German Johann Winckelmann, visited and wrote about the sites. Architects had been basing their buildings on Roman ruins for centuries; now for the first time they could also derive their interior decoration from classical domestic designs. But it was only in the 1860s that enough of Pompeii was uncovered to map the street pattern of the Roman town and start extracting the evidence it contained about the lives of its citizens. For Pompeii had been buried by a prolonged shower of volcanic dust from the explosion of Vesuvius

in A.D. 79, rather than the torrent of mud that engulfed smaller Herculaneum. So Pompeii's covering was comparatively easy to remove and, apart from roofs burned or crushed by the weight of volcanic matter, preserved the buildings and even the body shapes of many of the inhabitants.

Pompeii was not an especially important town in Roman times, but it was an ancient one, dating from long before Rome started to spread her empire. The settlement may already have existed before the Etruscans from the north arrived in this area, Campania, in the sixth century B.C. It flourished after 400 B.C. when a tribe called the Samnites occupied the region and came into contact with the civilizing influence of a string of Greek colonies along the coast. Later, it became an independent town within the ambit of Roman power. Then in 89 B.C. the great general and future dictator of Rome, Sulla, captured the town. Nine years later it was made a self-governing colony and many of his trusted soldiers were settled there. From then until its destruction by Vesuvius nearly 160 years later, Pompeii prospered as a centre of trade, of fertile farmland and as the largest town along the southern part of the Bay of Naples, where rich Romans built almost as many seaside villas as their present–day Italian successors.

Pompeii lay along the top of a ridge of volcanic rock a little way inland from the sea. Vesuvius rises 8 kilometres (5 miles) to the north–west, dominating the view from the upper part of the town – but in Roman times the volcano had been dormant and completely silent for centuries, so that everyone presumed that it was extinct. The mountain, on the flat plain of Naples, was considerably higher than it is now, and the vines that produced its famous wine grew on the rich volcanic soil right up to its peak.

Below the hill on which Pompeii stood, the river Sarno flowed easily towards the sea. The river was navigable to the ships of the time, so the quays along its banks provided a safe harbour. From these quays a steep road ran up the hill to the Sea Gate, or Porta Marina, the south–western entrance of Pompeii. The town walls, which were built in the Samnite period, can still be seen.

From the Porta Marina gate, now the main entrance with a museum beside it, there is a wide view over the Bay of Naples. Beyond the gate the road goes

A pedestrian crossing, beside a public fountain (one of seven discovered) in Pompeii, designed not to impede wheeled traffic and to keep the walker above the mud or puddles of the Via di Stabia.

The courtship of Venus and Mars as explicitly shown in a Pompeian wall painting. Glue and wax were used to give a shiny surface to the treated limestone plaster.

Late nineteenth century excavations at Pompeii. Systematic excavation was begun in 1860 by Giuseppe Fiorelli, the personal choice of King Victor Emmanuel I of Italy, and he had no fewer than 512 workmen the next year. It was Fiorelli who in 1864 devised the plaster injection method of preserving the shape of victims of the Vesuvius eruption.

on climbing, its stone surface rutted by carts of the Roman Empire. On the right there are the remains of the Temple of Venus, protector goddess of the town. The temple had been felled by a violent earthquake 17 years before the great eruption of Vesuvius, but the Pompeians had not restored it by the time their destruction came.

At the top of the slope the entrance road passes along the flank of the Basilica (the town hall and law court, where meetings of the citizens and of the leading businessmen were held) and emerges into the long main square, the Forum. This open space, some 137 metres (450 feet) long and 36.6 metres (120 feet) wide, was the town centre and used for many public activities. The ruins of the chief public buildings can still be seen around it, all of them already historic buildings in Roman times, for they were built before Rome took over Pompeii. The Romans, however, enriched the Forum in many ways. All around it, except where the Temple of Jupiter rose at the north end, stood a two-tier colonnade of limestone columns, Doric below and Ionic above, running in front of the public buildings and creating cool dark spaces for people to use during the heat of the day. The pavements under these colonnades would be crowded with businessmen discussing their transactions, travelling salesmen offering their wares and peasants displaying their produce from the surrounding farms—the Macellum, or main market, lies just off the Forum. On festival days, crowds would gather in the square to hear orators speaking from a platform in the middle of the west side of the colonnade. In the evenings, the Forum would be full of family groups parading up and down—a practice still almost universally observed in Mediterranean towns—among the columns and the many public statues along the sides of the square, with the view dominated by the green cone of Vesuvius towering over the Temple of Jupiter at the north end.

The greater part of the Forum colonnades no longer exist but there is a short two-level section and many columns and plinths for statues have been re-erected from the jumble of stones excavated from the volcanic ash —enough for the mind to recreate the scene as it must have been nearly 2000 years ago. Even the shape of Vesuvius itself at that time needs to be imagined, for the explosion that destroyed Pompeii and subsequent eruptions (the last went on during 17 days in 1944) have removed the whole top of its high cone which soared up between the two gentler peaks visible today.

Heading north from the Forum in the direction of the volcano, past the Temple of Jupiter, the Forum Baths can be found in the next block. These were one of several public bath-houses in Pompeii. The Forum Baths are not the largest in the town, but the rooms are well preserved and grandly decorated. The Romans were educated to be aware that bodily cleanliness was very important to health—their standards of hygiene were less rigorous than ours in some ways, but they were probably cleaner than any earlier European peoples. The general view was that a bath should be taken every nine days. Moderately prosperous citizens would take a slave and walk or be carried in a litter to their favourite bath. There was an entrance fee to pay, though the state built many simpler free bath-houses for the poor. Inside the baths, men and women were divided. Each had their own dressing–rooms, with seats for waiting if the bathrooms were too crowded. The slaves would be left to guard the clothes, while their master or mistress went through the slow process from the cold *frigidarium* to the *tepidarium*, then to the steaming heat of the *calidarium*. In the Forum Baths at Pompeii the ambitious architecture and wall paintings can still be seen in these rooms, and it is clear that bathing was a social occasion as well as hygienic and pleasurable. People would sit and talk while enjoying the heat. Finally, the bather would return to his slave or a professional masseur for an enjoyable massage before going home.

The streets in this part of the town doubtless bustled during the day with the activities to be seen in some of the wall paintings. Many shops opened onto the roadsides—some can still be seen—and street vendors of food and drink pushed their way among the shoppers, shouting out to attract customers. In other areas there are eating–houses of many standards and wine shops—one advertises a cup of ordinary wine for one *as* (a low coin), a better wine for two *asses* and real Falerno wine for four *asses*. There are cheap hotels, too, intended perhaps for travelling salesmen, but also used by lovers—one has a simple memorial scratched on a wall, 'Romula lay here with Staphyclus.' Less romantically, a building a little farther north has a stone pay-booth at its entrance, a room where girls waited for their customers, and many little cubicles with pornographic paintings and graffiti.

Yet, only a few metres away from the noise of the shops, baths, taverns and brothels, the wide band of Pompeii's secluded houses starts. Most of these now stand uncovered, but some still have parts of their original roofs, while others have been restored. The typical town house of a prosperous Pompeian was built around internal courts with nothing but the main gate opening on to the road. So, however noisy the street, one could step through the vestibule into the *atrium* and find stillness.

The *atrium* was at the core of the Roman house—statues of the household gods stood there and the lady of the house lay in it while organizing the work of the slaves. It was usually a square space, roofed except for a central opening to give daylight (sometimes the open roof was in the next space, the *cavaedium*). Beneath this opening was a pond to catch the water when it rained, and this was treated as an ornamental pool in houses of the wealthy. Many of the main rooms of the house opened directly off the *atrium*, the living rooms (including the formal reception room called the *exedra* and the owner's study or *tablinum*) also looking out on to the *hortus*, a formal courtyard garden surrounded by a peristyle or colonnade. At Pompeii, scientists were able to identify the preserved seeds of many of the cultivated plants, so that houses such as that of Marcus Lucretius (in the via di Stabia, north-east of the Forum) and that of the Golden Cupids (farther north in the same street) have complex little gardens of sculpture and flowers much the same as in Roman times.

Right *The Temple of Apollo's altar and steps with a replica of the god's bronze statue (as an archer) in front of the second century* B.C. *colonnade which has 48 Doric columns. The Ionic column of Phrygian marble in the foreground had a sun-dial on top (according to old drawings) and an inscription on the opposite side records that it was put up by the* duoviri *(town magistrates) L. Sepunius and M. Herennius.*

Below *The* atrium *of the House of the Faun (named after the dancing bronze faun) with the* tablinum *(living room) behind flanked by dining rooms. Beyond is the garden peristyle, behind which was a room containing the famous Battle of Issus (333* B.C.*) floor mosaic depicting Alexander the Great fighting Darius III of Persia.*

The buildings of these two houses, as well as their gardens, are fairly well preserved and impressive. But the most famous grand houses of Pompeii are perhaps the House of the Vettii (a wealthy family), for the impressive state of preservation of its many decorated rooms—though the artistic quality is patchy—and the House of the Faun, where the sheer spacious beauty of the architecture is so dramatic that the crumbled state of its ruins hardly seems to affect it.

The Romans used quite a range of furniture in their houses. The forms found at Pompeii, including the low couches and the tables with animals' legs, are familiar to us. For European neo-Classical furniture makers of the late eighteenth century produced copies of Pompeian designs in huge quantities

A girl about to be whipped in the Dionysian Mysteries while a naked Maenad dances in triumph; one of the life-size paintings of c. 60 B.C. in the Villa of Mysteries. These ten scenes are on three walls of the 7-metre (23 ft) by 5-metre (16 ft) Room of the Great Fresco in the owner's private apartments.

Small statue of a gladiator in the Pompeii Museum. The eruption caught a party of gladiators at a tavern in the Via di Nola; they fled, leaving half-finished drinks and some trumpets. In the Gladiator Barracks 63 died, leaving 15 helmets and 6 shoulder guards to be discovered.

when the excavations revealed the range of Roman interiors. The low couches were used for eating as well as for sleeping, and that brings us to the main preoccupations of the wealthy citizens of Pompeii. For good eating and drinking—together with money and sexuality—come up time and again in the ruins.

Agriculture was thus a very important feature of Pompeian life. The main crop of the farmers around Pompeii was wheat, though in that area grapes were almost as important. The farmers also grew other cereals (barley and oats) as well as beans, peas, chick peas, lentils and olives in large quantities. These, together with meat such as pork or poultry, formed the basis of most meals for wealthy Romans. For the poor, meat was rare and their largely vegetarian diet included much turnip and beet as well as the beans and lentils.

In the houses of Pompeii the day started with a breakfast of bread, perhaps soaked in wine, and sometimes fruit or cheese. At noon there was a light meal, usually eaten without even gathering at the table. But the main meal of the day was dinner or *cena,* eaten at about three in the afternoon in summer and later in winter, when people did not start work so early. A small number of guests might be invited for *cena,* but if a larger party was planned, that would normally involve a light supper late in the evening when much wine would be drunk. All meals were eaten with the fingers from bowls or plates.

Families were dominated by the father, who had absolute power in his own household, though by the late first century B.C. there was increasing sexual equality—the traditional power of a man to divorce or repudiate his wife was increasingly shared by wives eager to get rid of their husbands. Before these egalitarian trends emerged, a father could indeed be tyrannical. When one of his children was born, the father viewed it and, if he picked it up, it was part of his family. If not, one of his slaves would abandon it at a crossroads to die unless a slave-merchant collected it. The historical reason behind this practice was the poverty from which the Romans emerged to form their empire—a child too many, or a weak or deformed child, could make a crucial difference in a community fighting for survival. But the practice took a long time to die out.

Once taken into the family, children of conscientious and reasonably prosperous parents were put through a serious education. This was started by the father himself and continued by a literate slave before the child was sent to one of the schools increasingly established by the state as the Empire developed. Apart from the accumulation of knowledge, *gravitas,* morality and public spirit were important in Roman education, but we can see in the streets of Pompeii that human nature often rejected the standards taught during childhood. The search for pleasure and entertainment drew most young people when they emerged from the virtuous schooling of their youth.

The public entertainment centres of Pompeii lie in the south and south-east parts of the city. There, in the Large Palestra, the young men practised their athletic talents—racing, wrestling, jumping and hurling javelins. Much of the colonnade around three sides of this open space still survives. The fourth side is open towards the splendid Amphitheatre, built in 80 B.C. by two city magistrates at their own expense soon after the Roman occupation of the town, and the first of the Pompeii structures to be cleared after its rediscovery in 1748. It could seat 20,000 people, most of the population of the town at its later height, and is perhaps the earliest surviving Roman amphitheatre. Various sports and pastimes entertained the citizens here—animals were goaded to a pitch where they would fight each other, men fought against ferocious beasts, trained gladiators faced each other ready for armed combat, sometimes to the death. An outbreak of hooliganism at a gladiatorial show of

A.D. 59 in which Pompeian spectators killed and wounded visitors from neighbouring Nuceria caused the Emperor Nero to ban all shows for ten years.

Farther west lies the open square surrounded by colonnaded buildings that, from Nero's time onwards, acted as a barracks for the gladiators. The men and their families lived in the quarters around the open area, which was used for practising their spectacular fighting. Beside the barracks stand the two theatres of Pompeii—the larger for open-air performances in summer, the smaller a covered theatre of great beauty built in 75 B.C. for around a thousand people to see the bawdy comedies that did well in Pompeii.

In the small triangular forum beside the open-air theatre is a strange neighbour for the centres of entertainment. The Temple of Heracles and Pallas Athene dates back to a time before 400 B.C. when Pompeii was ruled for a while by the Greek colony of Cumae, north of Naples. The Romans inherited much of their religion from the Greeks, but a more exotic temple survives in fairly good condition on the other side of the large theatre—the small Temple of Isis on its high brick podium. A doorway behind the altar in the main chapel (*cella*) leads to a chamber, which originally held a pool of Nile water.

Isis was a protagonist in one of the central myths of Egyptian religion. It was Isis who collected the pieces of her murdered husband, the god-king Osiris, and gave him life again, at the same time conceiving the sky-god Horus. Her separate cult flourished in the New Kingdom of Egypt and spread into other countries, sometimes under different names but always with some of the characteristics of the Great Goddess whose worship goes back earlier than many. To the Greeks, she was their goddess Demeter—to the Romans, Ceres. All were goddesses of fertility and renewed life. From about 100 B.C. when her first temple at Pompeii was built, she gathered an increasing number of Italian worshippers under her original name. When the earthquake in A.D. 62 tumbled most of the Pompeian temples, Isis' shrine was rebuilt immediately by her adherents.

Completing the circuit of the town and returning to the main Forum, the principal group of temples is all around. The Temple of Venus was still in disorder after the earthquake. The Temple of Jupiter (which also acted as the Capitol of the town, at the north end of the Forum) was being rebuilt. The Temple of Apollo (on one side of the Forum, and the original sacred site of Pompeii in the fifth century B.C.) was apparently in a good state. Outside the walls to the north-west, the sinister rites of the cult of Dionysus—involving phallic worship and flagellation—can be seen in the wall paintings of the Villa of Mysteries. The variety of practices in the town reveals a culture that had evolved far from the unifying religion of creation myths, god-kings and fruitful temple-mountains typical of early civilizations. But old gods or new, the volcano buried the sanctuaries with the rest of the town.

Most of the inhabitants of Pompeii left soon after Vesuvius erupted and escaped destruction. However, the remains of at least 2000 people were found by later excavators. In the museum on the site, there are gruesome plaster casts of many of these people. Some made the mistake of sheltering in their cellars and died of sulphur poisoning. Others were overcome by the fumes as they waded through the deepening ash in the streets. Some priests of Isis, clutching their holy treasures, lay under columns in the Forum, which had fallen on them as they struggled towards the Sea Gate. When the last people were gone or dead, the rain of volcanic dust continued to pile up in the streets until it rose over the roofs of the buildings. The ash buried the city for some 1800 years in an almost unparalleled state of preservation until the spades of excavators let the sunlight fall on its streets and houses again.

Part of the family of Obellius Firmus overwhelmed by Vesuvius' sulphurous fumes. The homes of more than 500 Pompeians have been identified.

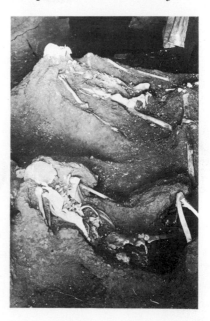

AVEBURY AND STONEHENGE

Prehistory's Great Stone Circles

FROM NORFOLK IN the east of England a track wanders south-west, keeping to the highest ground it can find—once to avoid the marshes and robbers of the valleys—and avoiding modern London to cross the river Thames at Goring. Much of that stretch of the track—known as the Icknield Way—has been built over during recent centuries, and the long footpath marked today by the Countryside Commission had to be made up of paths that run as near to the Icknield route as possible. But beyond the Thames crossing, across the chalk land of southern England, the original road can be traced as it continues high on the backs of the downs. Here, for 80 kilometres (50 miles), is the famous stretch of the Ridgeway through the part of England called Wessex. It is a route that men and women have used since they returned to Britain as the perpetual snow of the last Ice Age retreated northwards in about 10,000 B.C. At its south-western end, the Ridgeway divides into a path that goes on to the South Coast in Dorset and another heading westwards towards Bristol.

During the period when early farmers built the great stone circles of Britain, the Ridgeway was a trading road, particularly important for bringing the flints from the mines of Norfolk to the prosperous settlements of Wessex. Most of the central 80-kilometre part of the route, through Berkshire and Wiltshire, is a rough track today, impassable to motor cars. And so it is a special track for walkers—the oldest and perhaps the most beautiful road in England. Winding south-west along the tops of the long chain of downs around Marlborough, many of the hilltops crowned with small rounded woods, the traveller looks down on to a wide valley on his right. Among the lower hills ahead a green flat-topped cone appears. It vanishes behind the swelling flank of a hill, then appears again as the track tops the next rise. It is Silbury Hill, one of the greatest of all man's prehistoric earthworks, and the traveller is approaching Avebury, the centre of ancient England.

Avebury disappeared from people's consciousness for over 3000 years until an English antiquary called John Aubrey came upon it while out hunting a few days after New Year's Day in 1649. Aubrey and, a century later, William Stukeley wrote about the Avebury circles and avenues of standing stones and brought them to the attention of scholars. More than that, they recorded the monuments as they were in their time and some of our knowledge depends on their descriptions and plans. For in the following years the local farmers decided that the huge standing stones were pagan obstacles to their agriculture and many were destroyed by uprooting and heating over fires until they cracked into fragments. Stonehenge, the most famous of English monuments, lies 32 kilometres (20 miles) south of Avebury and well off the Ridgeway. But it was near a later highway and attracted interest throughout history. Roman travel writers mentioned it and the early seventeenth-century architect, Inigo Jones, wrote a book about it, concluding that it had been built as a Roman temple.

Stukeley's books on Avebury and on Stonehenge started a keen public interest in the megaliths, which produced a stream of theories about the builders and dates of the massive structures. The speculation continues today, but with the excavations of the twentieth century, and the recent development of radiocarbon dating, some parts of the story can at last be established. For the rest, the recognition that the megalith builders may have had considerable knowledge of astronomy has opened up a new field of conjecture, while the relationship of their works to those of the world's other early cultures remains fascinating.

After the last Ice Age, Britain was reinhabited by hunter-gatherers of the Middle Stone Age (Mesolithic) for many centuries before organized farming

Previous pages Avebury stone circle at sunset. The western half has the vast majority of the still standing sarsen stones (28 of the 100 originally in the Great Circle).
The chapter symbol is West Kennet Long Barrow.

Right An artist's impression of Avebury from the north (aerial view) in around 2300 B.C.

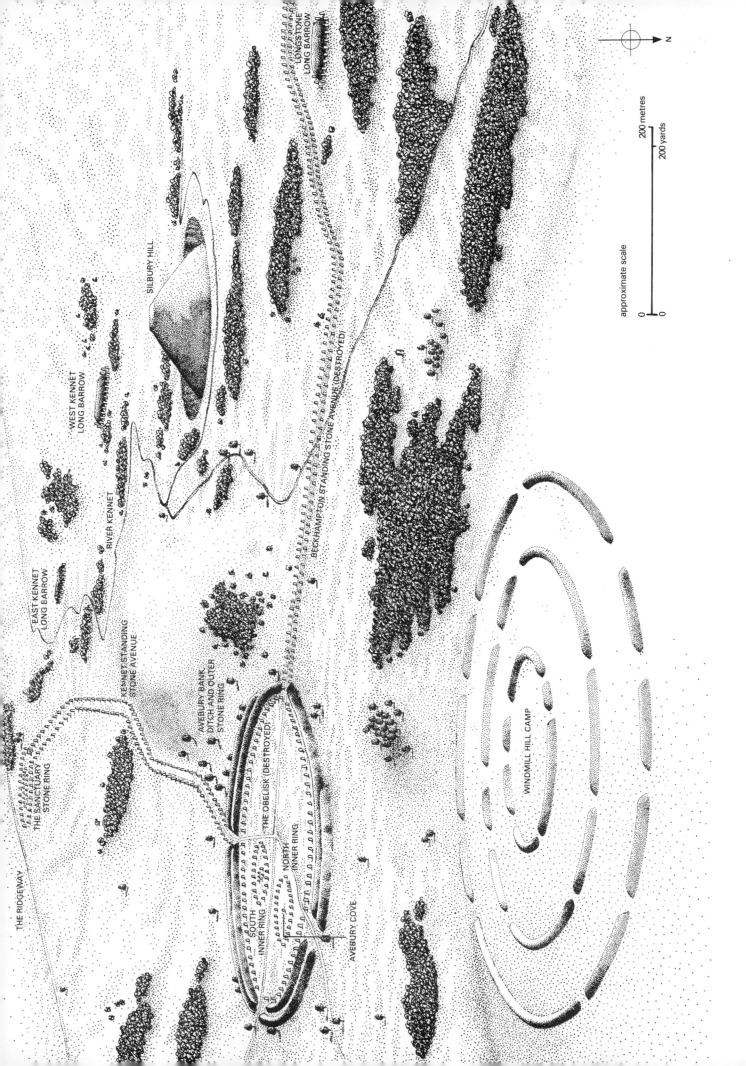

THE RIDGEWAY

THE SANCTUARY STONE RING

KENNET STANDING STONE AVENUE

EAST KENNET LONG BARROW

WEST KENNET LONG BARROW

RIVER KENNET

SILBURY HILL

LONGSTONE LONG BARROW

BECKHAMPTON STANDING STONE AVENUE (DESTROYED)

AVEBURY BANK DITCH AND OUTER STONE RING

NORTH INNER RING

SOUTH INNER RING

THE OBELISK (DESTROYED)

AVEBURY COVE

WINDMILL HILL CAMP

N

200 metres

200 yards

approximate scale

0   0

was started. The new settled agricultural ways were introduced at some time in the millennium following 5000 B.C. and, as in all western European countries, the first large-scale earthworks and megalithic structures were built by the farmers a few hundred years later. By 4000 B.C., the first big earth-banked camps were in use and the earliest chambered mounds with collective burials followed after a century or two. In some areas of England, the round mound, with a passage leading to a stone chamber, was the accepted form (as it was in the earliest megaliths of around 4500 B.C. in France and Spain). In other areas, including south Wales and central England, the usual monument was the long barrow.

Avebury's importance began with the construction there, before 3000 B.C., of one of the biggest of the Neolithic earth-banked camps and of the famous West and East Kennet long barrows. The camp was on Windmill Hill, north-west of the modern village of Avebury.

Windmill Hill is best visited in the very early morning of a fine summer's day. A narrow lane runs up the slope from the outskirts of Avebury, but the last stretch has to be walked. The hilltop meadow has a notice about the prehistoric camp at the gate, but in the field there is nothing to be seen. Or almost nothing, for there are some small barrows—much later than the Stone Age camp—and some very slight undulations in the level of the turf. One of the little barrows is right on the top of the hill from where one looks over the treetops of Avebury to Silbury Hill and to the cloud shadows chasing across the surrounding slopes. To the left, the Ridgeway runs along the chain of downs. At this point one is in fact just outside the centre of the great camp.

The remains of most of the causewayed camp lie underground behind one, spread over 8.5 hectares (21 acres) around the top of Windmill Hill. Thousands of years of ploughing have flattened the three concentric rings of earth banks and filled up their ditches, so that it is hard to trace their outlines now. But excavations in the 1920s and subsequent digs have revealed a great deal about the community that used the camp. The place was inhabited by farmers of the late stone-using period from 3700 B.C. onwards. In about 3250, these people built the three rings of earthworks around the hill. Their purpose is still not proved, but it was not for defence, for they left wide earth causeways across the ditches at many points. Some archaeologists have seen the camp—and its equivalents in other parts of Wessex—as a residence for the farmers of the region and their beasts, sheltered by the banks from the winter winds. But the winters in 3000 B.C. were less severe and less damp than those of today, and other scholars believe that the camp was a market and a meeting place for people at the time of the year's major festivals. It has also been suggested that the camp was the capital of one of the first chiefs to organize the Stone Age farmers of his area into any sort of political entity.

The human remains at Windmill Hill and its burial place show that the people were of the long-headed North European kind and that many of them suffered from arthritis. Beyond that, it is difficult to imagine the details of the men and women who brought their cattle to the camp. They probably wore well-stitched clothes of softened leather, and perhaps of a sort of felt matted from the wool of their sheep and the flax which they grew, but we do not know the shape of their garments. Not even the foundations of their houses have survived, as the soil has been eroded below the level that would have held shallow post-holes, and it may be that the camp contained many simple houses of the kind traced elsewhere, constructed around light timber frames.

So our picture of the people who moved around Windmill Hill and of their dwellings is dim. But we know much about what they farmed and ate. Their principal crop was a primitive sort of wheat called emmer, from which they

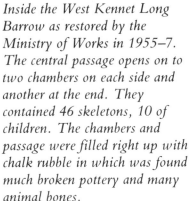

Inside the West Kennet Long Barrow as restored by the Ministry of Works in 1955–7. The central passage opens on to two chambers on each side and another at the end. They contained 46 skeletons, 10 of children. The chambers and passage were filled right up with chalk rubble in which was found much broken pottery and many animal bones.

Silbury Hill, the largest artificial hill in Europe, is more than 39.6 metres (130 ft) high and 167 metres (550 ft) broad with an area of 12.2 hectares (5½ acres). The silted up ditch was once 36 metres (120 ft) wide by 9 metres (30 ft) deep and is crossed by two causeways, one being visible on the left. The work, according to modern calculation, took 18,000,000 man-hours or 500 men 50 years for three months a year. Even all-year construction would have taken 15 years.

may have made bread, or a sort of porridge, after grinding the grain in stone querns. They also grew some barley and gathered quantities of crab–apples and a certain number of hazel–nuts. Most of their meat came from their large herds of cattle, but they kept sheep and pigs too, as well as a few goats. Their rough ploughs were of antler or wood, their sickles and hunting weapons of finely-worked flint; the wild animals they hunted included deer, fox, wild cat and wild horse. Many domesticated dogs of a sort rather like a fox terrier helped with their hunting and perhaps played with their children. The families had large pots with simple decoration for cooking and storage—they probably cooked on open fires outside their houses, for English weather was often warm and clear between 4000 and 1400 B.C.

On the far side of Avebury valley from Windmill Hill, 4 kilometres (2½ miles) away, lay the religious centre of these people. The most spectacular monument of that centre today is the West Kennet long barrow, whose horizontal outline can be seen from the causewayed camp just to the left of Silbury Hill (which was built several centuries later). Long barrows are a type of sanctuary found in many parts of northern Europe—from western Wales across England, and in varied forms from Scotland across into Holland, northern Germany and Denmark. They contained places of collective burial in a megalithic chamber at one end of the barrow, but it is improbable that their hugely extended mounds were built only as funerary monuments. All the evidence from the megalithic period in western Europe points to ceremonies being enacted here that were very much concerned with the well-being of the living and that the presence of dead ancestors in the burial chamber only strengthened the effect of these rites. The earliest round-chambered mounds in Europe have passages that face towards the point of the midwinter sunrise, the time when the old year died and the new was born. The long barrows are slightly later—some are oriented on the midwinter dawn, some of them in continental Europe point towards the *midsummer* sunrise, but many of the largest point due east-west towards the rising point of the sun at the equinox. The big long barrow on the hill above East Kennet village is aligned on the midwinter sunrise. It has not yet been excavated, but its even larger neighbour at West Kennet faces due east.

The West Kennet long barrow lies at the end of a brisk walk uphill of a few hundred metres from the Great West Road (the modern A4) of recent centuries. Like the Windmill Hill camp, this barrow was built in about 3250 B.C. It is the largest long barrow in England and Wales—which speaks of the importance of Avebury—100.5 metres (330 feet) long, with a structure of boulders covered with chalk dug up from two ditches (now ploughed flat) on its flanks. John Aubrey's illustrations of the seventeenth century show these flanks of the mound with a curbing of mighty standing stones, but these have been removed by farmers. At its eastern end, the megalithic burial chamber survives almost complete. It consists of a central east-west passage with five cells opening off it—46 skeletons were found here when Professor Stuart Piggott excavated the barrow in 1955 though others had been removed by a Marlborough doctor in the 1680s for grinding into a popular medicine. But even if there had been a hundred burials in the cells, it seems that only a select group or family was buried here during the 1200 years that the place was used as a tomb.

In front of the burial chamber at the east end of the barrow there is a forecourt with a curving screen of standing stones—the three huge stones in front of the entrance were only placed there when the tomb was finally closed off in about 2000 B.C. Before that, the forecourt was probably the focal point for ceremonies at the equinox, a major festival for the Avebury people. For at the equinox, day and night are equal—in perfect balance with each other—an expression of the stability and continuity of the fertile seasons, which were apparently so important to these early farmers. In this, the West Kennet long barrow, oriented east-west, is related to countless other early sacred structures all over the world that are aligned on the cardinal compass points. It is perhaps not too fanciful to imagine the people from the farms around Avebury gathered in the forecourt and on the top of the great barrow in about 3000 B.C., awaiting the equinoctial dawn in spring and, again, in autumn. As the sun rose, it could be seen directly along the line of the long barrow by those on top, and it would penetrate down the passage into the burial chamber. There, or in the forecourt, the leaders or priests of the community peformed their unrecorded rites to ensure the continuity of the farming cycle for another year.

A few centuries later, a little before 2600 B.C., a new symbol of Avebury's stability was started 550 metres (600 yards) to the north of the long barrow. This was Silbury Hill, built of compacted chalk blocks in four stages over a fairly short period. For many years archaeologists, hoping that the hill would fit in with old-fashioned ideas about these ancient monuments, tried to find a burial chamber in the huge mound, but the most thorough investigations revealed no chamber and another purpose for Silbury has to be sought. This purpose must be close to that of the ziggurats, temple-mountains and pyramids of other cultures all over the world, which have been described elsewhere in this book. Deep under Silbury Hill, a primary mound of turf was found, which may stand over the earliest sacred place in the Avebury area. A simple mound or outcrop of rock was the first shrine of countless early farming communities, probably linked to the legendary mountain dwelling of the gods at the centre of the universe, and to the widespread creation myth of the mound originally established on the formless oceans. The people of Avebury started to build around this mound in about 2600 B.C., forming a stepped cone that rose 39.6 metres (130 feet) in six levels of circular sloping walls, made of chalk blocks, to a flat top. The resemblance to the step pyramids of Egypt at this stage is obvious. But then the Avebury builders levelled off all the steps except the top one (which can still be seen) with compact chalk, to form smooth sloping sides. So, at the time, Silbury Hill was a huge gleaming white cone, with a flattened top and a circular platform around it a few metres lower down.

Many theories have been put forward about its use as a centre for seasonal rites, but it is likely that—as with the temple-mountains of Cambodia, the stupas of India and the pyramids of Egypt—its very existence ensured prosperity in the minds of the people who lived around it. As it happens, the volume of Silbury Hill is almost the same as that of the smallest of the three pyramids at Giza, and Silbury was probably built about 50 years before the first of those three, the Great Pyramid. It is reasonable to see common roots in the ancient religious ideas that inspired the builders of these monuments, but it is unlikely that there was any greater similarity than that between their distant cultures.

Only a century or so after the completion of Silbury Hill, the stone and antler tools of the Avebury people were turned to their most famous monument—the great stone circles and avenues around the modern village of Avebury itself. Although we have very few clues about the developing political organization of the farming communities at this time, it is likely that widespread links of some kind were being formed. For just at this period around 2500 B.C., the earlier idea of the causewayed camps seems to have been developed into building a chain of circular earthworks, usually called henges, and giant circles of standing stones—a chain that runs, whether by accident or by design, down the centre of Britain. There are other big stone circles, and nearly 900 smaller ones in Britain, but those combining circle with henge seem to have been very special. Eleven of these henged great circles were built—two in Orkney, Cairnpapple near Edinburgh, Long Meg and her Daughters in Cumbria, two in Derbyshire, Arminghall in Norfolk (where the circle was of tree trunks, rather than stones), the Devils Quoits in Oxfordshire, Avebury and Stonehenge in Wiltshire, and the Stripple Stones in Cornwall. Several of them have now lost their stones, but all the henged earthworks can still be seen. Of these, Avebury and Stonehenge are the most celebrated and the largest.

To understand the purpose of the henged circles, it is best to return to the

Ridgeway and recall that it was a trading route. At the point where the old track crosses the modern Great West Road (A4) a fence encloses a small area of grass sprinkled with circles of modern concrete marking posts. These indicate the position of a vanished monument now called the Sanctuary. During the years when Silbury Hill was being built, a small circle of posts was put up at this place. In the next two centuries, these were replaced first by a larger circle of timbers and then by five concentric rings of wooden posts. Finally, two concentric circles of standing stones were erected on the site in about 2300 B.C.

The Sanctuary clearly had a key role of some sort, and the most obvious clue is that it was the point at which people left the Ridgeway to go to Avebury. From the Sanctuary, a long double row of standing stones—the Avenue—snaked north-west over the brow of the hill, down to the valley near the Kennet river and rose again to reach the great stone circles 2 kilometres (1½ miles) away. The route can be followed today, though only for the last few hundred metres are the stones of the Avenue still to be seen. On the west side of the Avebury circles, another avenue of standing stones ran through the fields to what is now the hamlet of Beckhampton, but only two stones of this survive.

The most impressive moment of a visit to Avebury is the entry through the high earth bank to the outer circle of megalithic stones. The houses of the present village straggle into the 11.5-hectare (28-acre) enclosure, and many tall trees grow within its area. In all directions one sees the steep banks and ditch, and the curving lines of huge rough boulders. The outer circle is by far the largest stone ring ever built in Britain—even the two stone circles within it are larger than any other except the Ring of Brodgar in Orkney (which has the same diameter as these two). In one of these inner rings a strange formation of small stones on the plan of an irregular D can be seen; there was a large stone pillar exactly in the centre, but this was one of more than a hundred boulders smashed by farmers. The other inner circle, to the north, was originally two concentric rings, with a U-shaped setting at its centre of three particularly large stones (only two survive), called the Cove. Despite the missing stones, the place is still overwhelmingly grand and, more than that, has an extraordinary atmosphere—some find it upsetting, others deeply peaceful.

So what was all this built for? In the approach avenues to the Avebury circles, archaeologists have found bones and many pits containing ritual debris of various sorts, including broken potsherds. To judge from finds at many other megalithic monuments, the breaking of vessels containing some sort of liquid was an important part of these people's ceremonies. It would probably be a mistake to regard Avebury only as a temple, for politics, trade, farming and religion seem to have been inseparable to the megalithic builders in a way that is difficult for many of us to appreciate. It was not a city, for there are no signs of prehistoric dwellings on the site. But the grandeur of the monuments speaks of a centre of political power of some sort, perhaps the seat of great chieftains in the loosest of federations. The huge enclosure hints at large gatherings for special festivals, travellers spreading their wares on the grass for barter with visitors from places with different products. Some of the stones could have been used for astronomical observations, but not all. So, if the approach avenues and the inner circles are suggestive of processions—both joyous and funeral—and of the ritual celebration of the major festivals watched by the people at sunrise, the outer enclosure was surely used for other more worldly purposes and festivities. And this complex purpose was shared, on a slightly smaller scale, by the other 10 great henged circles that were built from the north of Scotland to Cornwall.

The circles and avenues of Avebury represent the highest point of the

Neolithic culture in England. They, and the other henged circles, were built in the years around 2500 B.C. In the meantime, 32 kilometres (20 miles) south of Avebury, an even more famous circle was developing towards its final unique form. Like Avebury, Stonehenge is the centrepiece of an area rich in megalithic monuments. Three kilometres (2 miles) to the north-east are the buried remains of a large causewayed camp called Durrington Walls—probably the secular centre of Stonehenge's builders, as Windmill Hill was to Avebury—and there are three long barrows to the north and west of the stone circle. Moreover, 1 kilometre (½ mile) to the north of Stonehenge lies the Cursus, one of those strange Wessex monuments consisting of a long man-made depression in the ground, deep and wide, and in this case running for over 1.6 kilometres (1 mile) almost east-west.

Stonehenge itself stands on a shallow spur running down east towards the modern town of Amesbury. What we see today is the surviving part of the last of several monuments built and rebuilt over a period of more than 1000 years, starting in 2800 B.C. Professor Richard Atkinson, who has conducted many of the important excavations at Stonehenge and Avebury during recent decades, has divided these works into five periods, which he has numbered I, II, IIIa, IIIb and IIIc. Since Professor Atkinson published his findings in 1960, Professor Alexander Thom and others have demonstrated how Stonehenge may have been used as a lunar and solar observatory.

The first monument built at Stonehenge was the henge itself, the circular bank surrounded by a ditch, with one level gap in the earthworks to provide an entrance causeway. This was built in about 2800 B.C. The only standing stones at this stage were a pair at the entrance causeway (the one survivor is now misleadingly called the Slaughter Stone) and the outlying Heel Stone, thought to have marked a lunar alignment. But around the perimeter of the circular enclosure, the builders bored 56 holes in the ground. These so-called Aubrey Holes never contained stones, but may have been positions for

Stonehenge in an aerial view from the south-west. On the left is the flat 'Slaughter Stone', the survivor of a pair of stones at the entrance causeway. The 56 concrete-filled Aubrey Holes (first discovered by John Aubrey in 1666) behind the ditch come next with two of the four Station Stones remaining (centre top, centre bottom). The second phase of building saw two circles of Welsh bluestones partially set up within the Aubrey Holes. They were then removed to make room for the 77 sarsen blocks (averaging 26 tons each) from the Marlborough Downs above Avebury 32 kilometres (20 miles) away. Three of the five trilithons (pair of standing stones capped by a third) of the inner horseshoe ring still stand, while six of the outer ring's 30 trilithons remain. Finally, the 79 old bluestones, 16 still upright, were put up inside each of the sarsen rings.

189

One of Stonehenge's inner trilithons. These hard sandstone (sarsen) blocks were shaped by stonecutters using tools of the same material. The round trip, from Marlborough Downs to Stonehenge and back, has been estimated as taking 14 days with up to 1000 men hauling the largest stones on rollers. In position a pit would be dug with one vertical and one sloping side. The stone would be levered in down the slope to rest against the stake-protected vertical side. It would be raised by a combination of ropes lashed round the top and levering from the entry side using a wooden platform as fulcrum. The pit was then packed tight with any available material including stone hammers. A 7-ton lintel stone was raised gradually using levers and successive layers of timber criss-cross supports until it was level with the top of the uprights and could be shifted into position to fit their projections in its holes. The lintels were shaped to form a circle and their height does not vary more than 17.7 cm (7 in) across the ring despite the sloping ground of the site.

movable markers. And in the earth beside the Slaughter Stone and the Heel Stone, Atkinson found curious patterns of holes as if posts had been pushed into the ground, then moved to a near-by position.

These traces, and the 56 Aubrey Holes, have been analysed to show that they may have been used to study the complicated movements and cycles of the moon. It has even been suggested that it was here, in this observatory of earth, stones and posts, that mankind first worked out that the moon's patterns have a main cycle of 18.61 solar years and confirmed its regularity by continuous observations through six successive cycles. This discovery would have been important for people who acknowledged the moon's divine influence—on the tides, the germination of seeds, the female menstrual cycle and the eclipses after which the reappearance of sun or moon was a dramatic form of rebirth. If the discovery was made at Stonehenge, it may account for the later glorification of the henge with standing stones.

The first stone ring at Stonehenge was erected in about 2400 B.C., a little later than the much larger stone circles at Avebury. The design was very different from that of any other great stone circle. The stones were of bluestone transported all the way from south-west Wales—rather slender columns that rise only 1.5–1.8 metres (5–6 feet) above the surface when placed in the ground. They were arranged in two concentric circles. The Altar Stone, now lying under tumbled sarsen stones in the middle of the circle, is also of Welsh rock, which must have been credited with special powers. At the same stage, the earthwork avenue was raised—it points towards the midsummer sunrise, then curves east to end near the Avon river. Within the henge, the four Station Stones were erected, forming an oblong with diagonal lines that point to midwinter and midsummer sunrises and with sides that point to moonrises at important stages in its cycle (at any other latitude, that oblong would have to be distorted into a parallelogram to combine these properties).

At this point in prehistory, about the time of the building of Stonehenge II, a new people appear in England. At first they seem to have come in small numbers, bringing the first metal-working techniques, perhaps weaving and certainly a new sort of pottery with them. We do not know their name, so they are called the Beaker people after their most favoured sort of pot. Nor do we know where they came from—some archaeologists have argued that they were from the metal-working cultures of east-central Europe, others believe they arrived from southern Germany or even from Spain. Whatever their origins, they spread all over western Europe around 2400 B.C. And in England, it appears that they took over the leadership of the native people from the old Neolithic chieftains by 2300 B.C. Despite the unprecedented achievements of the Stone Age builders during the previous two centuries, the rulers of Avebury and other centres seem to have been helpless against the metal weapons, and perhaps the greater knowledge, of these newcomers.

For a time, it appears that the new leading caste let the people continue with their established ways. There were signs of activity as late as 2000 B.C. in the Windmill Hill camp and burials of the same period in the West Kennet long barrow. But then the Beaker people closed off the long barrow with three huge stones, still to be seen and the causewayed camp was abandoned.

Around Stonehenge, there was no sign of Beaker pottery in some structures of 2400 B.C. at Durrington Walls camp, but the Woodhenge monument just outside the banks of Durrington has produced evidence that it may have been built a little later by the Beaker people. Putting all the available clues together, it seems likely that before 2000 B.C., the Beaker People—or another group that took political power—decided to transfer the centre of importance from Avebury to Stonehenge.

The great dressed stones and trilithons, which make Stonehenge a unique monument, all date from its rebuilding in about 2100 B.C. The builders, under the orders of their rulers, dug up the circles of bluestones and piled the rocks to one side. Then they carved much larger sarsen rocks from the Marlborough Downs above Avebury and transported them overland to Stonehenge. There they erected the ten largest blocks in pairs, with a carefully shaped capstone over each to form five trilithons, in an inner enclosure with a horseshoe-shaped plan open towards the midsummer sunrise and the Avenue. The other big sarsens were erected as an outer ring of standing stones, each linked to the next by a continuous line of capstones.

The strangest thing about Stonehenge is that it is the only monument built by later people that can compare in size with the Neolithic great stone circles—indeed, it outstrips them all in the size of the stones and their smooth dressing. After that, Beaker folk or others made hundreds of stone circles in various parts of Britain—probably to pursue their study of the moon and other celestial bodies—but most of them are small and none are on this scale. It is clear that Stonehenge was built for a special purpose, and that purpose was probably to move the power centre of southern England. Although there are later Bronze Age barrows around Avebury, their numbers cannot compare with the huge cemetery of small barrows in the countryside around Stonehenge.

Two more stages of Stonehenge remain to be described. In the first, perhaps built around 1900 B.C., some of the magic Welsh bluestones were put up again in a two-layer spiral that wound round the outer sarsen ring. Finally, the bluestones were uprooted again and set, two or three hundred years later, in a pattern that almost echoes the plan of the big sarsens. One group formed a second horseshoe within the sarsen horseshoe, the other formed a ring inside the tall outer circle. Again, it seems that the particular qualities ascribed to the bluestones were more important than their size. This combination of the two kinds of rock is the arrangement that we see today, though a good many of the stones have fallen or disappeared. It seems that the monument in this state was not used as a working celestial observatory, but as a setting for rites at key moments of the year to enhance the progress of the sun and the seasons for the benefit of the farmers and their land.

This last alteration of Stonehenge may have been made as late as 1600 B.C. and that brings the story close to the end of megalithic building in northern Europe. For between 1500 and 1400 B.C. the overall weather pattern changed from the comparatively dry warmth and clear skies of the Sub-Boreal period, as the weather historians call it, to the cool and rainy climate of the Sub-Atlantic period, which is still with us. For the farmers who built the megaliths, this change was disastrous. The high and open areas, such as Salisbury Plain or Bodmin Moor, which had been pleasant regions in Sub-Boreal weather, were now exposed to wind and drizzle, and a blanket of peat moss started to grow up over them. The skies, which had been clear for the people's observations of sun and moon and stars for so many centuries, were now clouded over much of the time. The latest date traced for the building of a megalithic structure in northern Europe is 1400 B.C. for one dolmen (stone tomb) in France. For the people of those times, it must have seemed that the divine order of things, which their rites had aimed to keep stable, was overthrown and the power of their deities lost. Some of the largest monuments, including Stonehenge, may have been adapted for use by the priests of later beliefs. But most of the megaliths were useless now. The farmers were driven to seek land in lower places more suited to the times, leaving their chambered mounds and stone circles deserted on the moors.

Two daggers and an axe carved on Stonehenge's south trilithon. There are five other carvings on trilithons, three being of Irish bronze axes traded at that period (c. 1600–1400 B.C.). The daggers have been compared with those of the contemporary Mycenaean civilization in Greece which once lent support to the discredited theory that Stonehenge was the work of foreign architects.

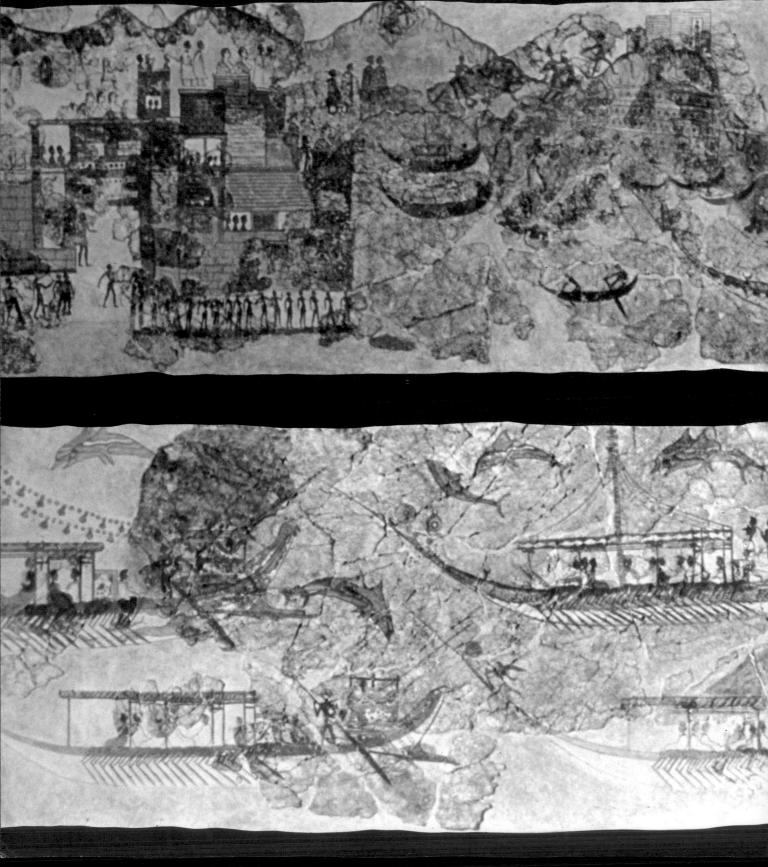

ATLANTIS

The Greatest Mystery Of All

THE PROTOTYPE OF lost worlds is of course Atlantis. According to Plato's Dialogues, the great lawmaker of Athens, Solon, visited Egypt a few years after 600 B.C. and met a priest in the city of Sais, who claimed that he too had Athenian ancestors. This priest told Solon the story of a great civilization that developed on an island in the ocean 9000 years earlier 'beyond the narrows called the Pillars of Hercules (Gibraltar and, nearly opposite it, a mountain on the north African coast), and from there it was then possible for a ship to sail to other islands and on to the continent enclosing the ocean which bears its name. . . . On this island, which was called Atlantis, there was a powerful and magnificent kingdom, which occupied the whole island, as well as other islands and parts of the continent beyond. It also ruled Libya, up to the Egyptian border, and part of mainland Europe as far as Italy.'

The priest continued with a description of the mainland of Atlantis. 'A beautiful plain spread from the sea to the middle of the island. A mountain rose there, sloping down evenly in all directions. On top of it had lived a man called Euenor, who had grown from the earth at its creation, with his wife Leucippe and their only daughter Cleito. When Cleito grew up, Euenor and Leucippe died. The sea god Poseidon thought her beautiful and became her lover. The god made defences for Cleito's mountain at the centre of Atlantis by making channels of water around it in the land, so that it was surrounded by three circles of water and two of land, each equal width; thus the mountain could not be reached, for there were no boats at that time. In the centre of the island Poseidon made two springs from the ground, one of hot water, the other of cold, and the earth produced good crops of many sorts. And Cleito bore the god five pairs of twin sons.' The first of these sons was called Atlas, who was made king while the others became governors of provinces marked out by Poseidon. Later the governors became ten kings, who shared the powers among themselves.

As the people multiplied, they began to build. 'Their first work was to make bridges across the three circles of water and to build a palace for the kings on Cleito's mountain abode, to which each king added a new part until the royal palace was astonishingly large and beautiful. Then they cut a canal for large ships 6 miles long from the sea to the outer circle of water and on to the inner circle . . . the central island, within the circles of water, with the royal palace on it was about 600 yards wide; both this and the outer side of the largest circle were surrounded by stone walls, with towers and gates. . . . The outer wall was encased in melted bronze, the inner with tin.'

The priest went on with a description of the royal palace on the acropolis of the central mountain. 'In the very centre of the palace was the temple of Poseidon and Cleito, encircled by a fence of gold and forbidden to most people, for it was there that the original ten princes had been conceived. Once a year, people from all ten provinces of Atlantis gathered there to make offerings.' The temple was covered with silver, with some features of gold, and it contained a statue of Poseidon.

As for the island itself, the plain was oblong in shape—about 340 miles (547 kilometres) long by 220 miles (354 kilometres) wide—open to the sea in the south, but otherwise ringed with mountains which sheltered the land. (These dimensions make it evident that the central mountain was not at the *geographical* centre of the island, for that could not have been reached by a canal 6 miles (9.66 kilometres) long. Either this is simply a mistake or the word 'central' is used in some other sense, perhaps symbolic.) The description continued with an account of Atlantis' political system and just laws, its power and prosperity. But later, the society began to degenerate and was obsessed by greed and evil deeds. The Atlanteans set out to conquer the whole world, and

Previous pages The ships of Atlantis? This intriguing Minoan frieze dating from the sixteenth century B.C. adorns a house in Akrotiri, capital of the volcanic Aegean island of Santorini (Thera). More than 7 metres (23 ft) long and 40 cm (1¼ ft) high it depicts a naval expedition perhaps to North Africa and thus is the first visual evidence for the sea-based empire of King Minos. Among the tantalizing details are dolphins, ceremonial rigging, two ports, deck cargo, ornate bowsprits, and strange stern projections usually interpreted as gangways. The ship under sail has been estimated to be of 16–19 tons displacement and 24 metres (78 ft) long. The chapter symbol repeats the Cross of Atlantis described opposite.

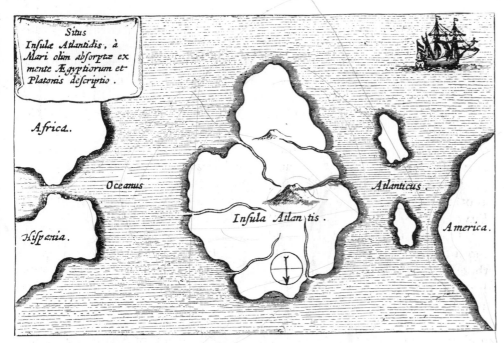

Situs
Insulæ Atlantidis, à
Mari olim absorptæ ex
mente Ægyptiorum et
Platonis descriptio.

Africa.

Oceanus

Hispania.

Insula Atlantis.

Atlanticus.

America.

The position of Atlantis according to Athanasius Kircher's 1655 map; north point to the south. Kircher was a German Jesuit who gave up teaching maths and Hebrew at the Jesuit College in Rome in favour of archaeology and hieroglyphics in 1643.

only Athens prevented their success. Destruction followed soon after this defeat for Atlantis. 'Zeus, the supreme god and ruler by eternal laws, saw how this fine race of men were corrupted and, calling the other gods together on their high dwelling at the centre of the universe, decided on their punishment.' And so 'when terrible earthquakes and then floods occurred, the whole brave population was buried in the earth and the land of Atlantis was drowned under the sea. It vanished completely in one terrible day and one terrible night.'

Plato's account of Solon's story is the sole basis for thinking that Atlantis may have existed, though a similar legend with different names is told in two very old epic poems of India. Within 50 years of Plato's death in 348/7 B.C., the long debate began. Aristotle, who opposed many of Plato's teachings, dismissed the Atlantis story as an idealistic fiction of the sort that we would nowadays call utopian. Plutarch's *Lives* confirms that Solon, the great lawmaker, did indeed travel to Sais in Egypt in about 571 B.C. and wrote an account of Atlantis in the memoirs, now lost, that he wrote at the end of his life. In the fifth century A.D. the philosopher Proclus wrote in his long commentary on the relevant dialogues of Plato, the *Timaeus*, that in about 270 B.C. a Greek called Crantor actually saw the story of Atlantis carved in hieroglyphs on the walls of the temple of Neith in Sais. But Sais and the temple are now buried under the mud of the Nile delta.

After Proclus, nothing more is heard of Atlantis during the long centuries of the Dark Ages and medieval Europe. For the scholars of those times, Aristotle was the ultimate authority of antiquity and his dismissal of Plato's story made Atlantis uninteresting. Then in 1553, 61 years after Columbus had first crossed the Atlantic, the Spanish historian Lopez da Gomara pointed out that the West Indies and American continent fitted astonishingly well with Plato's account of the lands beyond the lost continent. And that started the arguments that have continued until our time. Among many others, Francis Bacon's *Nova Atlantis* of 1614–18 held that the lost land lay between Gibraltar and Brazil, while Athanasius Kircher's *Mundus Subterraneus* of 1655 thought that the Azores were the peaks of the mountains of Atlantis. Such ideas stayed close to Plato's description, but later the locations ranged far more widely. The submerged country has been detected in Sweden, South Africa, Nigeria, Armenia and many other places by various authors. According to one recent

Below The so-called Cross of Atlantis, an ancient symbol based on the layout of Atlantis as described by Plato. In the centre is Cleito's original island broken into four quadrants by water (black) for the purposes of the symbol. Then comes the inner harbour (first black ring) surrounded by the lesser zone of land which, in Plato's description, had two temples, two underground docks and a guardhouse on the south side next to the 9.6 kilometre (6 mile) long ship canal where it enters the second circular harbour. The outer and major band of land had gardens, a stadium and gymnasia with four underground docks and another guardhouse by the ship canal's exit into the great harbour (outer black circle).

count, around 20,000 books about Atlantis have been published.

Was the kingdom factual? If so, where was it? Or was the story a moralizing fable? If so, was it a fable of Plato's, or of Solon's, or of the Egyptians? Unless an underwater continent is found, with ruins and of a size corresponding to Plato's description—or unless some new written proof one way or another emerges—these questions cannot be answered conclusively. But as long as they remain unanswered, more theories will be added to the thousands already put forward, for something deep in the human psyche responds to the idea and *wants* Atlantis to be true.

In 1882 an American Congressman called Ignatius Donnelly wrote a book which became the basic text for a new field of study, Atlantology. Donnelly's *Atlantis: the Antedeluvian World* produces a huge range of evidence to show that a continent had once existed in the Atlantic Ocean whose culture had spread both to east and west of it, thus accounting for the pyramids that occur on both sides of it and for many other similarities. Donnelly thought that Atlantis had vanished under the sea when continental drift parted America from Europe and Africa. Even more colourful was a 1912 article by Paul Schliemann, grandson of Heinrich Schliemann. In *How I discovered Atlantis, the Source of all Civilization* Schliemann claimed that his grandfather had left him an envelope containing all the information he had about Atlantis and telling how, during his work at Troy, he had found a superb bronze bowl inscribed 'From King Chronos of Atlantis'. The bowl was proved to be a fake but there was no stopping the tidal wave of speculation. In the 1920s, an American clairvoyant named Edgar Cayce started to record a series of trances in which he saw that

This unique bust has been claimed by some writers to be an Atlantean priestess. It comes from Elche, a small town 32 kilometres (20 miles) south-west of Alicante in Spain. Here a doctor found the bust in his garden in 1897. No other clues were found as to the Lady of Elche's origin. Only on stylistic grounds has the weighty jewellery been dated to the fourth century B.C. when Carthage held sway in southern Spain.

A fisherman from Santorini (Thera), one of the most favoured candidates for the site of Atlantis. Is he wearing seaweed in his hair? This Minoan fresco of c. 1500 B.C. comes from the West House in Akrotiri, the Aegean island's capital on the south-west peninsula.

Another Santorini (Thera) fresco to come from the revelational excavations since 1967. In this oldest representation of boxing, two children battle it out. To judge by shoes, bracelets, and girdle the boxer on the left has richer parents than the one on the right but both just have a single glove.

the Atlanteans had had powered flying machines and nuclear energy—which had destroyed their civilization in the end, though some of them had escaped to take their architecture and some science eastwards to Egypt and westwards to Mexico.

Cayce also foretold that Atlantis would appear again in about 1968 near the Bahamas, and indeed during that year the American zoologist, Dr. J.M.

Plato (428/7–348/7 B.C.), the Athenian philosopher, who described the Atlantis legend in his Dialogues Timaeus *and* Critias. *The latter, Plato's cousin, says on three occasions that it was true and Socrates himself is cited as to its veracity. The geographer Strabo preserved the Stoic philosopher Poseidonius of Apamea's (c. 135–50 B.C.) record of Plato saying 'It is possible that the story is not an invention'. But the latest modern study suggests that Plato's main interest in Atlantis was as a moral tale to warn Dionysus II of Syracuse when he was tutor to that Sicilian tyrant in the 360s B.C.*

Valentine, found extraordinary structures of huge stone blocks deep in the sea off the island of Little Bimini. The island is within the famous Bermuda Triangle, an area of sea in which ships have disappeared inexplicably and other strange things have happened. So far, nobody has disproved that these structures under the water may be the remains of Atlantis, but most archaeologists remain sceptical.

The year before Valentine's discoveries, a Greek archaeologist named Spyridon Marinatos found remains of an advanced culture on the volcanic Aegean island of Santorini, which had exploded with titanic force in about 1500 B.C. Marinatos' theory was that Atlantis was the Minoan civilization of Crete, whose ports were probably all destroyed by the tidal wave—estimated at 192 metres (630 feet) high—caused by this, the most violent of all volcanic explosions in the last few thousand years. The explosion would, literally, have been heard in northern Egypt and, with the Cretan ports demolished, the Minoans would have vanished as far as the Egyptians were concerned. And this, Marinatos believed, may have been the basis of the story told to Solon by the priest 900 years later.

The most recent explanation that must be mentioned is that of Dr Otto Muck, an eminent German scientist who was, among other things, the inventor of the U-boat schnorkel. Muck's carefully researched book *The Secret of Atlantis* was published posthumously in 1978. After working out the shape and position of Plato's island in the mid-Atlantic by scientific detective work, he proposes that it was destroyed by the shocks and tidal waves of a giant asteroid that fell from space into the Atlantic, east of Puerto Rico, in about 8500 B.C.

None of these theories can actually be proved unless submarine archaeology reveals hard evidence, so there are probably centuries of debate and new ideas on the subject to come. Meanwhile, I believe another approach altogether is worth considering. Plato's account of the origins and description of Atlantis, summarized at the beginning of the chapter, have remarkable resemblances to some of the visions of the universe found among ancient people in other lost worlds described in this book. The quadrangular plain largely ringed by mountains, with the ocean beyond and a sacred mountain at its centre—all this is very close to the cosmos as seen by Chinese, Indian and other cultures. Atlantis' central mountain itself, dwelling place of gods, has strong echoes of Mount Olympus, of Mount Meru of the Hindus.

It may be that they all have their roots in that creation myth found most commonly, though in many variants, throughout the globe—of the female hill or mound floating on the primordial oceans until it was pierced and held in one place at the centre of the world by the staff of a male divinity, thus establishing the order of our existence in many dimensions. And the mysterious man-made mounds of early Europe, the pyramids of Egypt and Mexico, the ziggurats of Mesopotamia, the *stupas* of India, the temple-mountains of Cambodia and the similar monuments of other countries may well all be local re-enactments of that central mythical mountain, still built by god-kings far apart from each other and from the original unknown source of the idea. Many scholars are working along these lines and their researches may shed light on the legendary drowned country too. For other features of Plato's Atlantis also remind us of early mankind's symbolic pictures of the universe. And it has been pointed out earlier in this book that the fact that the apparent world can be proved to be unlike the mythical world, centred on Mount Meru, is meaningless to a Hindu. Truth has many levels, and the symbolic can be just as real as the physical in the minds of men and women, and just as strongly necessary.

199

GEOGRAPHICAL CIRCLES

⊕ **ATLANTIS** 9600 B.C. ?

MALTA 3500-3000 B.C.

AVEBURY AND STONEHENGE 3500-1500 B.C.

UR 3000-300 B.C.

TROY 3000-1100 B.C.

EGYPT'S PYRAMIDS 2700-2200 B.C.

MOHENJO-DARO 2500-1700 B.C.

PERSEPOLIS 520-330 B.C.

SOLAR SYSTEM

NORTH POLE

NORTHERN OCEAN

GREENLAND

Nova Zembla

LAPLAND

SWEDEN

RUSSIA

SIBERIA

MOSCOVY

EUROPE

GERMANY

POLAND

FRANCE

SPAIN

Baltic

TURKEY

Black Sea

WESTERN TARTARY

EASTERN TARTARY

ASIA

KAMSCHATKA

Sea of Kamschatka

Sea of Corea

PEKIN

CHINA

TIBET

EASTERN

MEDITERRANEAN SEA

BARBARY

MOROCCO

ALGIERS

TRIPOLI

DESART OF BARBARY

ZARA

PERSIA

MOGOLS

INDIA

Bay of Bengal

G. of Siam

PHILIPPINES

OCEAN

Marian Isles

NEGROLAND

AFRICA

GUINEA

NUBIA

EGYPT

ETHIOPIA

EMPIRE of Monomotapa

Ceylon I.

Sumatra

Java

Molucca I.

New Guinea

Ireland

INDIAN OCEAN

CONGO

MACOKO

Angola

Monomugi

MADAGASCAR

Mauritius I.

Cocos

NEW HOLLAND

NEW SOUTH WALES

CAFFRARIA

Cape of Good Hope

Natal Pt.

Kerguelins Land

Diemens Land

Tasman I.

SOUTHERN OCEAN

Fields of Ice

Fields of Ice

⊙	**POMPEII** 500 B.C. - A.D. 79	⌂	**GREAT ZIMBABWE** A.D. 1300-1440
⊙	**CHICHEN ITZA** A.D. 700-1200	⊙	**MACHU PICCHU** A.D. 1450-1570
⊙	**ANGKOR** A.D. 800-1431	⊙	**EASTER ISLAND** A.D. 1600-1862
⊙	**BENIN** A.D. 1200-1897		